DA
145
.W2
1971

Ward,
The Roman era in
  Britain.

DATE DUE			

THE ROMAN ERA IN BRITAIN

THE ROMAN ERA
IN BRITAIN

BY

JOHN WARD, F.S.A.

WITH SEVENTY-SEVEN ILLUSTRATIONS BY THE AUTHOR

KENNIKAT PRESS
Port Washington, N. Y./London

THE ROMAN ERA IN BRITAIN

First published in 1911
Reissued in 1971 by Kennikat Press
Library of Congress Catalog Card No: 79-118507
ISBN 0-8046-1255-2

Manufactured by Taylor Publishing Company   Dallas, Texas

PREFACE

SEVERAL years ago, I was desired by the Editor of this series to write a volume on Roman Britain, but I soon found that the subject was too large and complex to be treated comprehensively, and at the same time to place the reader *en rapport* with the results of the systematic excavations of the last twenty-five years. These have vastly increased our knowledge of Roman Britain, especially its " major monuments " —the towns, forts, public buildings, and houses—and to these I confined myself in *Romano-British Buildings and Earthworks*, of this series.

It was felt, however, that the series demanded a general work on the era in Britain. This was now feasible, as the subjects which came within the restricted purview of the above volume could be treated in a more condensed manner than would be otherwise· desirable. In spite of this, however, the question of space has been a difficulty. Two chapters which could best be spared—a short history of the era, and practical hints upon archaeological exploration—had to be cut out ; and a third upon our public Romano-British collections, which was contemplated at the outset, and for which much material was collected, had to be abandoned. In obtaining this material I am indebted to the hearty co-operation of many museum curators, and although the proposed chapter had to be given up, their labour has by no means been in vain in the production of this volume.

The book does not cover as much ground as I wished, but to have included more would have entailed an undesirable curtailment of several of the chapters. But, with all its deficiencies, I hope it will prove to be of service to those—now a large number—whose interest in Roman Britain has been awakened by the prolific results of the systematic excavations of late years.

I am indebted to many for various services rendered, and especially to Mr. A. G. Wright of Colchester, Mr. T. W. Colyer of Reading, Mr. Oxley Grabham, M.A., of York, Mr. Robert Blair, F.S.A., of South Shields, Mr. J. H. Allchin of Maidstone, and Mr. Frank King, who has superintended the excavations at Caerwent for some years, for photographs and particulars of objects in the museums of those places. Most of the objects illustrated are in public museums, and each group is, as far as possible, drawn to a common scale.

JOHN WARD

Cardiff

CONTENTS

LIST OF ILLUSTRATIONS

THE ROMAN ERA IN BRITAIN

CHAPTER I

INTRODUCTION

POLITICALLY, the Roman era in Britain began with the Claudian Conquest in A.D. 43, and ended with the isolation of the country from the rest of the decaying empire consequent upon the passing of northern Gaul into the hands of the Trans-Rhenish barbarians in A.D. 406–410. But Roman influence through intercourse with the Continent preceded the former event, and Britain continued to be Roman after the latter event, remaining so, harassed by foes from without and probably by dissensions within, until the English conquest. Broadly speaking, the Roman era lasted 450 years.

To gauge what four-and-a-half centuries may mean in the history of a country, let the reader contrast the times of Henry the Sixth with our own. England then was without the printing-press, the newspaper, and a cheap literature ; without steam-power and almost without machinery ; without a postal system, railways, steamships, telephones, and gas and electric lighting ; without cotton, porcelain, vulcanite, and a host of other familiar inventions. It helps one to realize what four-and-a-half centuries mean, when one recalls the fact that since that time twenty-three sovereigns have sat on the throne of England ; and that during the interval the population has increased well-nigh tenfold, America has been discovered, our political system has been evolved, and a vast colonial empire founded. We cannot doubt that under the Romans, the greatest organizers of the ancient world, enormous changes were also wrought in this country, and this is confirmed by the verdict of both history and archaeology.

The more we contemplate the remains of Roman Britain, the more we are impressed with the high culture they betoken. But at the outset, let the reader who confines his attention to this local phase of Roman archaeology, guard himself against a mischievous bias in favour of his own country. Britain was but a small province on the fringe of a great empire, and before its conquest was probably as little known to Italy as central Africa was to us a quarter of a century ago. To the average Roman, his empire was his world, and if he troubled to think of Britain at all, he thought of it as an unexplored land on the confines of creation, wrapped in the mists of the earth-engirdling ocean, and only known through the reports of traders. From no ordinary campaign, in the estimation of his countrymen, did Claudius return in A.D. 43, to be acclaimed the Conqueror of the Ocean. " His father, Drusus Germanicus, had sailed past Friesland to visit the Baltic and to search for ' fresh Pillars of Hercules ' : ' our Drusus,' said the Romans, ' was bold enough, but Ocean kept the secret of Hercules and his own.' But now it was feigned that the farthest seas had been brought within the circuit of the Empire. ' The last bars have fallen,' sang the poets, ' and earth is girdled by a Roman Ocean.' ' The world's end is no longer the end of the Empire, and Oceanus turns himself to look on the altars of Claudius.' " [1]

As a province, Britain was never as thoroughly Romanized as Gaul. It never attained the wealth and refinement of Italy. Its architecture was crude compared with that of Rome. Its mosaic floors and wall - decorations lacked the elegance and delicacy of those of Pompeii. It had not the background of eventful history and high culture of many of the eastern provinces : it was a land wrested from nations whom the Romans were pleased to regard as barbarian. In a word, our country contrasted with the heart of the empire, much as some of our less-developed colonies contrast with England and London to-day.

As a study, the Roman era has a peculiarity which distinguishes it from other eras through which our country has passed. Our knowledge of pre-Roman Britain depends almost wholly upon the researches of the archaeologist—he is there supreme.

[1] Elton, *Origins of English History*, p. 307.

On the other hand, the part played by him in the elucidation of medieval times is subsidiary to that played by the historian : he illustrates the statements of history, much as the plates of a book illustrate the text. But the Roman era differs from both. The literary remains relating to Britain are too few and, as a rule, too incidental and ambiguous, for the historian to weave them into a continuous narrative ; whereas the archaeologist has a growing wealth of material to work upon. It is a domain in which neither can dispense with the other ; and in one highly important branch of the study—the inscriptions of tablets, altars, and tombstones—their provinces overlap. Broadly speaking, what we know of Roman Britain is the outcome of the joint labours of the two, and the student who approaches the subject in the capacity of the one will soon find himself compelled by force of circumstances to supplement his conclusions with those of the other.

The researches of the geologist and the statements of early explorers and Roman and later writers converge to indicate how wild a country was Britain at the period of the conquest. The regions under cultivation were but a fraction of the whole, and they lay mostly towards the Continent. Dense forests in which roamed wolves, bears, wild boars, and wild cats and other animals that still survive, alternated with bleak moors and swamps. The atmosphere was more humid and the rainfall heavier, than at present. " The fallen timber obstructed the streams, the rivers were squandered in the reedy morasses, and only the downs and hilltops arose above the perpetual tracts of wood " (Elton). The Domesday Book bears witness to the extensive wastes in its day ; and as recently as the reign of Elizabeth about one-third of England was still in the primeval state of nature. In medieval times the Andreas Wold of the Weald still stretched with few breaks from Kent to Hampshire, and the New Forest may be regarded as its western outlier. To the north of the latter lay the forests of Speen, Savernack, and Selwood ; west-ward were the marshes of Sedgemoor ; and farther to the north-west, between the Severn and the Wye, was the forest of Dean, " great and terrible." In Warwickshire was the forest of Arden, of which it has been said, that " even in modern times a squirrel might leap from tree to tree for nearly the whole length of the county." In Worcestershire was Wyrewood, and stretching from Flintshire to Snowdonia were the forests of Denbigh. The wastes of Peakland, the forests of Sherwood and Elmet, and the marshes of the Humberhead Level, well-nigh shut off Northumbria from the south; while East Anglia was similarly isolated by the Fens, then vastly larger than at present, and by a belt of forests through Cambridgeshire and Hertfordshire. So dense were the forests in earlier times that they, more than other natural features, isolated the British tribes, and even the Roman engineers sometimes found it necessary to swing their roads out of their direct courses to avoid them.

Perhaps even more remarkable are the changes which have affected the configuration of the island since the Roman era. Here, the shore has receded in consequence of the erosive action of the waves, or the depression of the land. There, where the land has risen, or low-lying stretches of silt have been deposited, it has advanced beyond the Roman line. What was a Roman port may have long since succumbed to the encroachment of the sea; or it may now be miles inland. The rivers, too, in their meanderings through alluvial tracts, have wandered from their old courses, and the declining rainfall has reduced their volume.

The map (Fig. 1) presents the physical features of the era; and how these determined the distribution of the civilian population is indicated on the second map (Fig. 2). Here the shading represents the regions of densest population—the regions where towns, villages, and houses abounded—and it roughly coincides with the lowlands except where occupied by forests and marshes. The population and wealth of the country were thus chiefly concentrated in the southern counties from Kent to Devonshire, in the Thames basin, in Essex and the country of the Ouse and Nene, in Somerset and Gloucestershire, and about the lower Severn. This distribution differed remarkably from that of the present, as indicated in our third map (Fig. 3). *Now* the most populated regions are the Metropolitan area; Lancashire and Yorkshire as far east as the Don, with its constellation of large manufacturing towns, Liverpool, Manchester, Preston, Oldham,

Leeds, Bradford, and Sheffield; the southern prolongation of this region from Sheffield to Derby and Nottingham; the

FIG. 1.—Physical Map of Roman Britain, showing the Forests, Marshes, and Elevations exceeding 500 ft.

Potteries; the Birmingham district; Glamorgan and East Monmouthshire; the Bristol district; East Durham; and the belt of country between the Clyde and the Forth, dominated by

Glasgow and Edinburgh. These regions, with the exception of the Metropolitan, are where coal is found, and nearly all these

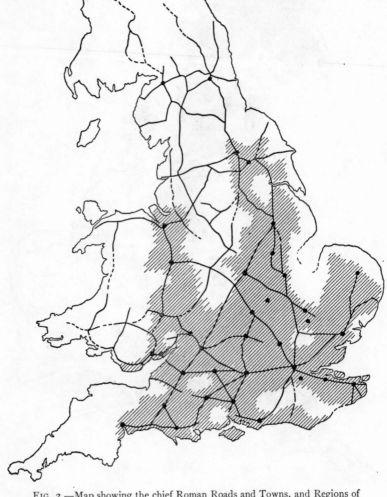

FIG. 2.—Map showing the chief Roman Roads and Towns, and Regions of densest Romanized Population

towns were little more than villages two centuries ago. This shift of population is a modern phenomenon dating from the economic revolution of the 18th century. We are pre-eminently a manufacturing people to whom coal is of vital importance. The Roman-Britons were essentially an agricultural

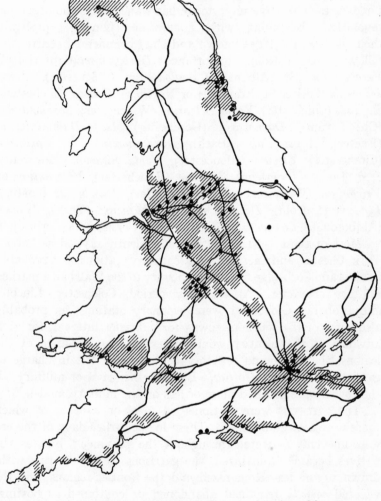

FIG. 3.—Map showing chief Railways, Towns, and Regions of densest
Population at present

people, and the few manufactures they engaged in did not depend upon this fuel, although its use was not unknown ; hence to them the rugged coal-fields were of little value.

The Roman towns, as will be observed on our second map, were with few exceptions confined to the more fertile lowlands and they still remain towns, although, with the exception of London, their relative importance has waned since the economic revolution. Beginning with *Londinium* (London), probably then, as now, the largest town and chief commercial centre, the following were of Roman importance : *Durovernum* (Canterbury), *Verolamium* (St. Albans), *Camulodunum* (Colchester), *Venta Icinorum* (Caister St. Edmunds or Norwich), *Calleva* (Silchester), *Regnum* (Chichester), *Venta Belgarum* (Winchester), *Sorbiodunum* (Old Sarum), *Durnovaria* (Dorchester), *Isca Dumnuniorum* (Exeter), *Aquæ Sulis* (Bath), *Durocornovium* or *Corinium* (Cirencester), *Clevum* (Gloucester), *Venta Silurum* (Caerwent), *Isca Augusta* (Caerleon), *Magnae* (Kenchester), *Viroconium* or *Vriconium* (Wroxeter), *Ratae* (Leicester), *Durobrivae* (Castor), *Lindum* (Lincoln), *Deva* (Chester), *Eburacum* (York), *Isurum* (Aldborough), *Luguvallium* (Carlisle), and *Corstopitum* (Corbridge).

Most of these towns may be conveniently classed as ' civil.' York, Chester, and Caerleon were legionary stations, and probably Carlisle and Corbridge from their vicinity to the Wall had a marked military character. At an early period, Colchester, Lincoln, and probably Gloucester were legionary stations, as probably also some of the southern towns for a briefer interval, for each advance of the frontier would necessitate an advance of the legions, the conquered territory behind being left in charge of garrisons to maintain order. But, whether civil or military, all the towns were planned more or less on the military model.

The garrisons were stationed in forts or *castella*, of which there were a large number. These in the earlier days of the era were unevenly scattered throughout the province ; but, as the natives became Romanized, the garrisons were as a rule withdrawn to the less Romanized and the frontier regions, and the vacated *castella* remained abandoned or continued as posting-stations and developed into small towns. Some of our old towns, as Manchester and Newcastle, were originally Roman *castella*. In later times the garrisons were distributed chiefly in the north, especially along and in the vicinity of the Wall of Hadrian, and on the eastern and southern coasts, to protect the province from external enemies ; hence in these regions the military remains are conspicuous.

The Roman hold upon the country once established, the great works which had in view the development of its natural wealth were immediately put in hand, and chief of these was a magnificent system of durable roads and posting-stations. Under the security of the imperial rule the rural population rapidly increased, and the zenith of prosperity was reached in the Constantine period. The houses of the country squires—spacious, comfortable, and now and again on an almost palatial scale—were a marked feature of the fertile lowlands, each with commodious farm-buildings, and, like the medieval manor-house, the centre of a community of peasantry. Villages there were, and the sites of some have been excavated. That wheat was grown in abundance is indicated by an incident of the 4th century. Agriculture in the Rhenish countries being interrupted by the barbarians, the Emperor Julian arranged for the import of corn from Britain, and no less than 600 vessels were employed for its transit. The rearing of sheep and the manufacture of cloth from the wool were important industries, and contributed to the export trade of the country. British cloth was widely esteemed, and its importation into the East is referred to in an edict of Diocletian.

The mineral resources were early exploited. In the quantity and quality of its lead, Britain stood second to no other province. Its chief mining centres were the Mendips in Somerset, the Peak of Derbyshire, Shropshire, and the district of Holywell in Flintshire, in all of which are extensive ancient workings. More definitely the inscribed pigs of lead, which have been found in and around these regions, bear witness to Roman enterprise. The earliest dated examples show that lead-working was in full swing on the Mendips in A.D. 49, and in Flintshire fifteen years later. The mines were the property of the state and were at first worked by the officials, and subsequently—sometime in the 2nd century—were leased to private individuals. Curious circular pigs of copper with Roman inscriptions prove that this metal was worked in North Wales and Anglesey, apparently at first under the same conditions as lead. Gold was obtained from the quartz rocks near Lampeter in West Wales. Inscribed silver ingots found in London and Richborough, and the remains of a silver-refinery at Silchester testify to the production of that metal, which was probably obtained by the cupellation of copper and lead. There is also evidence that tin was worked in the Roman era in Cornwall, especially in the 3rd and 4th centuries. Iron was used in abundance for a great variety of purposes, and its chief sources were the Forest of Dean and Sussex, where immense deposits of slag bear witness to an enormous output of the metal. Coal was also used, for it has been frequently observed on Roman sites, and coal-pits apparently of Roman age have been noticed at Werneth, Lancashire.

Pottery was manufactured on an extensive scale in the Nen Valley in Northamptonshire, along the south side of the Medway between Sheerness and Chatham, and in and about the New Forest ; and in many other parts of the country have been found the remains of kilns and other evidences of pot-works. Whether the fine wares of the Nen and Medway potteries were exported is uncertain ; but there was a considerable importation of pottery from Gaul and the Rhine, and this included the well-known red-glaze or 'Samian' ware, which is found on almost every Roman site. Traces of glass-works have been noticed at Wilderspool near Warrington. In the production of bronze and silver brooches and other small objects, and in the art of enamelling, the British worker probably excelled his Continental brother ; and in the 4th century, British artisans were engaged upon public works in Gaul on account of their superior skill.

Most of the towns were British *oppida*, remodelled on Roman lines. At Colchester, St. Albans, and Silchester may still be traced the British defences enclosing larger areas than the Roman towns which succeeded them, and we know that these *oppida* were respectively the 'caputs' of the Trinobantes, Catuvelauni, and Atrebates. The Roman names of some other towns, as Venta Belgarum, Isca Dumnuniorum, Venta Icinorum, Venta Silurum, and Isubrigantum (a variant of Isurium), indicate that they were respectively the chief towns of the Belgæ, Dumnonii, Iceni, Silures, and Brigantes.[1] The British *oppidum* was

---

[1] Not necessarily on the sites or within the lines of the British *oppida*.

not a town as we understand the term. It was a fortified tribal camp, but it probably contained a small settled population whose huts tended to cluster round the house of the chief or regulus. The Romans adopted the tribal territory as the unit

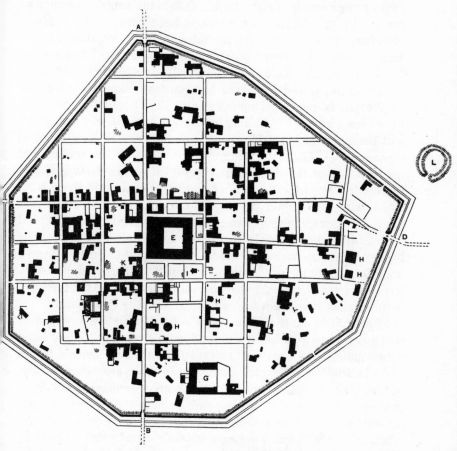

FIG. 4.—Plan of *Calleva Atrebatum*, Silchester

of administration, and with it the tribal capital. Thus was kept up a link with the past, and to this was due in great measure the rapid acquiescence of the natives in the rule of their conquerors. How far the old machinery of administration was modified is uncertain, but undoubtedly it received a Roman form.

The systematic excavations at Silchester, during the last twenty years or more, have afforded an insight into a Romano-British town. Calleva was surrounded with a strong wall, in which were four principal gates and several posterns. Its streets were in two sets cutting one another at right angles, as in many a modern American town. In the centre was a magnificent forum and basilica ; elsewhere, four temples, public baths, a large hospitium, and a small church. Unlike a modern town, as also Pompeii and ancient Rome, its houses were not packed closely together, but were, as a rule, separated by yards and gardens ; and they were of rural type and mostly of a goodly sort. The population probably never reached 3000. Although planned early in the era, there still remained considerable spaces unbuilt upon at its close, and there is no evidence of extramural suburbs. A few trades, and notably that of the dyer, were carried on within the walls, and there were shops for the sale of commodities around the forum, which with little doubt presented an animated scene on market days. Calleva, however, can hardly be called a commercial centre : it rather appeals to one as a residential town. The basilica with its courts and offices was altogether on too large a scale for the municipal needs of so small a place, but probably large enough to have included the administration of the territory —the *Civitas Atrebatum*—of which Calleva was the capital.

Venta Silurum (Caerwent) was a smaller walled town, with two great and two lesser gates, one main street, and many lanes which divided the area into rectangular *insulae*, a central forum and basilica, and a temple. Houses and shops crowded the sides of the main street, many of them with verandas or porticoes that covered the side walks, and behind these were houses, several of a size and sumptuousness such as would befit the officials of the local government and other substantial folk attracted by the social conditions of the local capital. Here an imperfect monument has been unearthed, which was erected *ex decreto ordinis respublica civitatis Silurum*—by order of the senate of the state or canton of the Silures — to an Imperial legate. The forum, basilica, and public baths—an extensive group of buildings—have been opened out on the site of Viroconium (Wroxeter) ; and the exploration of Corstopitum (Corbridge) is bringing to light public and other buildings of unusually strong and good construction.

Britain shared in the religious complexity of the Roman world at large. For this side of our subject we have to rely chiefly upon the testimony of the monuments—especially the inscriptions of altars and tablets—and in less degree upon that of the better-known conditions on the Continent. But as the monuments were mostly raised by the soldiers, who at first were a foreign element in the population, worshipping under the toleration of the empire the gods of their native lands, their testimony is necessarily one-sided. With the conquest came the invocation of the gods of the Græco-Roman pantheon, but many altars are inscribed to deities bearing Celtic and other barbaric names. We know too little of the religions of pre-Roman Britain to estimate how far the latter deities were indigenous and how far imported by the military. As polytheism has unlimited elasticity, these barbaric deities were identified with the Roman. The expansion of the empire favoured syncretism. It brought the subject-peoples into closer touch with one another, and with Roman civilization. The men who were levied in every province officially recognized the Roman state gods and raised altars to their own wherever their lot was cast, and thus the surrounding provincials were familiarized with strange gods and cults, and soon learned to recognize that the same god might be worshipped in different lands under different names. " The altars and images were used indifferently by worshippers under many creeds ; the titles of Jupiter covered gods as far apart as ' Tanarus,' the German thunder-god, and Osiris, ' the nocturnal sun,' who ruled the world of the dead. . . . Apollo represented all bright and healing influences, and under the name of Mars, the soldiers from every province could recognize their local war-god " (Elton). At Bath, Sulis, the nymph-goddess of the hot-springs, was invoked as Sul-Minerva, and in the north, the Celtic Belatucadrus, ' the brilliant-in-war,' as Mars Belatucadrus.

The Roman state worship had little power to satisfy the intellect or to inspire devotion, but it had less when laden with a multitude of new gods and cults ; and this paved the way for the widespread acceptance of various cults of eastern origin, which by their monotheistic strain, their underlying mysticism, and their offer of divine illumination through penitence and expiation, promised a satisfaction which the current paganism failed to give.   Chief among these was Mithraism, of which there are many traces in Britain, and almost as popular was the worship of the Egyptian Isis and of the Great Mother of Phrygia.   These in their turn paved the way for Christianity, itself an eastern religion, which undoubtedly had a firm hold upon Britain before the close of the era, in spite of conflicting evidence.

The map of Roman Britain is in the main the outcome of a comparison of the evidence of the archaeologist with the statements of ancient geographical writers whose works have come down to us.   Five of these works are of special value.   The *Geography* of Claudius Ptolemy, who wrote about the middle of the 2nd century, is mainly a catalogue of places with their latitudes and longitudes, and considering that he had to rely upon the statements of travellers who were not provided with the various instruments that are now considered indispensable, his results remarkably approximate to the truth.   A map of Great Britain compiled from his data is on the whole easily recognized ; but Scotland is curiously turned to the east, and it has been suggested [1] that Ptolemy or a predecessor worked from sectional maps of the British Islands, and inadvertently placed that peninsula the wrong way.   In comparing maps from his tables with the modern, it is necessary to remember that his degrees of longitude are one-sixth less than ours ; also that the degrees are divided into twelfths.   Some of the bays, estuaries, promontories, and cities are easily identified ; and the latitudes and longitudes of others give their approximate positions ; but his blunders and the possibilities of textual corruption must be constantly kept in mind.   The *Peutinger Tablet* is a 13th-century copy (now preserved at Vienna) of a Roman *itinerarium pictum* or pictorial road-chart.   It depicts in diagrammatical form the ancient world, greatly elongated to suit a narrow roll of parchment and to display the roads with panoramic effect, the distances being inserted in

[1] *Archaeologia*, xlviii, p. 379.

numerals ; but unfortunately only the south-east portion of Britain is shown, the extreme left section of the roll being lost. The *Itinerary of the Provinces of Antoninus Augustus* is a list of roads, or more strictly routes, giving the names of places upon them and their distances apart. In the British section, fifteen routes are given, most of which can be identified by existing remains. Its title connects it with one of the four emperors who bore the name of Antoninus (A.D. 138–222). The *Notitia Dignitatum* is an official register or calendar of the civil and military establishments of the empire, and is a document of high historical value. Its topographical information is incidental, consisting mainly of the names of the places where the garrisons were stationed, forty-six of which are given in the portion relating to Britain. This return appears to have been drawn up about the beginning of the 5th century. The *Ravenna Chorography* was the production of an anonymous writer of the 7th century, who described the world, which he regarded as extending from India to Britain, with much rhapsody and appeal to Scripture. In the British section he enumerates the various cities, rivers, islands, etc., probably taken from some Imperial road-chart like the Peutinger Tablet, but he gives them in little apparent order, and his spelling is very corrupt.

In these works over five hundred names of towns, stations, bays, promontories, and rivers are given ; but probably not more than a seventh or eighth have been located with any degree of certainty. This is owing to three chief defects—the ambiguity of the writers, their blunders, and the corruption of their text in its transmission to us. Many of the names lack any hints as to their whereabouts ; and the whereabouts of others—and this represents the majority—are vague. We can assign, for instance, a series of names to a certain region, but beyond this we cannot go. The archaeologist may point out a number of sites in that region, but we have no means of identifying the several names with the several places. Textual corruption is responsible for such vagaries in the spelling of the names that the collation of the various lists presents insurmountable difficulties. Still, the data supplied by these writers are of inestimable value.

The modern bibliography of Roman Britain is very copious. From Camden downwards, the remains have engaged the continuous attention of antiquaries, and never more critically than during the last half-century. For reasons already given, it is hardly possible to pursue the archaeological side of Roman Britain without invading that of the historian, consequently the works that are wholly confined to one or the other province are comparatively few. A full list of the works that are especially useful to the archaeologist would greatly exceed our space, but a short notice of some of the more important will be helpful to the beginner. It is almost unnecessary to say that some which will be referred to are both costly and difficult to obtain. Still, most of them are to be found in our chief provincial libraries, and if these fail, there remains that *dernier ressort* of the literary man, the British Museum Library.

The *Archaeologia* of the Society of Antiquaries, and the *Journals* of the Archaeological Institute and of the British Archaeological Association, are grand repositories of papers on Roman Britain; as also are some of the publications of the provincial societies. The *Index of Archaeological Papers* from 1665 to 1890, and its annual continuations from the latter date, published under the direction of the Congress of Archaeological Societies in union with the Society of Antiquaries, places the student *en rapport* with this valuable source of information. The late Charles Roach Smith's *Collectanea Antiqua*, 1848–80, contains many important articles on the subject.

The works that treat of Roman Britain in general are few. Foremost among them is Horsley's *Britannia Romana*, a valuable conspectus of knowledge at its date, 1732, and still a useful book of reference. The last edition of Wright's *The Celt, the Roman, and the Saxon* is useful, but is disappointing in some respects. Scarth's *Roman Britain*, 1885, is also disappointing; and its successor, Conybeare's *Roman Britain*, 1903, leans more to history. The Roman section of Traill's *Social England*, 1902–4, should be carefully studied. The following are useful works of reference—Stukeley's *Itinerarium Curiosum*, 1776; Gough's *Camden's Britannia*, 1789; King's *Munimenta Antiqua*, 1799–1806; the *Gentleman's Magazine*

Library (Romano-British Remains), 1887 ; and Clark's *Military Architecture in England*, 1884. Among the many works which treat wholly or partially on Roman Britain, but less from an archaeological point of view, the following may be especially mentioned—Elton's *Origins of English History*, 1889 ; Coote's *Romans of Britain*, 1878 ; Petrie, Sharpe, and Hardy's *Historica Britannica*, 1848 ; Mommsen's *Provinces of the Empire*, 1886 ; Babcock's *Two Last Centuries of Roman Britain*, 1891 ; Bury's *Gibbon's Decline and Fall of the Roman Empire*, 1896 ; Rhys' *Celtic Britain*, 1904; Hogarth's *Authority and Archaeology*, 1899 ; Oman's *England before the Conquest*, 1910. The works that treat of some particular phase of Romano-British archaeology are more numerous. Hubner's *Inscriptiones Britanniae Latinae*, which forms a volume of his great and costly work on the epigraphy of the empire, is of such importance that no reference library can be said to be complete without it. For inscriptions overlooked or discovered since its date, 1873, recourse must be had chiefly to the papers of the late Mr. Thompson Watkin and subsequently to those of Dr. Haverfield, in the *Archaeological Journal*. McCaul's *Notes on Roman Inscriptions, found in Britain*, 1862, is useful, but scarce. Morgan's *Romano-British Mosaic Pavements*, 1886, the only manual on the subject, contains much information, but fails to attain the promise of its opening paragraphs. Lyson's costly *Reliquae Britannicae Romanae*, 1813–15, and other works, including his *Woodchester*, 1797, are noteworthy for their sumptuous plates of mosaics ; as also is Fowler's scarce series of twenty-six plates. The roads are the subject of Codrington's *Roman Roads of Britain*, 1905, and of Forbes and Burmeister's *Our Roman Highways*, 1904, two useful and inexpensive books.

But the largest, and on the whole the most important element in the bibliography, is the topographical literature. The Wall and its contiguous Roman remains have been and are still a fertile theme of inquiry. Warburton's *Vallum Romanum*, 1753, was the first important monograph on the subject. Bruce's *Roman Wall*, of which there have been several editions, the last and largest, that of 1867, being one of the chief descriptive works on English archaeology ever produced, but naturally some of its conclusions are rendered untenable by recent researches. His *Handbook to the Roman Wall*, the last edition of which was revised by Mr. Robert Blair, F.S.A., is essentially an abridgement. Maclauchlan's great works, *The Roman Wall*, with its *Memoir*, 1858, and his *Eastern Branch of the Watling Street in Northumberland*, 1864, are especially noteworthy for their engraved plans. Hodgson's *History of Northumberland* is a mine of valuable information, and the volume treating on the Roman remains was published separately under the title of *The Roman Wall and South Tindale*, 1841. Neilson's *Per Lineam Valli* is one of the best of the more recent works, 1891. Hutton's *History of the Roman Wall*, 1802, is worth mentioning for its quaint and gossipy reading. Dr. Haverfield's *Reports on the Five Years' Excavations on the Roman Wall*, conducted by the Cumberland and Westmorland Archaeological Society, 1894–99, can be obtained as reprints with a summary, and are valuable for the new light thrown on the history of the Wall. Dr. Budge's *Roman Antiquities in the Chesters Museum*, 1903, is more than a catalogue : it contains chapters on the whole subject of the Wall.

Scotland has given rise to several important works—Gordon's *Itinerarium Septentrionale*, 1726 ; Roy's *Military Antiquities of the Romans in North Britain*, 1793, which is particularly valuable for its large plans of camps ; Stuart's *Caledonia Romana*, 1845 ; and the *Antonine Wall Report*, an account of the excavations made by the Glasgow Archaeological Society, 1899. The *Proceedings* of the Society of Antiquaries, Scotland, contain reports on the exploration of Scottish Roman forts, and Curle's *Roman Fort of Newstead*, shortly to be published, promises to be a highly important work.

Lancashire and Cheshire are fortunate in the late Thompson Watkin's *Roman Lancashire* and *Roman Cheshire*, two thorough works on their Roman remains up to the years of their issues, 1883 and 1886. Whitaker's *History of Manchester*, 1773, devotes much space to these remains in the vicinity of that city. Roeder's *Roman Manchester*, 1900, and Bruton's *Roman Fort at Manchester*, 1909, bring Whitaker and Watkins up to their dates. Smith and Short's *History of Ribchester* gives much information

of the Roman remains there. The excavations at Wilderspool
are the subject of May's *Warrington's Roman Remains*, 1904.
Roman York is treated on in Drake's *Eboracum*, 1785, and Well-
beloved's *Roman York*, 1812 ; and Aldborough in H. Ecroyd
Smith's *Remains of the Roman Isurium*, 1852. Derbyshire has
yielded *Melandra Castle*, 1906, edited by Prof. R. S. Conway.
Lincoln, considering its Roman importance, has not given rise
to much literature. The Roman city at Wroxeter, Shropshire,
was the theme of several pens in the ' sixties,' and these were
followed by Wright's *Uriconium* in 1872. Gloucestershire and
Somerset, from their richness in remains of this age, have yielded
a considerable output, as Lyson's *Woodchester*, already
referred to ; Bathurst and King's *Roman Remains in Lydney
Park*, 1879 ; Buckman and Newmarch's *Illustrations of Roman
Art in Cirencester*, 1850 ; Beecham's *History of Cirencester and
the Roman City of Corinium*, 1886 ; and Witt's *Map and Archaeological Handbook*, 1880 (?). Bath is treated in Scarth's *Aquae Solis*,
and Lyson's *Two Temples and other Buildings discovered at Bath*,
1802. Monmouthshire was the scene of much archaeological
activity in the middle decades of the last century, and this
resulted in Lee's *Delineations of Roman Antiquities found at Caerleon*,
1845, and *Isca Silurum*, 1862, a well-illustrated catalogue of the
museum there ; and in Omerod's *Memoir of British and Roman
Remains illustrative of Communications with Venta Silurum*, 1852,
and *Strigulensia*, 1861. Ward's *Roman Fort of Gellygaer*, 1903,
is an illustrated report on the exploration of that site in Glamorgan. A. C. Smith's large and detailed map with its accom-
panying *Guide*, 1884, presents the British and Roman remains
of a hundred square miles round Abury in North Wiltshire ;
and this county was the scene of most of the excavations of
General Pitt-Rivers, which are described in his four profusely
illustrated volumes.

Roman in common with other early remains in Dorset are
described in Warne's *Ancient Dorset*, 1872 ; and the mosaic
pavements at Frampton are the subject of one of Lyson's monographs. The Isle of Wight has contributed Nicholson's *Account
of the Roman Villa near Brading*, 1880, and Price's *Description
of Roman Buildings at Morton near Brading*, 1881. The excava-

tions at Silchester during the last twenty-one years have resulted in a series of important reports in *Archaeologia*, most of which may be obtained as reprints.

The Roman coast-forts of Kent and Sussex—Reculvers, Richborough, Lympne, and Pevensey—were ably described by C. Roach Smith, both in his *Collectanea* and in separate works, *Excavations on the Site of the Roman Castrum of Lymne in* 1850, *Excavations at Pevensey in* 1852, and *Antiquities of Richborough, Reculver, and Lymne,* 1850. From the same pen issued *Illustrations of Roman London,* 1859, with many plates. Roman London was also the theme of several well-illustrated monographs by J. E. Price—*Description of the Roman Tesselated Pavement found in Bucklersbury,* etc., 1870 ; *Roman Antiquities discovered on the site of the National Safe Company's Premises,* 1873 ; *On a Bastion of London Wall,* 1880. Various excavations at and in the vicinity of Chesterford and Audley End in Essex about the middle of the last century were described by the Hon. R. C. Neville, afterwards Lord Braybrook, in his *Antiqua Explorata,* etc., mostly privately printed, and scarce. Much about Roman Colchester is to be found in Strutt's *History and Description of Colchester,* and in Buckler's and in Jenkin's *Colchester Castle,* 1869 and 1877, respectively. The coast-fort of Burgh Castle is the subject of Ive's *Garianonum of the Romans,* 1803 ; and Castor and its Roman potteries are illustrated in Artis's *The Durobrivae of Antoninus,* etc., 1828, now very scarce.

In the *Victoria History of the Counties of England,* descriptive articles on the Roman remains of the following counties have appeared—Berkshire, Buckinghamshire, Derbyshire, Hampshire, Herefordshire, Northamptonshire, Norfolk, Nottinghamshire, Somerset, Staffordshire, Leicestershire, Warwickshire, Worcestershire, and Shropshire. These are all, except one, from the pen of Dr. Haverfield, and are of inestimable value to the student.

We turn now to another important source of information about Roman Britain—museum collections. Most of our museums contain objects of Roman age, and these, as a rule, have been found in the districts of their present resting-places. As might be expected, the chief collections are in or near the sites of the more important Roman towns and populous regions, so that their distribution somewhat coincides with the distribution of the civil and military population. The Romano-British collections of the York Philosophical Society and of the Reading and the Colchester museums are large and varied. That of Reading is mainly derived from Silchester, and its value is enhanced by models of some of the buildings of the ancient city. The exploration of Caerwent has given rise to another important collection, most of which is stored in a temporary museum on the site, the residue being in the Newport Museum. The numerous objects found at Wroxeter are in the Shrewsbury Museum, and those found at Bath, Caerleon, and Cirencester are in the museums of these places, all being important collections. The City of London has been fruitful in finds of Roman age, and most of these have gravitated to the Guildhall Museum. The British Museum collection is not so large as would be expected, but it contains many rare objects from various parts of the country. The Grosvenor Museum, Chester, is notable for its tombstones and other lapidary remains, and these are also a conspicuous feature in the Leicester Museum. In the Wall country are three important collections, those of Tullie House at Carlisle, of the Blackgate Museum at Newcastle-on-Tyne, and of the Chesters Museum, the last being a model of good arrangement and exhibition. The notable feature of the collection of the National Museum of Antiquities at Edinburgh is the finds from the exploration of Roman forts and other sites in Scotland.

Besides the museums just named, those of South Shields, Warrington, Taunton Castle, Bristol, Maidstone, Devizes, Gloucester, Cardiff, Canterbury, Dorchester, Chichester, St. Albans, Oxford, Sheffield, Hull, Norwich, Durham, and some others contain Romano-British collections of greater or less interest.

CHAPTER II

ROADS, BRIDGES, FORDS, AND MILESTONES

WITH comparatively few exceptions, the indications of a Roman road can only be appreciated by the experienced eye. A slight rise here, a hollow there, a difference in the colour of the herbage, or, in the absence of these, a length of road still used, a hedgerow, or a parish boundary which coincides with the conjectured line—*these* are the hints from which the archaeologist puzzles out the course of a Roman road. But if these roads are regarded as a whole—as a network of communications—no remains impress us more with the thoroughness of the masters of the ancient world and their high sense of organization. They are more akin to our railways than to our country roads, except such as happen to perpetuate a Roman course or to be the product of a modern engineer. They exhibit, too, in their distribution, their relation to the country at large, and their directness, the impress of a single authority, imperial in its comprehensiveness. We cannot conceive that the semi-isolated British tribes could ever have elaborated such a road-system ; on the other hand, this system, once established, must have powerfully operated in breaking down their mutual antipathies and hastening their acceptance of Roman rule. These roads represent the most useful of the great works raised by the conquerors, and they are the most enduring in their effects ; indeed, it can scarcely be doubted that our island never possessed finer roads, until the revival of road engineering under Telford and his contemporaries in the reign of George III.

Many of our Roman roads are still used, but these rarely show signs of their Roman origin beyond certain peculiarities of their courses, which will be referred to later. Many, on the

other hand, fell out of use at an early period, probably owing
to the changed conditions brought about by the English conquest.
These disused roads have in a wholesale manner been levelled
by the plough and plundered of their materials ; but in most
counties of England and Wales there are fragments that have
escaped.   If Nature may have been unkind to these fragments—
if the roots of trees have loosened their structure and the moisture
of the ground has softened their concretes—she also has gently
buried them under a protective mantle of vegetable mould.
Thus buried they continue, sometimes as perfect in form as
when they were abandoned.

These intact roads usually show as low, rounded ridges,
varying from a few inches to a foot or more in height and from
15 to 30 ft. in width ; but these limits are sometimes not reached,
or are exceeded.   For instance, the Erming Street in Lincolnshire and the East Riding, the road from Silchester to Bath,
and the 'Achling Ditch' between Old Sarum and Badbury
Rings, occasionally attain a height of 5 ft. or even more.
On the other hand, the ridge may be so low as to be scarcely
discernible.   The actual roadway is rarely seen, as it is usually
covered with turf, and as this is generally thinner on the summit
than at the sides, it has the effect of softening the contour and
reducing the relative height.   Another feature may sometimes
be noticed—side ditches.   These, in rare instances, retain much
of their original size ; but usually they are so far obliterated
as to show only as gentle and ill-defined hollows, less apparent
in themselves, than in their effect of accentuating the relief
of the ridge.

The structure varies greatly, even in the same road.   It may
be anything from a mere spread of gravel on the old natural
surface to a causeway of Vitruvian complexity.   The differences
of construction are not susceptible to any satisfactory classification.   We know that there were various kinds of roads—*viae
militares, viae vicinales, viae agrariae,* etc.—and maintained in
different manners ; but we cannot say whether these were distinguished by any peculiarities of form and construction.   No
doubt the art of road-making underwent some change during
the centuries of Roman rule.   No doubt, also, the by-ways were

less carefully and strongly constructed than the principal thoroughfares.   But it is certain that the chief cause of structural differences
lay in the nature of the materials used.   The ancient road-makers
depended, with rare exceptions, upon materials near at hand,
and as these varied considerably, the mode of construction varied
also.   The differences are more noticeable in the treatment of
the surface than in the under-structure.   Where hard or massive
rocks abound, paved or pitched roads preponderate ; whereas in
other districts, especially those of cretaceous or tertiary formation,
gravelled roads are the rule.

The ' Fen Road,' which threads Fenland from east to west,
is an example of simple construction.   Dugdale described it as
" a long causey made of gravel about three feet in thickness and
sixty feet broad, now covered with the moor, in some places three
and in others five feet thick." [1]   The road between Badbury and
Poole Harbour in Dorset is similar.   Near Corfe Hills, it consists
of gravel, $1\frac{1}{2}$ ft. thick and 18 ft. wide at the base, resting on the
old heath.   Sometimes the gravel was mingled with larger
stones, as in a road cut through at Manchester in 1765, which
was $4\frac{1}{2}$ ft. thick and 42 ft. wide.[2]   In chalky districts, the roads
were often of chalk and flints mixed together, as the ridge of
the Watling Street on Barham Down, described by Dr. Stukeley.[3]
More often the finer materials rest on a platform or foundation
of large stones.   The Watling Street near Rugby, for instance,
has 3 ft. of gravel on a layer of large cobbles laid on the clayey
subsoil.[4]   A section of the Akeman Street at Woodstock, in 1898,
presented a ridge 17 ft. wide with a small ditch on either side,
which was constructed of two well-defined layers—a lower, 10 in.
thick of Stonesfield slates naturally split and laid sloping in the
direction of the road with a few placed flat on the top, and an
upper, of 6 in. of the local gravel.[5]

Two cuttings made by the late General Pitt-Rivers across
the Roman road between Old Sarum and Badbury at Bokerly
Dyke in 1889, indicated a more complex structure.   The
second section shown in Fig. 5 presents a central agger with a

---

[1] *History of Imbanking and Draining*, p. 174.
[2] *History of Manchester*, i, p. 120.   [3] *Itin. Curiosum*, p. 127.
[4] Codrington, *Roman Roads*, p. 73.   [5] *Proc. Soc. Antiquaries*, xvii, p. 333.

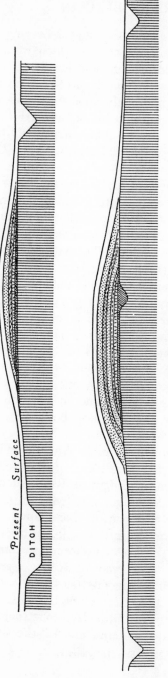

BOKERLY DYKE

MURAL ROAD AT WHITE CROSS

FIG. 5.—Sections of Roman Roads at Bokerly Dyke, Dorset, and at White Cross, Cumberland.   (6 ft. to 1 in.)

convex summit, 25 ft. 6 in. wide at the base and between 3 and 4 ft. high in the middle, between two ditches which were not visible before excavation, the width over all being 87 ft. The agger was constructed as follows : Upon a spread of nodular flints, about 3 in. thick and resting directly upon the old natural surface, were laid, in ascending order, 6 in. of rammed chalk, 10 in. of gravel, 6 in. of rammed chalk rubble, and finally 6 in. more of gravel, the last forming to actual road-surface. Over this had accumulated 5 in. of humus.[1]

Some drainage operations at Strood, Rochester, in 1897, disclosed a fine section of the Watling Street, which presented, in addition to a similar stratified structure to the last, the unusual feature of a timber foundation. The land here was formerly a marsh, and in order to provide a suitable bottom, the Roman engineers first drove two rows (14 ft. apart, the width of the intended road) of stout oak piles into the mud, and spanned the intervening space with timber beams. Upon the platform thus formed, were deposited the following : 3 ft. 6 in. of large pieces of flint and Kentish rag with a few broken tiles ; 5 in. of rammed chalk ; 7 in. of finely broken flints ; 9 in. of small pebble gravel and earth, rammed ; and finally the pavement of Kentish rag in irregular pieces, and jointed together with fine gravel. This pavement had worn wheel-tracks, a single one on one side, and three close together on the other, the outermost being 6 ft. 3 in. distant from the first.[2]

Examples of road-structure might be multiplied indefinitely, but we must further consider the treatment of the surface. That of the Roman equivalent of Edgware Road, London, which was cut through a few years ago, was found to consist of large nodular flints laid with their smooth faces upwards on a bed of rammed gravel, and grouted into a rock-like mass, the whole being about 24 ft. wide. Such roads were not uncommon where flints were obtainable. We read of roads elsewhere being paved with boulders, cobbles, moor-stones, etc. Others are better described as pitched. The surface of the Foss Way near Ilchester was, according to Dr. Stukeley, constructed of flat quarried stones laid edgeways, and resembled " the side of

[1] *Excavations*, iii, p. 74.   [2] *Proc. Soc. Antiquaries*, 2, xviii, p. 36.

a wall fallen down." [1] A mile west of Ponty、 ɔol is a small Roman road, the pitching of which is of the local Pennant grit packed on edge, like the granite settings of our street-crossings (Fig. 6, C).[2]

Others again, as indicated above, were metalled with gravel ; but it is probable that in some cases the gravel was the agglomerate of concrete, the limy constituent of which has perished. In other cases, the fine superficial material may be the bedding from which paving or pitching has been stripped. From many of our Roman roads the surface stones have been removed in a wholesale fashion for building purposes.[3]

Where suitable stone abounded, the roads were often confined with kerbs. The military way of the Wall of Hadrian has edgings of large rough stones, as indicated in Fig. 5, a section made in 1894 at White Cross. This road is peculiar in having a double row of large stones bedded in it along the middle, possibly to support a fence to prevent the commingling of troops travelling in opposite directions. The kerbs of the Maiden Way are similar but roughly squared.[4] A neater kerb, and one that would better withstand the thrust of the agger, was a line of flagstones planted on edge in the ground. The road near Pontypool, referred to above, has kerbs of this description ; so also has a Roman road at Blackpool Bridge in the Forest of Dean. This road, which is barely 9 ft. wide, is formed of a rough spread of stones, and the kerbs are supported externally by a row of blocks, as indicated in Fig. 6.[5] Piles occasionally take the place of stone kerbs. A good example occurs near Chats Moss, Lancashire, where the whole structure, consisting of a pavement of large stones, 18 ft. wide, a layer of sand, and a foundation of brushwood, is supported along the sides by stakes driven into the peat below.[6]

In marshy places, the roads sometimes consisted of a ' corduroy ' of oak logs. Such roads have been found near Ambleside and Gilpin Bridge, Westmorland, the latter resting on three longitudinal lines of logs, and kept in position by stakes

[1] Codrington, p. 67.   [2] *Itin. Curiosum*, p. 155.   [3] Personal Observation.
[4] *Cumb. and Westmor. Archaeo. Soc.* xiv, pp. 196, 461.
[5] Personal Observation.   [6] Watkin, *Rom. Lancashire.*

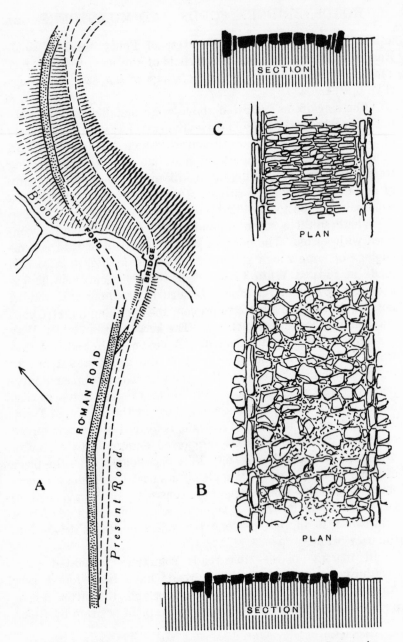

FIG. 6.—Roman Roads.   A and B, Blackpool Bridge ; C, near Pontypool.
(Plan 100 ft., and details 4 ft. to 1 in.)

28

at intervals.[1] The Danes Pad, near Fleetwood, is probably a Roman footpath. It averages 20 in. in width, and is constructed of oak trees sawn asunder and laid end to end—a single piece, if wide enough ; if not, two or more side by side—upon transverse oak sleepers, through which they are pegged into the peat below.[2]

The Roman engineers were careful to give their roads the necessary convexity to ensure the rapid removal of rain-water, and they often, perhaps always, provided side ditches. These were sometimes small and bordered the actual roadway. In other instances, they were large and set back from the road-sides, as at Bokerly Dyke. On the Northern Watling Street, near High Rochester, they are 8 ft. wide and 34 ft. apart. The Roman road between Old Sarum and Badbury, near Vernditch Wood, is 6 ft. high and 16½ ft. wide, and the ditches are 60 ft. apart. Another road on Durdham Down, Clifton, was found a few years ago to be 20 ft. wide between two ditches 50 ft. apart. Even on the same road the distance of the ditches frequently varies. On dry ground, a mere gutter on each side sufficed to carry away the rain-water. On swampy ground, it was necessary to drain not only the agger, but the soil below, and for this purpose the ditches were larger and deeper. Prudence demanded that they should be at some distance, especially if the road was highly raised.

The popular belief that undeviating straightness is the distinguishing mark of a Roman road is not borne out by facts. The Foss Way nearest approaches this condition. Throughout its 200 miles between Lincoln and Axminster it never deviates more than 6 miles from a straight line joining these places. Its gentle sinuosities swing it from time to time across this line, but nowhere do road and line coincide. It provides a remarkably *direct* route, but not a straight one. On the other hand, in the hilly districts where such direct roads would involve impracticable gradients, they are notably winding, as in the case of the Northumbrian Watling Street and the Doctor Gate between Brough and Melandra Castle in Derbyshire. Another example of circuitousness is the Roman road between Lincoln and York. As the crow flies the distance between these places is 55 miles, but

[1] *Proc. Soc. Ant.* xviii, p. 268. [2] *Roman Lancashire.*

in order to avoid the swamps of Humberhead, the road swings inland, and this adds 17 miles to the route.

A characteristic of Roman roads, but one which they share with many other ancient roads, is a decided preference for high rather than low ground, due to the swampy and wooded condition of the valleys at the time. A more characteristic feature is the mode in which the deviations are laid out. In a modern road or railway, this is effected by curves ; in a typical Roman road, by straight lengths forming angles with one another. These angles generally occur on hills or other high landmarks ; less frequently at rivers and stations. Reaching a hill, where there is one of these bends, the spectator may expect the road to make a bee-line for some conspicuous point, be it a hill or a gap in the hills on the horizon. The road there may make a fresh bend, or it may continue in the same line until a suitable point is reached, from which the engineers of old were enabled to determine the next stage of their work.

This predilection for high ground and straight sections may be well studied on the Foss Way between Lincoln and Leicester. As already stated, this road crosses the country diagonally in a singularly direct course, nowhere deviating more than 6 miles from a straight line ; and the greatest deviation occurs in this portion. The road branches from the Erming Street about a mile and a half south of Lincoln, and instead of pointing to its destination approximately south-west by south, it takes a more westerly course, heading straight for Potter Hill, 8 miles away. This hill crests the watershed of the Trent and Witham basins. By this westerly trend, the road avoids the valley of the latter river, which it otherwise would follow for about 18 miles. To avoid the Trent, on the other hand, it now gently swerves somewhat to the south ; but after $6\frac{1}{2}$ miles of straightness, it again has a more westerly trend at Newark in order to reach that river at East Stoke, $2\frac{1}{2}$ miles farther, where a bridge carried a branch-road to the north-west. The road here makes a more decided turn towards the south, in order to gain the high ground behind the east side of the valley. For 8 miles it goes straight ahead, until an eminence near Cropwell is capped, when its course becomes still more southerly. Then after another straight course of $2\frac{1}{2}$ miles, the high ground of Cotgrave Gorse is reached, and here the road attains its maximum divergence from the ideal line. The configuration of the country is now favourable for a return to this line. Availing itself of the stretch of high land between the Devon catchment and that of several small streams which debouch into the Trent to the west, the road takes an $8\frac{1}{2}$ miles' almost due south course, and perfectly straight except for an easterly detour near Willoughby, probably a deviation from its original line. Six Hills, the highest point between Lincoln and Leicester, is then reached. Here a slight westerly bend directs the road more towards the latter city, and at the same time enables it, in its generally descending course to the Soar valley, to take advantage of the spur between the tributaries of that river on the west, and those of the Wreak on the east. After 7 miles of straightness, the Soar is reached at Thurmaston, then another slight westerly deflection directs it to Leicester, 3 miles distant. Throughout this 42 miles of the Foss Way, the road is made up of straight lengths, and the changes in the course take place on the hills and brows, but in no instance at the intervening stations, of which the sites of three are known.

These peculiarities in the setting-out of Roman roads render valuable corroborative service where the actual remains are doubtful ; and in the absence of such remains, will sometimes suggest the probable line. But it should be kept in mind, that the Romans did not always follow so exact a method in the setting-out of their roads as in the example just cited.

The distribution of our Roman roads now claims attention. If three maps of Britain, one showing the principal Roman roads, another the principal modern roads, and the third the railways, are compared, it will be observed that, in each, London is the grand centre from which the chief thoroughfares radiate. Further, it will be observed that many of these arteries follow similar courses on the three maps ; also, that most of the places where the Roman roads intersected—'junctions' in railway parlance—still fulfil the same function in the modern road and railway systems. The generally closer network of the modern communications and the multiplication of towns and villages, indicate a denser population, but the preponderance of the country's traffic still flows along the old lines ; and this in spite of the radical change in the distribution of the population referred to on page 4, and indicated on the maps (Figs. 2 and 3). That our highways should reflect the Roman system is not surprising, for many of them perpetuate Roman lines ; but that the railways should in any appreciable degree reflect that system, may seem extraordinary. The explanation lies in the paramount importance of London and the physical features of the country ; and as both the ancient and modern engineers have in the main followed the lines of least resistance, the results, not unnaturally, are also, in the main, similar. The Pennine Chain furnishes a simple illustration to the point. Both the ancient and the modern engineers have avoided it in their routes to the north. Our Great Northern and North-Eastern Railway route is along the lowlands to the east, through east Yorkshire, Durham, and Northumberland ; while the London and North-Western is through Lancashire, and the basins of the Lune and the Eden which divide the ' chain ' from its more mountainous outlier, the Cumbrian Mountains. The Roman routes were along almost identical lines. In both systems it was necessary to connect east and west by threading some of the transverse valleys of the ' chain.'

A comparison of some of the more important railway routes with the Roman will impress the reader's memory with not only the courses of the chief roads, but also with the places on them.

The Watling Street in its diagonal course across the country through St. Albans (*Verolamium*), Dunstable (*Durocobrivae*), and Towcester (*Lactodorum*), to Chester (*Deva*), may be regarded as the Roman London and North-Western main line, and its ramifications make the analogy all the more striking. Through Chester, the traveller could proceed to Carnarvon (*Segontium*) and the Menai Straits, by a route which the present Irish mail closely follows. Or, he could branch off *en route* for *Viroconium*, our Wroxeter, and there, as his modern representative does at Shrewsbury, ' book ' for Caerleon (*Isca Silurum*), *via* Abergavenny (*Gobannium*), by an almost identical route with present, only Newport would be the destination instead of the ' City of the Legion.' Or, if he wished to go to Scotland, there was a line of road through Lancashire, Westmorland, and Cumberland, which eventually reached the vicinity of Glasgow, by a route singularly prophetic of that traversed by the London and North-Western expresses of to-day. On this route *Breme-tonacum*, our Ribchester, stood for Preston, and Carlisle (*Lugu-vallium*) was the junction, as now, for the Roman ' North-Eastern ' for Newcastle (*Pons Aelii*). Or, again, the traveller could branch off for Manchester (*Mancunium*), either at Chester or a point farther south in the vicinity of Whitchurch, a Roman Crewe. This route continued, would conduct him to York (*Eburacum*), only without the modern detour by Leeds.

Perhaps, however, the traveller would prefer to reach Scotland by the more direct eastern route. Striking due north from London (*Londinium*), by the Erming Street, he would traverse for the first 90 miles a belt of country familiar to the passengers of the Great Northern Scotch expresses of to-day. The Roman, how-ever, bore eastwards to reach Lincoln (*Lindum*), and then by a counter swing crossed the present route at Doncaster (*Danum*), and continued his journey through Aldborough (*Isurium*), Catterick (*Cataracto*), Binchester (*Vinovia*), Corbridge (*Cor-stopitum*), and High Rochester (*Bremenium*), by the Northern Watling Street ; whereas the present expresses take a more easterly course through York and Newcastle.

The Great Western route from London to South Wales was remarkably anticipated. Silchester (*Calleva Atrebatum*) played the part of our Reading, and Speen (*Spinae*), of Swindon. At the second place, the Roman, like the modern traveller, could proceed by a northerly route *via* Cirencester (*Corinium*), and Gloucester (*Clevum*), or by a more direct one *via* Bath (*Aquae Sulis*) and across the Severn, only he negotiated the water by boat instead of tunnel. If he chose the former, he struck a little more inland on the western side of the Channel than the modern railway, and he joined his friends, who preferred the sea-passage, at Caerwent (*Venta Silurum*) ; thence the road threaded Caerleon, Cardiff, Neath (*Nidum*), and Carmarthen (*Maridunum*), much as the South Wales section of the Great Western Railway does to-day.

The Great Eastern perpetuates the Roman road from London

to Norwich, and as far as Colchester (*Camulodunum*) no railway more closely hugs an ancient route ; but the important Peddars Way, which connected Colchester with the north-west angle of Norfolk near Hunstanton, is quite unrepresented in the East Anglian railway system. The Foss Way, it may also be remarked, is another important Roman route which is similarly unrepresented.

The Watling Street, east of London, like its modern representative the London Chatham and Dover Railway, was the great highway for Continental traffic, and then, as now, Canterbury (*Durnovernum*) was the point whence branches radiated to east Kent ports, Dover (*Portus Dubris*) for one. The Stane Street from London to Chichester (*Regnum*), and Porchester, is tolerably well represented by the London and South-Western through Guildford and Petersfield.

Silchester was one of the most important ' junctions ' in the Roman road system. Having reached it, as indicated above, the traveller could turn southwards and proceed to Winchester (*Venta Belgarum*) and Southampton (*Clausentum*), just as the present railway passenger from Reading ; or he could proceed in a south-west direction through Old Sarum (*Sorbiodunum*) and Dorchester (*Durnovaria*) to Exeter (*Isca Dumnuniorum*) by a route almost as direct as our London and South-Western Railway.

The Midland Railway is less reminiscent of Roman communications ; but one limb of its X roughly coincides with the Rykneld Street through Worcester, Birmingham, Little Chester near Derby (*Derventio*), and Chesterfield, York-wards ; while the Derby and Manchester section of the other limb represents the Roman road between these places through Buxton whose warm springs were frequented, as at present.

FORDS AND BRIDGES

In a well-watered country as ours, fords and bridges must have been numerous, but remains of few have survived. The Roman fords were submerged portions of the roads, only more strongly constructed so as to resist the scour of the water. A good example

—perhaps the best of any—was one across the Trent at Little-borough near Lincoln, which was removed as a hindrance to navigation in 1820. It consisted of a pavement of large squared stones, the whole being kept in place between two rows of piles, which carried horizontal beams to serve as kerbs.[1] Dr. Stukeley mentions a ford on the Foss Way across the Ivel at Ilchester, and another across the Ebble at Bemerton near Old Sarum, both strongly paved.[2] Another paved ford, 20 ft. wide, crossed the Calder on the Roman road between Manchester and Ilkley.[3]

Although many small bridges are popularly regarded as Roman, very few of these appear to be so ancient. A small and narrow bridge of a single semicircular arch over the Cock near Tadcaster and on a Roman road to that place, was regarded as Roman by the late Mr. Roach Smith. Of Roman bridges of greater magnitude and importance, there are undoubted remains of several. Those of one over the North Tyne at Chollerford are noteworthy.[4] It was of four spans, and probably of timber, resting upon piers and abutments of fine and massive masonry, the length between the abutments being 184 ft. The existing masonry encloses the remains of a narrower and earlier bridge, possibly the work of Hadrian. When the ancient bridge over the Tyne at Newcastle was demolished in 1771, it was found that the medieval builders had availed themselves of portions of the piers of an older and Roman structure. Another Roman bridge, about 462 ft. long, with eleven waterways, crossed the Tyne at Corbridge, and its remains were examined and surveyed a few years ago. A Roman timber bridge on stone piers is known to have crossed the Nen near Caistor ; and the old timber and stone bridge at Caerleon, which was destroyed about a century ago, is said to have been Roman. Some remains of a timber bridge buried in silt at Wallasey near Birkenhead were regarded as Roman by the late Mr. Thompson Watkin. The plan of the Roman road at Blackpool Bridge (Fig. 6) presents an interesting example of a small road which crossed a brook by a ford and a bridge, of neither of which, however, are any traces left.

[1] *Arch. Journ.* xliii, p. 12.   [2] *Itin. Curiosum*, p. 154.   [3] Codrington, p. 108.
[4] For detailed particulars of bridges, see *Romano-British Buildings and Earth-works*, chap. ix.

The ford was the older, and subsequently a loop-road was made which crossed the brook by a bridge, the present bridge being on the site of the ancient one.

MILESTONES

The chief roads of Britain, as elsewhere, were equipped with milestones (*miliaria*). The Roman mile was 1000 paces, hence its name *mille passuum* (usually abbreviated to M.P.), and the pace was 5 ft.,[1] so that the mile was 5000 ft. It was thus considerably shorter than our mile, thirteen of the one being roughly equivalent to twelve of the other. The typical Roman milestone was a cylindrical shaft of stone about 6 ft. high, but square shafts were not uncommon in this country, and not seldom rough moor-stones of suitable sizes and shapes were used for the purpose. They were usually inscribed. The normal inscription set forth the name and titles of the reigning emperor, the number of miles, and the name of the place from which they were reckoned ; but one or both of the latter details were often omitted. The inscription is no evidence of the age of the road to which the stone appertained. On the so-called ' Via Julia ' in South Wales, for instance, *miliaria* to Diocletian have been found, yet the road was in existence at least one hundred and fifty years before his time ; and examples are known of old inscriptions replaced by those of later emperors.

In the British Museum, there is a good example of a cylindrical *miliarium* found at Rhiwiau Uchaf, near Conway, with the following inscription :—

IMP. CAES. TRAI
ANUS. HADRIANUS
P.P. COS III.
A KANOVIO
M.P. VIII.

' To the Emperor Caesar Trajan Hadrian, Father of his country, Consul for the third time. From Conovium, eight miles.' Another of similar form in the Leicester Museum was found on the Foss

[1] The Roman foot was a trifle less than the English, being about 11·65 of our inches.

Way two miles from that town, in 1771.   The inscription is
partially effaced :—

IMP. CAES.
DIV. TRAIANI PARTH. F. D(IV. NERV.)
TRAIAN. HADRIAN. (AUG. P.P. TRIB.)
POT. COS. III. A RATIS
II.

These two examples indicate how milestones sometimes prove
or corroborate the Roman names of places.   Caerhûn, near
Conway, and Leicester have long been identified as the Roman
Conovium and *Ratae* respectively, and these milestones found in
their vicinities confirm the identification.

A milestone found at Castleford about 1880 is an example
of a reinscribed one.   It was first inscribed to Decius Trajan,
and then was inverted under his successors, the joint emperors,
Gallus and Volusianus, and inscribed to them at the opposite end.

CHAPTER III

MILITARY REMAINS

CAMPS—FORTS—THE NORTHERN WALLS

THE military remains may be divided into ' temporary ' and ' permanent.' To the former division belong the various field-works raised during campaigns, whether to hold an army during a halt of a few days or to serve as its winter quarters, or a small detachment of the same charged with keeping open communications with its base, guarding some point of strategic importance, or affording protection to labourers engaged in road-making. To the latter division belong the great legionary centres of York, Chester, and Caerleon, the numerous stations of the garrisons which maintained order and defended the frontiers, and the great frontier lines of Hadrian and Pius ; and to these may be added the walls of towns. Broadly speaking, the works of the one set are distinguished by their slight construction, often so slight as to be scarcely discernible, and by the absence of buildings within their defensive lines ; whereas those of the other set rank among the most conspicuous and notable remains of Roman Britain.

I. CAMPS [1]

As the visible remains of Roman entrenched fieldworks are comparatively few and little is known of them, it will be helpful to hear what Roman writers have to say about the art of castrametation.

Two writers, whose works have come down to us, are pre-

---

[1] For more detailed particulars, see *Romano-British Buildings and Earthworks*, chap. i.

eminent for the fulness of their descriptions of Roman camps :
Polybius, the friend of the younger Scipio, in the second century
before our era, and the author of a treatise, *De Munitionibus
Castrorum*, who is usually called Hyginus, and who flourished
about the close of the 2nd century. The camp of Polybius
was simple and symmetrical (Fig. 7). The site being selected,

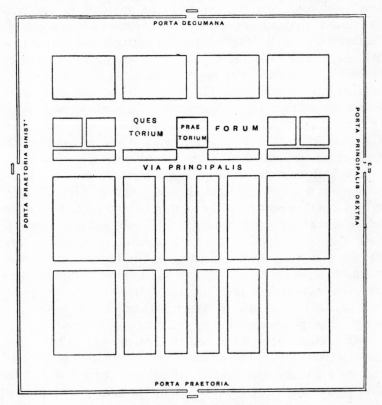

FIG. 7.—Plan of Polybian Camp

the position of the general's tent was fixed, and from this the
whole plan was developed. Through this point a line—the
decumanus maximus—was drawn, and at a certain distance it
was crossed by another—the *cardo maximus*—at right angles.
These served as the base-lines from which the general outline
and internal divisions were determined. The resultant figure

was a square, 2150 Roman feet each way, bisected in its ' length ' into two equal divisions by the *decumanus maximus*, and in its ' depth ' into two unequal divisions by the transverse *cardo maximus*. Along these lines ran the two chief thoroughfares, each passing through the rampart. The transverse thoroughfare was known as the *via principalis*, and the great square of the *praetorium*, containing the general's tent, occupied the middle of its side next the back of the camp. This square necessarily broke the continuity of the longitudinal thoroughfare, and that portion between it and the front of the camp was known as the *via pretoria*. A number of by-ways contributed to divide up the interior into rectangular plots for the tents, and around all, within the rampart, was a clear space or *intervallum*, 200 ft. wide, to facilitate the drawing up of the troops in marching order. The rampart itself was usually formed of the upcast from the ditch which constituted the outer defensive work.

Polybius mentions neither the number nor the names of the gates ; but it may be incidentally gathered from Livy and other writers that they were normally four, and were known as the *portae principales* (*dextra* and *sinistra*), the *porta praetoria*, and the *porta decumana* or *questoria*. Such a camp as described above was for a consular army consisting of two legions, and if there was need for two of these armies to be encamped within the same lines, Polybius directs that two such camps should be applied back to back with the intervening ramparts suppressed, the result being an oblong enclosure with six gates.

When the treatise attributed to Hyginus was written, some three centuries later, the military system had greatly changed, and, as might be expected, the Hyginian camp reflected the altered conditions. To us, this form of camp is of peculiar interest, as our Roman camps and forts are more akin to it than to that of Polybius. The Hyginian camp (Fig. 8) agreed substantially with that of Polybius. The chief differences were its oblong form with rounded corners, the narrower *intervallum*, the elongated praetorial space, and the altered disposition of the troops and smaller space they occupied, the last being all the more significant of the altered *status* of the common soldier under the empire, for while the number of men was nearly double, the accommodation for the officers had increased three-fold. The two transverse roads divided the Hyginian camp into three segments—the *praetentura* to the front, the *retentura*

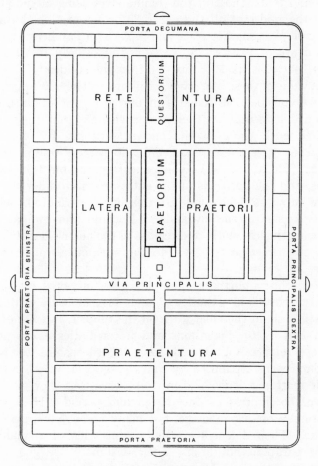

FIG. 8.—Plan of Hyginian Camp

to the back, the middle space being the *praetorium* and its *latera*, in which were quartered the general and his chief officers.

In a graphic sketch of a Roman camp, Josephus describes " the towers at regular distances " ; the four gates, " one at every side of the circumference," wide enough for " the entrance of the beasts " and " for making excursions if occasion should require " ; the rampart like a wall ; and " the engines for throwing arrows and darts, and for slinging stones." Within are streets and tents, those of the commanders being in the middle, and in the midst of all the general's own tent, " in the nature of a temple " ; a market-place and " place for handicraft trades," and a court of justice. So rapidly and orderly is all accomplished that it is like " a city built on the sudden ! "

The value of these literary descriptions will be best appreciated when we consider the remains of our forts, for in the case of our camps it is only in their defensive lines that they can be compared with those of the ancient writers. In some cases the agreement is close : more often it is more or less remote. A few exceed the sizes of Polybius and Hyginus, but the majority are less, and the positions of the gates are often different. The remains of these field-works are unevenly distributed, being of rare occurrence in the lowlands of England and comparatively frequent in the less cultivated regions of the north—a distribution due in some measure at least to the unequal advance of agriculture.

About thirty northern examples were surveyed by General Roy a century and a half ago, and his elaborate plates and notes still remain the chief work on the subject, in spite of some inaccuracies as to dimensions and uncertainties as to details. Of these, eighteen scattered from Aberdeenshire to Northumberland were attributed by him to Agricola, whether rightly so little matters : it is sufficient to observe that they all appear to have the impress of one design and period. These camps are normally oblong in shape, but many are oblique, and some irregular. Their defences are slight, consisting of a small rampart or parapet and ditch. Their entrances are guarded by straight traverses—a characteristic of the Polybian camp, and their number, as shown on the plates, range from one in the smaller camps, to four, five, or six in the larger. But a comparison of their positions leaves little room for doubt that in all, except the smallest, the original number was six, one at each end, and two on each side (A, B, Fig. 9). The six entrances recall the double Polybian camp—the two consular camps

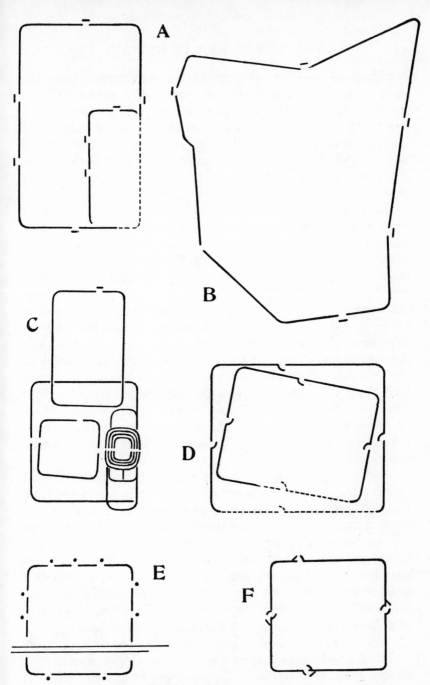

FIG. 9.—Plans of Roman Camps.   A, Towford ; B, Raedykes ; C, Chew Green ;
D, Pigwn ; E, Rey Cross ; F, Dealgin Ross.   (Approx. 800 ft. to 1 in.)

43

combined in one—but they could not have arisen from the same cause, as some of these camps are vastly smaller than the double Polybian. The sizes vary greatly. Three range from 116 to 130 acres each ; one is of 86 acres ; seven range from 50 to 58 acres ; and the rest from 6 to 42 acres. Since Roy's day more of these ' Agricolan ' camps have been noted. There are about eight in the vicinity of the Wall of Hadrian, and two of these near Haltwhistle Burn were trenched in 1908.

Leaving out certain small posts, the other camps described by Roy are of smaller sizes than most of the above, more symmetrical and as a rule of stronger construction, but they especially differ in their entrances. In several they are apparently simple unguarded openings ; but in most they are covered by curved guards or traverses, joined to the rampart at one end (D and F), the advantage of this arrangement being that the defenders on the traverse were not isolated, but could pass at will from the rampart. Some of the camps have four entrances, and the smaller have three or two. But three are remarkable for their number and distribution, a camp at Rey Cross in Westmorland (E),. for instance, having apparently eleven, three on three sides and two on the fourth, and another at Birrenswark, three on one side and one on each of the others. A precisely similar arrangement to the last may be seen in a large camp at Ratby in Leicestershire.

A camp on a well-chosen site was likely to be reoccupied by the army on its return or by another marching along the same line. If, however, the second comers were more numerous or fewer than the first, the general rule was to make a new camp. The smaller of two camps at Pigwn in Breconshire is within the larger, and it is hard to understand why two sides of the larger were not utilized for the smaller, as in A. A curious example is at Ardoch, where two camps intersect one another, and the constructors of the second, whichever it was, did not trouble to level those portions of the first which lay within its lines.

General Roy gives plans of a number of small strongly entrenched posts ranging from about 60 to 160 ft. square, and mostly with one entrance. Several are associated with his ' Agricolan ' camps ; others appear to be quite isolated. From

their strength—they all have several ditches—it is reasonable
to think that they were intended for a more or less protracted
occupation. That their use was to keep open communications
between the army in the field and its base and to overawe the
conquered territory, is equally reasonable.

There is a good example of the Roman adoption and modification of a native camp at Hod Hill in Dorset. The Romans
cut off a rectangular portion within the north-west corner,
utilizing the old lines for the north and west sides, and completing
the enclosure by their own, on the south and east. The remains
were partially destroyed many years ago, when many Roman
relics were found, including coins ranging from Augustus to
Trajan.

II. FORTS

We now tread upon firmer ground. The sites of the garrison
stations are usually well-defined and easily recognized. The
ridges of their ramparts, whether of earth or of built-stone,
are frequently conspicuous. The ditches are rarely filled to
such a degree that their hollows are not visible. The positions
of the gates generally show as breaks in the continuity of the
ramparts. If the interiors have not been subjected to the
plough, the lines of the chief thoroughfares and the sites of the
buildings may often be traced ; and now and again these surface-
indications may be sufficiently pronounced to admit of plans
showing all the salient features. Their distribution is, as stated
on page 8, uneven. There is evidence that the forts were not
so strongly constructed at first as was customary at a later date.
The coast-forts, as a rule, have certain peculiarities, not wholly
confined to them, however, which represent a departure from
traditional lines and a development in the art of fortification.
One of these peculiarities is the presence of bastions, and for
this reason we will call them ' bastioned forts,' and distinguish
the ordinary type as the ' Hyginian.' This type we will consider
first.

Many sites of forts of the latter type have been system-
atically explored, wholly or in part, during the last quarter of a
century. Four of these are notable for the complete plans

they have yielded,—Housesteads one of the Wall forts, Birrens
in Dumfriesshire, Gellygaer in Glamorgan, and Newstead in
Roxburghshire. These are closely followed by Rough Castle,
Castlecary and Bar Hill on the Antonine Wall, Ardoch in Perth-
shire, Chesters and Great Chesters, two Wall forts, and High
Rochester and Haltwhistle in Northumberland. Excavations

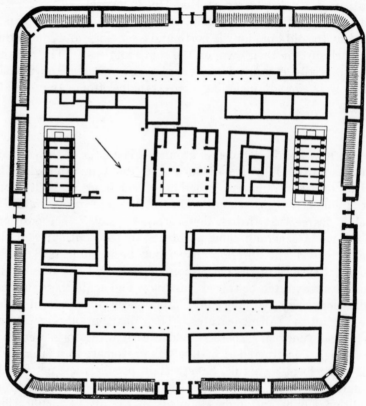

FIG. 10.—Plan of Roman Fort, Gellygaer. (100 ft. to 1 in.)

at Camelon in Stirlingshire, Lyne in Peeblesshire, Birdoswald on
the Wall, Hardknott in Cumberland, Ribchester in Lancashire,
Castleshaw and Elslack in Yorkshire, Wilderspool in Cheshire,
Melandra Castle and Brough in Derbyshire, Caersws in Mont
gomeryshire, and Coelbren in Glamorgan, have yielded less, but
still valuable results. These investigations, as also many on the

Continent, have proved that with the exception of the bastioned forts, the Roman garrison stations were all of one pattern, although differing in details, and that this pattern was substantially that of the Hyginian camp. In fact, we may regard them as translations of that camp into stone or other durable materials, provided they are looked upon as free, and not as literal renderings.

They are symmetrical, usually longer than broad, with the corners rounded off, and four or exceptionally six gates. They have usually one or two ditches, but if one or more sides are more vulnerable than elsewhere, there may be more. Their planning recalls that of the Hyginian camp, presenting two principal streets arranged cross-wise and stretching from gate to gate. The continuity of the longitudinal street is similarly broken by a central building, which has on either side others of diverse shapes, the whole range corresponding with the Hyginian *praetorium* and its *latera*, and similarly dividing the rest of the interior into a *praetentura* and a *retentura*. The buildings in these divisions are mostly of long and narrow shape, and they recall the *strigae* of the tents in the camps. The plan of the fort at Gellygaer (Fig. 10) well illustrates these various features, and it is all the more useful for preliminary study, as it is simple and free from confusing alterations and re-buildings.

RAMPARTS AND ACCESSORIES

The ramparts vary considerably. In the 'earth forts,' of which Birrens and Ardoch are notable examples, they are usually of great size and width ; but the term 'earthwork' fails to express their intricate construction. There is usually a pavement-like foundation of stones, or, as at Coelbren, a 'corduroy' of logs. The rampart itself is more or less stratified, seams of clay, earth, gravel, and decayed sods being of common occurrence, as also bonding-courses of branches or brushwood. In several instances, and perhaps in all, the face was of clay. Ramparts of sods or turves laid in definite courses are not uncommon, and may be regarded as a connecting-link between earthwork and masonry. Those of Rough Castle and Bar Hill are good examples, and like that of Birrens, rest upon stone bottomings. The Antonine Wall is of the same construction, only on a larger scale.

In the 'stone forts' the face at least is of masonry, serving as a strong retaining-wall for an earth-bank behind. Gellygaer furnishes a good example of one of these 'composite' ramparts. The wall is from 3 to 4 ft. in thickness, and the bank behind, including a thinner retaining-wall at the foot of its slope, makes up a total rampart-width of about 20 ft. The material of the bank is derived from the ditch and the trenches for the foundations of these walls. The rampart of Caerwent, which, however, was a town, not a *castellum*, is similar, but on a larger scale. Its

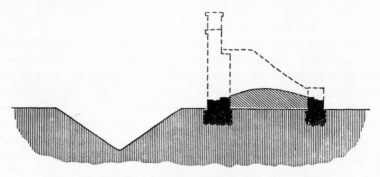

FIG. 11.—Section of Ditch and Rampart at Gellygaer, showing restoration of latter.
(15 ft. to 1 in.)

wall has a thickness of nearly 11 ft. at the base, and in one place, where it remains to the height of 24 ft., this is reduced to 6 ft. 6 ins. at the summit by off-sets on the back, the front being, as is usual in Roman work, vertical. The bank attains almost the same level. In most other 'stone forts' of the Hyginian type, the bank is less conspicuous or is apparently absent. At Housesteads, the wall is somewhat thicker than at Gellygaer, and remains to a greater height; and there are scarcely any perceptible traces of a bank. But here, as also at Chesters and Great Chesters, are indications that the bank was reduced or removed in Roman times. At Caerwent, there is evidence that the rampart was originally of earthwork only, the wall being a late addition, and this may have been frequently the case;

at Gellygaer, on the other hand, the masonry appears to have immediately followed the throwing up of the bank. As time went on, more reliance seems to have been placed in walls of masonry—thicker, loftier, and stronger ; and in some of the later bastioned forts, the wall alone appears to have intervened between defender and assailant, there being apparently neither ditch in front nor bank behind.

The ditches are almost invariably of an open V-shaped section, with an average width of 19 or 20 ft. and depth of 6 or 7 ft., and there is always an interval or berm between the ditch and the rampart of a few feet or more, the chief use of which was to

FIG. 12.—Fortification Turrets on Column of Trajan

ensure the safety of the latter by giving it a firmer foothold. A single ditch was often deemed sufficient, and perhaps as often there were two. Where the defences were naturally weaker than elsewhere, there were sometimes more ; for instance, the more assailable end at Birrens is sheathed with five additional ditches, and the corresponding end at Ardoch presents a remarkable complex of intricate ditches and ravelins. The upcast from a ditch was sometimes partly or wholly used to form a low glacis-like mound along the outer side, the object of which was apparently to increase the height of the counterscarp, but never to such an extent as to afford cover for the enemy. In the walls of Antoninus and Hadrian the whole of this upcast was so utilized.

Turrets were a usual feature of the ' stone forts ' and probably also of the ' earth forts.' The remains of their basements are well seen on the Gellygaer plan, attached to the inner side of the wall, and with doorways to the *intervallum* ; but in many forts they were confined to the corners. Ancient writers, as Josephus, for instance (page 41), refer to them in connection with fortifications ; and they are represented on the Column of Trajan, two of which are shown in Fig. 12, the one within the rounded corner of a fort and apparently constructed of wood and roofed, and the other a stone one with a flat top. Both stand a storey above their respective rampart-walls and are entered

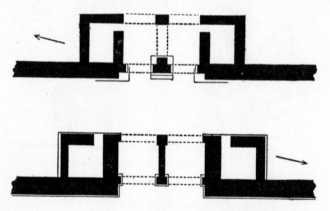

FIG. 13.—Plans of Gates, Housesteads and Birdoswald.   (30 ft. to 1 in.)

from the parapet walks by doorways. No traces of kindred structures have been found in the ' earth forts,' but if, as is probable, they were of timber their remains might easily escape detection.

The gates varied considerably : some were of stone, some of timber, and a few of both materials ; some had a single passage, others two ; and the larger were provided with guard-chambers. The gates of the ' stone forts ' of the Hyginian type were normally double ones, that is with two passages each, side by side, and between two guard-chambers which did not project beyond the face of the rampart. The gates at Housesteads and Birdoswald (Fig. 13) are typical examples. The portals were arched and

were provided with doors of two leaves, the lower pivots of which
turned in iron-sheathed stone sockets in the angles between the
jambs and the side walls of the passages. Those with a single
passage were of similar arrangement and construction, but they
rarely had guard-chambers. The smaller gates at Birdoswald
and Chesters were of this character, and simpler ones may be seen
in several of the mile-castles of the Wall of Hadrian. It is note-

FIG. 14.—Fortification Gates on the Column of Trajan

worthy, however, that the gates of the Scottish forts seem
invariably to have been single-passage ones with or without guard-
chambers, and the great *castellum* of Newstead is no exception
in this respect.

These structures are in too ruinous a condition to supply
definite information as to their upper work, but the sculptures
of the Column of Trajan will again be helpful. In Fig. 14 are
shown four examples of gates therefrom. The first two, it will
be noticed, have no upper chambers, and in the second of these

is shown the wooden parapet of the continuation of the rampart-walk over the gate. The second two have upper chambers with window-like openings, and lateral doorways from the rampart. The arched openings of the fourth example imply a stone structure. There are several Continental Roman gates—notably at Rome, Turin, Verona, Autun and Treves—which still retain their super-structures, and their façades present one or two storeys of arched openings of considerable size over their portals. A gate-building on a mosaic in the Avignon Museum so elucidatively fits in with the remains of the double gates described above, that we repro-duce a sketch of it by the late Mr. C. Roach Smith (Fig. 15).

The gates of the Scottish earth forts were wholly or mostly

FIG. 15.—Gate of Town or Fort, from Mosaic in the Avignon Museum

of timber, and their remains are consequently slight and often indefinite. In most cases they appear to have had single passages, and masonry, if used, was confined to their sides, perhaps more for the purpose of retaining the ends of the rampart than anything else.

The approaches to the gates varied. The ditch was either continued in front of the gate and was crossed by a bridge, or it stopped short on either side, leaving a causeway-like approach. Gellygaer provides an example of each. The sides of the ditch in front of the south-west gate are stepped out evidently to receive two rows of supports of a timber bridge; while in front of the south-east gate the ditch is simply discontinued. The causeway approaches were usually simple and direct; but in some of the Scottish forts they were devious, and at Ardoch there is evidence of timber palisades along their sides and transverse structures to prevent the entrances being rushed.

The bastioned forts differ from those of the type described above, not only in having bastions or external towers, but in their thicker and loftier walls, and their gates being fewer, more strongly defended and of a single passage each—these apparently never exceeding two in number, any additional entrances being posterns. These forts also show a decided tendency to depart from the traditional rectangular form. They certainly indicate a change in the principles of defence. The above modifications

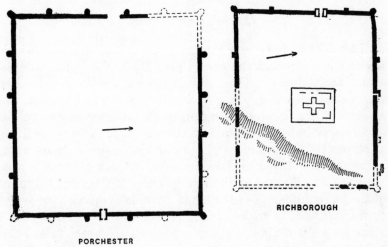

RICHBOROUGH

PORCHESTER

FIG. 16.—Plans of Roman Forts, Porchester and Richborough. (300 ft. to 1 in.)

had a twofold effect : they increased the passive resistance against attack by the greater strength of structure and the restriction of entrances, and they increased the active resistance by providing means of enfilading both walls and gates by the introduction of bastions. The remains of *castella* of this type may be seen at Burgh Castle, Bradwell-juxta-Mare, Richborough (Fig. 16), Lympne, Pevensey, Porchester, Bitterne, and Cardiff —all coast-forts, the first six or seven belonging to the series which about the close of the 4th century was under the control of the 'Count of the Saxon Shore.' The bastions vary in shape and projection. At Cardiff and Richborough they are of slight projection, those of the former being polygonal, and of the latter rectangular, with circular ones capping the corners. At Burgh Castle, Lympne, Porchester, and Pevensey, they boldly project and have rounded fronts and straight sides. These *castella* are undoubtedly late, and can hardly be assigned to an earlier date than the latter part of the 3rd century.

The walls of some inland forts and towns had bastions— the multangular tower at York is a well-known example—but in some of these, as at Caerwent, the bastions were added to work of an earlier period.

INTERNAL BUILDINGS

The chief building in a Roman fort was a central one, which is generally known as the *praetorium*, also as the *forum* from its forum-like planning. There is no evidence, however, that either was its ancient name. It is probable that it was known as the *principia* ; for inscriptions recording the erection or restoration of *principia* have been found on the site of the central building at Rough Castle, and in its vicinity at Lanchester. In any case, it can safely be called the headquarters, for such it certainly was.

The plan (Fig. 17) of the headquarters at Chesters is typical of the larger buildings of the kind. A wide doorway gave access to its yard, nearly 50 ft. square, paved, and surrounded with a stone gutter, while in one corner was a well. On each side of this yard was a wide portico supported on square piers, and next the street, a narrower one or passage with openings to the yard, probably arched. The pavement of the porticoes was slightly higher than the yard. Along the back was the front wall of a second main division, having five openings, all probably arched, the end ones being somewhat smaller and providing direct access from the side porticoes. The transverse space behind was also paved, but it lacked a marginal gutter. It had on its nearer side a portico or aisle supported on four piers, and at each end of this was a side-door into the building. On the farther or opposite side of the space were five rooms or offices, of which the middle was the largest, and this and the two adjoining rooms had wide openings, all probably arched. The end rooms were entered from the contiguous ones by doors in the intervening walls. In the middle room were steps descending into an arched vault under the room on the left ; while the corresponding room on the right had a central square of flagstones.

The headquarters at Gellygaer was smaller but simpler, the chief differences being the absence of a portico or aisle in the transverse space behind the yard, of side entrances, and of a vault at the back. In the first two differences, the present example is typical of most of the smaller buildings of the kind.

We can in some measure reconstruct one of these buildings. The yard was certainly open to the sky, and it usually contained a well. The porticoes had pentice roofs sloping to the yard, and the gutter below caught the rain-water from the eaves. The transverse space behind is generally regarded as an inner courtyard ; but there are reasons for thinking that, in this country at least, it was roofed, one being that in no instance has it a marginal gutter. The offices at the back were normally five. The middle room was the most important, and when its remains are sufficiently

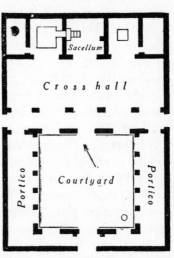

FIG. 17.—Plan of Headquarters, Chesters. (50 ft. to 1 in.)

intact, they invariably show a wide opening to the cross-hall. This opening at Housesteads retains its sill, which is chased to receive the bottom of stone or timber parapet or screen with a central gate or door. In most forts, this room has a vault or other underground receptacle as at Chesters, and there is good evidence that this structure was of late introduction. The two adjoining rooms, when sufficiently defined, have also wide openings, too wide to have been fitted with doors, and probably they had screens or parapets. The end rooms, on the other hand, were entered by narrow doors from the contiguous rooms or from the cross-hall.

The resemblance of these headquarters' buildings to a common type of forum-group in the towns, of which that of Silchester is a good example, is noteworthy. The yard with its porticoes is the counterpart of the forum-proper ; the cross-hall, that of the basilica ; and in both there is a range of rooms at the back, the basilica, however, usually having one at each end as well. It is well known that some of these rooms were fenced off from the hall by screens (*cancelli*) of wood or other material, and that they were used as courts for the administration of justice and for other public purposes ; this is also a common arrangement for shrines or *sacella*. There is practically no doubt that the corresponding rooms in the forts were used for administrative purposes, or, as we should say, were orderly rooms, the middle one being the *sacellum*, the place where honours were paid to the genius of the emperor and of the regiment, and to the standards. The shrine would, according to ancient usage, be the treasury—hence the vault or other underground receptacle found in most of them. It is interesting to note that almost invariably these underground structures are of *late* work, and from this it would seem that in the declining days of the empire, the growing lawlessness necessitated stronger protection for the treasure (probably kept in a chest in earlier times) than that afforded by the sanctity of the spot.

Near the headquarters was another important building, in some of the larger forts, two. These buildings varied considerably, but all of them had a house-like plan, and for this reason they have been identified as the residences of the commandants of their respective forts, and may have included rooms for the chief members of their staffs. They usually consisted of a number of rooms gathered round a small courtyard, an arrangement which is well seen on the Gellygaer plan. In some of the larger forts, one or more of their rooms were heated by hypocausts, and in one or two instances baths were attached.

Another essential was one or more oblong buildings of very distinctive character and remarkable for their thick and buttressed walls. Two at Gellygaer, one near each lateral gate, will be easily recognized on the plan. Two was the usual number, but occasionally there was only one in a fort. Rarer still there

were more than two—at Birrens there were three, and at High
Rochester, four. They were built singly or in pairs. They
varied in length considerably, from 54 ft. at Hardknott to 130 ft.
at Newstead, but rarely exceeded the limits of 22 ft. and 25 ft.
in width. A comparison of the remains shows that these buildings had two features in common—a raised or suspended floor
supported on dwarf-walls or pillars, and openings in the side
walls below their floor-levels ; but the actual floors have disappeared except at Corbridge, where they are of flagstones
spanning the intervals between the dwarf-walls. The remains of
doorways have been found in several instances, and invariably
at one or both ends of the buildings. The latter was the case
at Gellygaer, where their positions are indicated by the remains
of porches ; but in most, these appendages were lacking.

Little can be inferred as to the superstructures. There is no
evidence that the buildings were divided into rooms above the
floor-level, or that they had a second floor, although the buttressed walls could have carried one. It is probable that the
buttresses were carried up to the roof, and that the intervening
walls were pierced with openings for the admission of light and
air similar to those below the floor. The object of these lower
openings was to keep the floor dry by the free circulation of air
under it. That these curious buildings were granaries can
hardly be questioned. On the site of one of the pair at Corbridge
was an altar dedicated by the *praepositus* of the *horreum*. Inscriptions have been found in Roman forts—one in this country
at Great Chesters—recording the restoration of *horrea*, and on
the site of the building of this type at Camelon was a large
quantity of charred wheat.

On the plan of Gellygaer will be noticed six long L-shaped
buildings, four in the *praetentura* and two in the *retentura*. They
were approximately 145 ft. long, and their recessed sides had
verandas or porticoes supported on timber posts. Several
buildings of similar shape have been partially uncovered at
Chesters, which differed, however, in having stone columns instead
of posts, and in being divided into rooms by stone walls—
the ' heads ' into several of unequal size, and the ' limbs ' into a
series of equal size, each with a door to the portico. At House-

steads and Birrens, the corresponding buildings were of a long oblong shape divided into eleven or twelve rooms of equal sizes, and at the former place there are indications that each was sub-divided into a front and a back room. At Newstead, these buildings are represented by rows of eleven huts, each row being about 190 ft. long. There is little doubt that the Gellygaer buildings were divided into rooms as at Chesters, but by timber partitions.

These buildings, whether L-shaped or oblong, were certainly barracks. They recall the arrangement of the tents in the Hyginian camp. There, to each century, which at the time consisted of eighty men with a centurion and petty officers, was allotted a row of tents—ten for the men, and two, or a space equal to two, for the officers, the total length of the row being 120 ft. Usually two of these rows were placed face to face with a space between, the whole forming a *striga*; while a single row constituted a *hemistrigium*. At Gellygaer, there were two of the former and two of the latter. At Chesters and Housesteads, the number of rooms in each block, and at Newstead, the number of huts in each row, approximate to the number of tents in the *hemistrigium*; and in the first it is reasonable to think that the centurion had his quarters in the 'head,' and that some of the rooms there, were offices and one possibly the shrine of the century. Assuming that each block at Gellygaer provided accommoda-tion for a century, the six would represent an ordinary cohort, *cohors quingenaria*. At Housesteads, there were ten blocks which can be reasonably identified as barracks, and we know that its garrison—the First Cohort of Tungrians—was one of those entitled *miliaria*, nominally a thousand strong, and con-sisting of ten centuries. At Birrens, the plans of the buildings are less perfect, but there appears to have been a larger accommo-dation, and this may be feasibly explained by the fact that the garrison—the Second Cohort of Tungrians—was not only *miliaria* but *equitata*, that is, it included a small detachment of horsemen, for whose use stabling as well as additional barracks would be required.

On all the more complete plans of forts may be noticed other structures which cannot be classed with those described above, but we can only conjecture their uses. Each fort was the scene of many necessary operations—the corn had to be ground and the daily food prepared, and there must have been repairing shops of various kinds, as smithies, armouries, joineries, and so forth, and most if not all of these operations would require suitable buildings. In cavalry forts, and those containing both infantry and cavalry, the stables must have been an important element ; and perhaps in most of the infantry forts, a few horses were kept for scouting and dispatches—and horses imply the storage of fodder. Among the minor structures would be latrines, cisterns for the storage of water, ovens and other cooking arrangements, wells, drains, etc.

Of the arrangements for the preparation and cooking of the food for the garrisons, little is known. At Birrens, the remains of a row of four oven-like structures were found on the inner side of the rampart near the east gate. They may have been ovens, or they may have been fitted with cauldrons for boiling purposes. Similar structures have been noticed at Newstead, Housesteads, Great Chesters, and Birdoswald.

The streets of the forts were mostly of gravel ; less frequently they were paved with cobbles. The larger usually had a gutter on either side ; the smaller, sometimes only one along the centre. The drainage was always well considered and carried out. The larger drains had built sides and were covered with large slabs, the floors being often paved, and the smaller were often constructed of flagstones.

A plentiful supply of water for drinking and cleansing purposes was one of the first considerations. A well has been found in most of the excavated forts, in each case in the headquarters' yard, but this seems to have been a precaution to ensure a supply of water in time of stress, the normal supply being derived from without. At Great Chesters, for instance, there are the remains of a small canal or aqueduct which conveyed water from Haltwhistle Burn, five miles away ; and at Birdoswald a culvert brought the water of a spring some hundreds of yards away to a large cistern near the centre of the fort. At South Shields and Chesters are inscriptions recording the construction of aqueducts. As at Birdoswald, so in several

other forts, large and well-constructed stone cisterns or tanks
to receive water have been found. Remains of latrines have
been uncovered at Housesteads, Castlecary, Bar Hill, and Gellygaer, in such positions that they could intercept waste water
and street drainage for flushing purposes.

EXTERNAL BUILDINGS

In the vicinity of many Roman forts may be seen the remains
of buildings and other indications of ancient human occupancy.
Housesteads is a notable example. To the east and south
are the foundations of streets and houses which were more conspicuous a century ago. Altars, statues, columns, and carved
stones have been turned up from time to time, and tell of temples
(one of which, a mythraeum, has been excavated), shrines, and
other goodly structures. There is no doubt that the suburbs
of *Borcovicus* were of considerable extent, and sheltered a considerable population, which presumably would consist largely
of the soldiers' wives and families, time-expired soldiers, traders,
and other civilians who served the garrison in various capacities.
In the vicinity of other forts along the line of the Wall of Hadrian
may also be discerned the indications of buildings. Hard by
those of Chesters and Great Chesters are the ruins of extensive
baths ; and similar remains may be seen, or have been revealed
by the spade, close by the Roman forts at Camelon, Newstead,
Slack, Binchester, Gellygaer, and elsewhere.

Some of the forts had attached to them enclosed spaces or
annexes, fortified, but, as a rule, less strongly so than the forts
themselves. Rough Castle, Castlecary, and Gellygaer, had
one each, defended by a ditch and a rampart. At Lyne, there
were two, one on each side, like two wings. At Camelon, there
were also two, a smaller, the original annexe, and a larger which
exceeded the fort itself in area, and was protected by a large
rampart and several ditches. At Newstead, there were three.
The spade will undoubtedly bring to light more annexes, but it
is almost certain that many forts lacked them ; no trace of
one, for instance, has been noticed along the Wall of Hadrian.

Little is known of the contents of these enclosures. That

at Castlecary contains the remains of the baths. The larger annexe at Camelon was traversed by two streets, and contains the remains of two large buildings, one apparently baths, and traces of others. At Gellygaer, the baths were also in the annexe, and in addition two large enclosures (one containing furnaces) and several small structures. Several annexes on the Continent, notably at Heddernheim and Saalberg, have been found to contain the 'civil settlements,' but whether this is the case in our country further exploration alone can prove. There is certainly no room for such a settlement in the Gellygaer annexe, but the spade may discover another annexe, or what is equally likely, prove that the suburb was not enclosed as at Housesteads.

III. THE NORTHERN WALLS

Few Roman remains in Europe have attracted more attention than the two Walls, the lower stretching from the mouth of the Tyne to the Solway, and the upper across the narrower isthmus between the indents of the Forth and the Clyde. The term *Wall* does not convey an adequate idea of these great works. Each was a complex of forts, continuous rampart and ditch, military roads and outlying posts, planned with consummate skill and on an imperial scale ; but in addition, the southern line has enigmatical features which have long been the subject of controversy.

Both lines appear to owe their inception to the military genius of Agricola. The strategic advantages of the upper isthmus were certainly recognized by him, for he held it by a number of posts ; and it is probable that some of the forts upon or near the Solway-Tyne line were also due to him. His immediate successors lacked his energy, and during the period of border unrest which followed, the Caledonians made at least one serious inroad into the Province. To remedy this dangerous state of affairs, Hadrian, in accordance with his policy of consolidation rather than expansion, constituted the lower isthmus the frontier in A.D. 120. It is almost certain that the Agricolan posts of the upper isthmus had already long been abandoned ; but twenty-five years after Hadrian's visit, and in consequence of further border trouble,

Antoninus Pius fortified that isthmus with a 'wall.' This may have been dictated by a return to the 'forward' policy of Agricola, the intention being the conquest of North Britain by successive stages; or the object may have been to place the natives of the intervening country under a protectorate and thus create a friendly buffer-state between the Province and the Caledonians. Under any circumstance, the barrier of the lower isthmus continued to be held, and in fact served as the base whence detachments were drafted to man the upper line. This duplication of frontier lines, however, was of short duration, and there is reason to think that the upper wall was abandoned at the time of the great Caledonian inrush of A.D. 180. The lower wall, on the other hand, continued to be the recognized frontier to the close of the Roman era.

THE ANTONINE WALL (Fig. 18)

This structure was about 36⅓ miles in length, and for most of this distance its rampart and ditch are still visible. Less conspicuous is an irregular mound or glacis on the northern side of the ditch ; and at a varying distance behind the rampart is the stony ridge of the military way. " The work is thus in its entirety a quadruple line, which, instinct with Roman greatness of design and thoroughness of execution, undulates across the isthmus with a course as direct as the strategic requirements of strength would admit. It skilfully takes advantage of high ground, commanding throughout almost its entire course a valley or low-lying ground in front." [1] Add to this ' quadruple line ' the remains of a dozen or more garrison stations and the traces of ' periodic expansions ' at the rear of the rampart, and the reader will have a general idea of the Antonine Wall.

Excavations between 1890 and 1893 proved that the rampart was constructed of turves or sods laid in definite courses resting upon a spread of rough stones between two kerbs of squared stones. The width of this foundation, averaging between 14 and 15 ft., indicates the original width of the rampart, which has spread under its own weight and the disintegrating effects

[1] *The Antonine Wall Report*, p. 2.

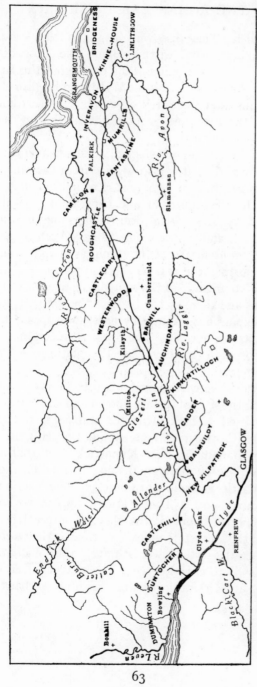

FIG. 18.—Map of the Antonine Wall. The known sites of Forts shown as solid squares; the uncertain or conjectural, as hollow squares. (6 miles to I in.)

of the weather. This discovery confirms the statements of
Julius Capitolinus, who, writing about the close of the 3rd
century, relates how Antoninus Pius conquered the Britons and
built a *murus cespiticius*. And the Welsh and English chroniclers,
Gildas, Nennius, and Bede, tell obscurely of a turf and a stone
wall between the Picts and Scots of the north and the civilized
population of the south.

The ditch is normally V-shaped, with an average width of
40 ft. and depth of 12 ft. Its distance from the rampart varies
from 18 ft. to 112 ft., but usually it does not overstep the limits
of 24 and 30 ft. The outer mound consists of the soil from the
ditch. It is very irregular in form, being sometimes flat, sometimes heaped up, and its use seems to have been to give greater
height to the counterscarp of the ditch, as the ground generally
slopes to the north. But it is nowhere so pronounced as to inter-
fere with the ' command ' of the rampart or to afford cover to the
enemy. Here and there at the back of the rampart are remains
of ' periodic expansions,' rounded bulges, so to speak, of the same
construction as the former. Their use is uncertain ; the most
plausible theory is that they were the platforms—*ballistaria*—
for military engines.

The garrisons were stationed in forts of the usual Roman
form, of which the sites of ten are known and those of six or seven
more are surmised. The known sites, starting from the east, are
Rough Castle, Castlecary, Westerwood, Bar Hill, Auchindavy,
Kirkintilloch, Balmuildy, New Kilpatrick, Castlehill, and Dun-
tocher. These are on the actual line ; but a little north of it,
near Rough Castle, is the fort at Camelon which may be regarded
as an advanced post. The stations appear to have been
tolerably evenly distributed, the shortest interval being about
1¾ miles, and the longest 3¾ miles. Normally, they were applied,
like the mile-castles of the lower isthmus, to the Wall, its rampart
forming their northern defence ; but that at Bar Hill, and
perhaps that at Kirkintilloch, were slightly set back from its
line.

THE WALL OF HADRIAN (Fig. 19)

This grand barrier extends from Bowness on the Solway to Wallsend on the Tyne, and is $73\frac{1}{2}$ miles in length. Like the Antonine line, it has a similar succession of ditch with glacis-like outer mound, a wall set back so as to leave an intervening berm-like space, and a military road behind ; also, at intervals, stations for the accommodation of the garrisons. But, unlike it, the wall is built of stone ; and the stations are in two series, one of greater and the other of lesser size, which may be distinguished respectively as forts and mile-castles. The most striking point of difference, however, is a ditch between two banks in the rear of the military road, and known as the Vallum. The lower barrier thus resolves itself into two sets of works, the Wall with its appendages and the Vallum (Fig. 20).

These two lines pass from sea to sea in close companionship as a rule, running parallel some 60 or 80 yds. apart for miles on the stretch along the lowlands of the eastern and western thirds of their course ; but in the intervening rugged region they seem at first sight to pursue independent courses, drifting apart here and there to the extent of half a mile or more. These divergencies in the middle third are due to the configuration of the country. The Vallum pursues the more direct course, while the Wall forsakes its companion for the higher grounds. In this region, where the hills have gentle dip-slopes to the south and craggy precipices to the north, the normal position of the latter is the crest ; that of the former, the slope behind. Between these great works, the Wall and the Vallum, the military road in the more hilly regions pursues a path which is parallel to neither, but which was determined with a view to the easiest possible route from point to point.

As already stated, the wall was of stone. Where best preserved, it remains to the height of 5 or 6 ft. ; but in those districts where the land has been long under cultivation, it is more often reduced to a mere ridge of foundation rubble, or has so completely disappeared that only the ditch remains to indicate its line. Where ascertainable, the thickness varies from 6 to $9\frac{1}{2}$ ft. The

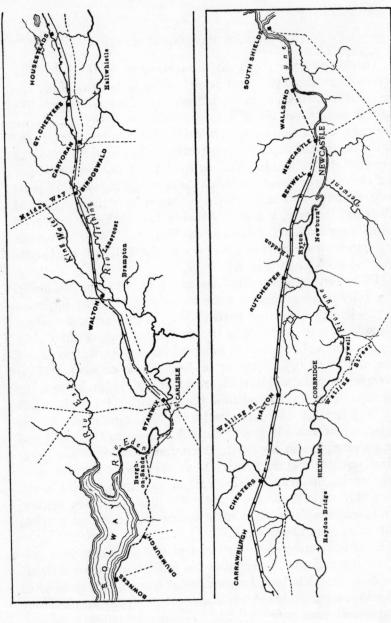

FIG. 19.—Map of the Wall of Hadrian. The Wall shown as a thick line; the Vallum, as a thin line; the Forts, as large squares, and the Mile Castles, as small squares. (6 miles to 1 in.)

66

ditch varies considerably in dimensions, but an average width of 36 ft. and depth of 15 ft. may be accepted as fairly correct. It accompanies the wall throughout its course, except along the edges of cliffs where it would be of no practical use, and for a mile or two west of Carlisle where the Eden takes its place. The upcast from it was used to form the glacis-like mound or spread as in the Antonine Wall.

Along the actual line, or in its vicinity, are the remains of the garrison stations. Of these, about nineteen are known, some still imposing though in ruins, others reduced to the barest traces. Their distances apart fall, as a rule, within the limits of 3 and 5 miles. Their plans, so far as they are known, are those of typical Roman forts. Some, including the three or more detached stations, were apparently constructed, not only before

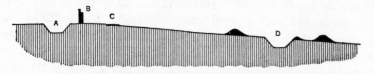

Fig. 20.—Diagrammatic Section of Wall of Hadrian.
A, Ditch; B, Wall; C, Road; D, Vallum

the wall, but before it was contemplated, and were subsequently woven into the mural scheme; the majority, however, were undoubtedly part of the scheme. The mile-castles were smaller than the stations, and were more numerous. They were all, so far as is known, of similar size and shape, and distributed at tolerably even distances apart. The sites of about fifty have been identified, but their remains are for the most part extremely slight, but in the wilder middle region some still present conspicuous ruins. These fortlets averaged 60 ft. by 50 ft., and were attached to the wall, that structure forming the northern side, the remaining three sides being of similar thickness and bonded into it. The free corners were rounded, and each fortlet had two gates, one to the north and the other to the south. In the lowlands they appear to have been as nearly as possible a Roman mile apart; but in the hilly region they are irregularly spaced, the engineers here relaxing their rule in order to select advantageous positions for them.   The original number of these structures was about eighty.

The remains of only a few turrets are known, but there is reason to think that they were numerous, and were placed where look-outs were needed.   They were small rectangular structures recessed into the back of the wall, with a narrow doorway to the south.

The mural road provided communication between the stations and the mile-castles.   Its stony ridge is best preserved in the hilly districts ; elsewhere it is mostly obliterated or buried.   Its usual position is from 60 to 100 ft. behind or south of the wall ; but here and there it recedes when it is necessary to do so in order to gain gentle gradients.   In serving the stations and mile-castles it necessarily clung to the wall, and thus participated in much degree in its sinuosities.   Hence in the hilly region where the wall zigzagged and curved considerably to the north, it was neither a direct nor an easy means of communication between distant points, and here it was augmented by a more direct route from lowland to lowland—the road now known as the Stane Gate.

The great earthwork, known as the Vallum, consists of a flat-bottomed ditch, about 30 ft. across the top, from 10 to 12 ft. across the bottom, and about 7 ft. deep, between two mounds formed of its upcast, each set back about 25 ft. from the brink of the ditch.   Where best preserved the mounds are still 6 or 7 ft. high.   Besides these there is, here and there, a smaller mound usually cresting the south brink, but occasionally the north one. In some places the Vallum is a conspicuous and imposing feature forming a great triple band of a total width of some 130 ft.   The small mound seems to be always on the side of the ditch which from the natural slope of the ground would be the lower, and its object is apparently to level it up to the height of the opposite side.   As the slope of the ground is nearly always to the south, this explains its usual position.

The behaviour of the Vallum to the stations has an important bearing on the question of its origin and use.   It is indistinct, or even obliterated, in the vicinity of the stations ; and this has given rise to the belief, reasonable enough, that whatever its

purpose may have been, it fell out of use at an early date, and
was intentionally levelled or allowed to be obliterated by the
gradual process of agriculture at these places, before the close
of the era.   This obliteration is responsible for some wrong
impressions as to its relation to the stations that stand across
its line or otherwise seem to touch it.   There are stations that
lie beyond its extremities, as Wallsend and Newcastle in the
east, and Drumburgh and Bowness in the west ; and there are
intervening stations that are entirely off its line, as Housesteads,
Great Chesters, Carvoran, and Chesterholm.   Of the residue,
Benwell, Rutchester, Halton, and Chesters are so placed that
their southern ramparts appear to be in line with the Vallum ;
while Carrawburgh and Birdoswald stand across it.   The old view
assumed that these two stations were in actual contact with it.
Excavations in 1896–97, however, have shown that in their case
the Vallum curiously and purposely avoids them by skirting
round them, and there is also reason to think that the mile-castles
were similarly avoided.

The purpose of the Vallum has long been a subject of controversy.   It has been regarded as a great pre-Roman barrier ; as
a Roman defence against the south, and particularly against
the Brigantes ; and as a sunken and fortified road.   But none
of these is consistent with the facts.   The curious manner in
which it deliberately goes out of its way to avoid the stations
which it otherwise would strike shows that it is part of the mural
scheme, and this tells equally against its being a pre-Roman
defence or a road, and, apart from this, excavations on its site
have failed to yield any evidence of a road either in its ditch or
elsewhere between the mounds.   With regard to the second
theory, high military authorities have pronounced against its
being a defensive barrier of any kind.   Professor Mommsen
suggested that it was a civil boundary—" that the Vallum
marks the southern or inside edge of the *limes* or ' frontier strip '
of the empire,' the two works, Vallum and Wall, being regarded as contemporary, but the one a legal, and the other a
military line.   Dr. Haverfield is of a similar opinion, but con-
siders that its purpose " was forgotten or ignored even in Roman
times," and in support of this, he instanced the evidence of the

early filling up of the ditch " where its presence may well have been inconvenient, as near a fort." The reader must draw his own conclusion as to the meaning of this " strange earthwork, the inscrutable Vallum " ; but it is safe to predict that his verdict will be that the last word has not been said upon it.

The discovery of the remains of a turf wall in 1895, " introduced," as Dr. Haverfield puts it, " a new factor into the whole Mural problem." It has long been observed that for about a mile west of Birdoswald, a ditch runs parallel to the Vallum at about 90 ft. to the north ; and this was usually regarded as a supplementary defence to that work. But a series of trenches disclosed the remarkable fact that it appertains, not to the Vallum, but to a former turf wall, from 10 to 15 ft. wide, which appeared to have been purposely destroyed, and evidence was forthcoming to prove that this work represented the original line of the Wall hereabouts. No trace of a turf-wall has been found elsewhere along the line ; but the discovery is strongly suggestive that the Wall of Hadrian was, like the Antonine Wall, originally constructed of turves, and was subsequently replaced by a stone wall, the builders of this stone wall finding it necessary for some reason or other to deviate from the old line in the vicinity of Birdoswald.

Enough has been said to show that the Wall embodies works and modifications of different times, all Roman, of course. The first emperor whose name appears in connection with it is Hadrian. In four of the mile-castles have been found inscribed tablets in his honour, and presumably similar tablets were placed in the others. Some of the stations may have been such of Agricola's camps as happened to be in the line of the projected wall ; but we cannot imagine a prior existence for the mile-castles—they are integral parts of the wall itself. If Hadrian erected these, that structure must have been already determined upon. It is true that no contemporary writer mentions his building a wall in Britain ; but a century and a half later, Spartian states that " Hadrian went to Britain and put straight many things which were crooked therein, and was the first to draw a wall eighty-thousand paces, to divide the barbarians from the Romans."

But the same writer tells us that Severus, more than eighty

years later, also built a wall—" The greatest glory of his reign is that he fortified Britain by a wall drawn across the island and ending on both sides with the ocean "—and this is reiterated by subsequent writers. But, as in the case of Hadrian, no contemporary writer records such a work on his part ; still more remarkable is it that both Dion Cassius, writing a few years after his death, and Herodian a little later, should describe his Caledonian campaigns in graphic terms, yet make no allusion to his wall-building.

That Severus had something to do with the barrier of the lower isthmus is, however, beyond question. It is true that no inscription to him has been found along the Wall ; but his name is inscribed upon Cumberland quarries, and upon slabs at Hexham, Risingham, and Old Carlisle. Between Hadrian's day and that of Severus there had been troublous times ; and it is likely enough that the second emperor found the Wall in a ruined condition, and that he not only restored, but strengthened it. If we accept this view of the part played by Severus, there will be little difficulty in also accepting as literally true the statement that it was Hadrian who " first drew a wall, etc." ; in other words, in assigning to this great emperor the initiation of the general scheme of wall, forts, mile-castles, and vallum.

CHAPTER IV

HOUSES [1]

'CORRIDOR' HOUSES AND 'BASILICAL' HOUSES

IT is hardly necessary to say that the remains of a large number of 'Roman villas,' as they are popularly designated, have been brought to light in this country. The term 'villa,' as thus used, is inaccurate. The *villa* was the Roman counterpart of the medieval manor—the estate of a landed proprietor. It comprised not only his residence, but those of his *villicus* or bailiff and of his servile and semi-servile dependents, his farm-buildings, and granaries. The estate was the villa; the residence of the *dominus* was the villa-house. Another misconception arises from the circumstance that most of the houses of the period which have been described were of the larger and more sumptuous sort. The result is a widespread notion that Roman Britain was studded with magnificent 'villas,' residences of foreign officials, in the midst of a native population which lived in cottages and huts; hence that the former were an exotic element in the land. It is likely enough that some of these large houses were official residences; but the officials could never have been so numerous as to have required all of them, the known remains of which can only represent a small portion of the whole number. It is more likely that the officials lived, as a rule, in the towns, and that the rural mansions were the seats of the country squires—native gentlemen who had adopted Roman tastes, and whose wealth lay in their broad acres and their crops and herds.

[1] For detailed particulars, see *Romano-British Buildings and Earthworks*, chap. vi.

The large country houses abounded in the fertile lowlands and vales of the southern half of England. Northwards their remains are found in Lincolnshire, and they practically cease with York and Aldborough. This distribution represents the portions of the island where the population was most Romanized and wealthy, and where the conditions of life were best and the land most cultivated. These houses were not fortified, nor were their sites selected for defensive purposes. The Romano-British proprietor, unlike his medieval successor, had little need to defend himself and his property. Roman Britain was not a land of castles and moated mansions. The houses were planned and designed for domesticity, with large rooms and wide corridors, contrasting in this respect with the cramped rooms and narrow passages of the feudal stronghold of a later age, in which comfort was subordinated to safety. Their sites were selected for convenience, agreeable surroundings, and pleasant prospects. These conditions bear witness to the general order and safety which the land enjoyed under the imperial rule. While garrisons watched the northern frontier, and strong *castella* and fleets barred the estuaries against descents from the seas, the natives prospered and slept in peace. The Pax Romana was not an empty name.

Eliminating mere cottages and huts, the houses were of two types of planning, and may be distinguished as 'corridor' and 'basilical' houses. The former were the more numerous, were of all sizes and degrees of sumptuousness, and were alike in town and country. The latter appear to have been confined to the country and to have been large farm-houses.

'CORRIDOR' HOUSES

One of the most valuable results of the systematic excavation of Silchester is the flood of light it has thrown on the houses of the era. The smaller and simpler Callevan houses consisted of a row of rooms with a corridor or veranda along one side which served as the normal means of communication between room and room. It was rare, however, that the corridor extended the full length of the block. The end room or group of rooms was usually wider than the rest, frequently overstepping the end of the corridor and forming a wing, as in Fig. 21. At this end of the house were the principal apartments, and in the larger houses of this simple planning, one of these was often heated by a hypocaust. The entrance was, at Silchester, usually at the opposite end of the corridor, but occasionally it was in its side, and this seems to have been the rule in the country houses. The corridor side of the block was its front, and it faced an open space which may have been a yard or a garden.

In the more complex plans, such a simple block usually

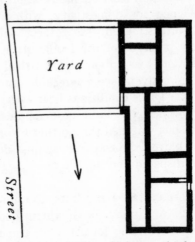

FIG. 21.—Plan of small House, Silchester. (40 ft. to 1 in.)

forms the main body or nucleus of the house, the extensions taking the form of adjuncts or outshoots. The wing may be extended. The opposite end of the corridor may be expanded into an entrance lobby, and this may be altogether removed from the main block and be connected with it by a transverse corridor along the street side. If many of these Silchester plans are compared, it will soon become evident that these extensions were on the front of the house, giving it somewhat an E-shaped plan, thus tending to enclose the open space in front. In some of the largest houses the fourth side was built upon, giving rise to what is known as the ' courtyard type ' of house.

The upper structures of the houses can only be inferred from their plans and their fallen débris. The corridor was normally an external feature with a pentice roof, and the frequency of small stone columns from 3 to 4 ft. long on the sites of Roman houses has led to the general opinion that they were used in the construction, the outer side of the corridor consisting of a dwarf-wall surmounted with these columns.[1] The corridor would thus be a portico modified to suit a cold climate. The main shell of the houses seems to have been of more than a single storey, and at Silchester the explorers frequently noted passage-like rooms which in their opinion contained wooden staircases.[2] Timber was certainly a prominent feature in the upper construction, taking the form of post-and-panel work with the panels filled in with 'wattle-and-daub,' such as may still be seen in many an old cottage. On the site of one of the Silchester houses pieces of the clay-daubing had been impressed with a zigzag pattern from a wooden stamp. The roofs were usually of large red tiles or stone slabs, both differing in shape from those now used.[3] The windows were glazed, as the scatterings of broken g'ass on the sites prove. The walls of the rooms were plastered and painted in gay colours, but little can be gleaned as to the patterns of the decoration.[4] Of the treatment of the ceilings nothing is known, but the upper floors were probably of wood.

Fig. 22 is the original portion of a house which was more than doubled in size by additions. It is a singularly perfect plan, almost every possible door on the ground-floor being shown, and it has all the appearance of being a single design and not the outcome of alterations and additions. The street door opened into a square lobby. From this, a short corridor led to the main corridor of the house, and passing the doors of the various rooms along its side, a short return at the end communicated with the principal rooms at the extremity of a wing almost as long as the main fabric. Both the lobby and the corridors had mosaic pavements,[5] and the main corridor a large door to the courtyard. The rooms showed a progression from the menial to the sumptuous. The first two reached from the street had had floors of mortar

---

[1] For a reconstruction of a corridor, see *Rom.-Brit. Buildings, etc.*, Fig. 51.
[2] *Ib*. chap. vi.   [3] *Ib*. Figs. 76, 78.   [4] *Ib*. chap. xi.
[5] For mosaic floors, see *Rom.-Brit. Buildings, etc.*, chap. xii.

or some other perishable material. The next had a plain mosaic floor, and served as the vestibule of a room behind with a simple cement floor, which probably contained the staircase. Then followed a large room and a narrower one divided into two by a cross-wall, all with plain mosaic floors, and the outer of the two small rooms had a fireplace. The last room of the range had a decorated mosaic floor, also a small fireplace. This has brought us to the wing, the first room of which had a pavement of similar character to the last. Between this and what may be termed

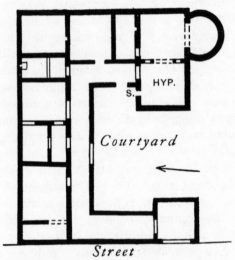

FIG. 22.—Plan of House at Silchester. (40 ft. to 1 in.)

the 'state apartments,' were two small rooms with plain mosaic floors, the one with a fireplace.

The 'state apartments' were two, communicating with one another by a large opening flanked with detached columns or piers, the one having a large semicircular recess or alcove, and the other a hypocaust. Both had rich decorated pavements. Perhaps it would be better to describe these apartments as a double-room or hall. From its large size, nearly 40 ft. long and 20 ft. wide, it was probably loftier than the other rooms of the house, and of a single storey. With little effort of the imagination one can form an idea of the interior. The pilasters and columns with the architrave they supported must have produced a pleasing break in the length, while the curved alcove must have equally agreeably contrasted with the straight lines of the main structure. Add to these architectural features, the strong patterns and quiet colours of the pavement and the lighter and brighter tones of the walls, and little of importance is left to complete the picture, except the windows, of which unfortunately we know nothing. It is reasonable to think that the opening between the pilasters was provided with curtains, which when drawn would shut off one division, and when thrown back would add artistically to the general effect. These double-rooms were a frequent feature of the larger Romano-British houses. They usually consisted of two square divisions or rooms, the one rather smaller than the other, with a simple large opening in the intervening wall. The latter division often contained a hypocaust, and both almost invariably had good mosaic pavements.

In many of the larger Silchester houses, the rooms enclosed the courtyard on three sides, the remaining side usually having a wall with a gate. Only one house—the largest in the town—completely surrounded its courtyard, and its remains proved that its final form was the result of several extensions.

The houses of Caerwent resembled those at Silchester; but considering that Venta Silurum was a smaller town, and that only about two-thirds of its area have been explored, it is remarkable that four or five of the houses already discovered were of the ' courtyard ' type, one of which is shown in Fig. 23. Another— if a private residence at all—was most unusual for this country, in having a peristyled courtyard (Fig. 24). The columns arose from the broad stone kerb of the ambulatory pavement, which was of red mosaic, and as they were about 10 ft. apart, the architrave must have been of timber. A stone gutter just within the kerb caught the rain-water from the peristyle roof of stone slabs, and drained the gravelled yard; but it was interrupted by a large stone water-trough in front of the middle intercolumniation of the east side, behind which was the entrance to the building. The peristyle was surrounded by rooms, many with doors opening upon it. There was a ' winter-room ' on the south side, also a large projecting latrine. The

floors were of mortar or fine brick concrete. Houses with peristyles were common in Italy, and were copied from the Greeks ;
but their open colonnades were ill-adapted for cold climates,
and this doubtlessly accounts for their rarity in the northern
provinces.   There are reasons, however, for thinking that this
Caerwent building was a *hospitium* or public guest-house.   It
resembles in several respects a larger Silchester building, which
is regarded as a *hospitium*, especially in the tendency of its rooms

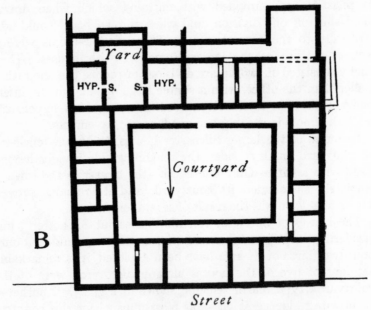

Fig. 23.—Plan of House at Caerwent.   (40 ft. to 1 in.)

to form sets, each with its own entrance, but it lacks the bath-
buildings which are a notable feature there.

The country houses, with the exception of those of ' basilical '
form which will be described presently, resembled the Callevan
houses in their general planning.   There were differences, but
they were less pronounced than the differences between town
and country houses to-day.   The houses at Silchester were
essentially rural houses adapted to the limited plots on which
they were built ; but these plots were relatively larger than

the building sites of our congested towns. House was not
built against house, except in rare instances. Each had its
garth in front ; most, an open space all round. If the house
came to the street side, it was by its back or end. If it fronted
the street, it was set back to allow of the usual courtyard or
garden. There is little doubt that Calleva was a veritable
' garden city.' Still, as the builders were limited as to space,
their houses, extended and straggling as many of them were,
were less so than most of the country houses. But the most
important difference lay in the fact that these were the seats

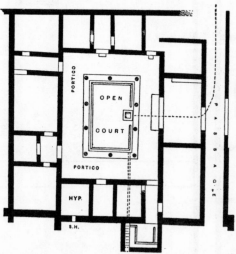

Fig. 24.—Plan of House at Caerwent. (40 ft. to 1 in.)

of landed proprietors whose wealth was derived from agriculture
and their flocks and herds, hence the residence had associated
with it farm-buildings, often on a large scale. The ' villa group '
clustered round an open space much larger than the town courtyard. Not seldom there were two such spaces, an upper on
which the residence looked, and a lower, usually the larger,
appropriated to the farm-buildings. Moreover, most of the
country houses had semi-detached or isolated baths ; the Silchester houses, never, as the town was well supplied with public
baths.

The remains of a house, excavated in Spoonley Wood, near

Winchcombe in Gloucestershire, in 1890, supplied a singularly complete plan of a medium-sized country house (Fig. 25). It was beautifully situated at the foot of a hill, from which issued

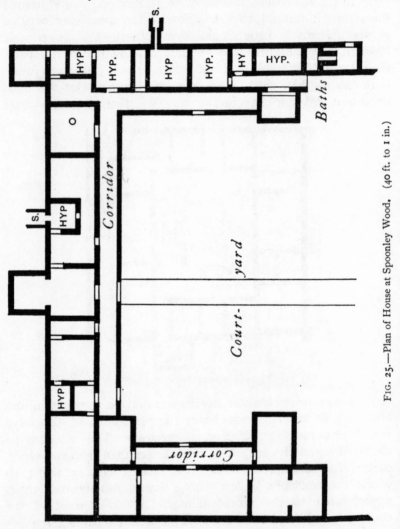

FIG. 25.—Plan of House at Spoonley Wood. (40 ft. to 1 in.)

a plentiful supply of pure water. It consisted of a main range with two wings, with its back to the hill and its front to a large courtyard or garden, enclosed partly by the house and its wings, and completed by a wall. In the centre of the wall, facing the house, was a gate with a paved walk leading to its front door in the centre of the main corridor. The principal rooms were served by this corridor, and a notable feature was the large central 'double-room.' The kitchen was near the right end of the range, and contained a well. The baths occupied the lower end of the right wing, and the servants' quarters were probably in the left wing. Many of the rooms were warmed by hypocausts ; and as usual, the chief rooms had decorated mosaic floors. Altogether this house is a good example of the corridored class, and was planned with a view to external symmetry. The main range, which was 190 ft. long, was probably of two storeys, and its staircase may have been in a narrow room on the left side of the spacious 'double-room.' Of farm-buildings one only, a barn prob-ably (Fig. 26), was discovered, and its situation renders it probable that there was a lower or base-court. It was an oblong structure, 47 ft. long and 28 ft. wide, and was divided into a nave and aisles by two rows of timber posts of which the stone bases remained—a type of building familiar to us in the large barns of the Middle Ages.

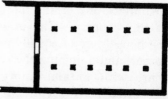

FIG. 26.—Barn at Spoonley Wood.
(40 ft. to 1 in.)

A grand example of a Romano-British house was excavated early in the last century at Bignor in Sussex, and it was of special interest, not only for its magnificent mosaic pavements, but because apparently the whole of its group of buildings was disclosed. The base-court was entered through a gate in its lower wall and a smaller on the left. On this side was a barn-like building, 128 ft. long and 56 ft. wide, and on the opposite side a smaller building with two others standing free in the court. These were evidently farm-buildings, and it is probable that there were also sheds of timber. The upper or house-court was 200 ft. long and 114 ft. wide, and was surrounded with a portico or corridor, the house and its adjuncts extending along three sides. The chief rooms were about the upper half of the

right side of the court, and most of them had rich mosaic pavements. One of these rooms was a large double one, resembling
that at Spoonley Wood. Each division had an elaborate mosaic
pavement, the central feature of the smaller being the Rape of
Ganymede in a medallion with enriched borders ; that of the
larger, a circle subdivided into six hexagonal compartments,
each containing a dancing nymph. In the centre of this circle
was an unusual feature—a hexagonal basin or piscina of white
stone, 4 ft. in diameter. Near this room was another large one
with an apse at one end. The mosaic floor was in a dilapidated
condition, but enough remained to show that it had a central
square of elaborate geometrical design flanked with two narrow
panels containing *amorini* engaged in gladiatorial combats ;
while that of the apse had a delicate scrolly border enclosing
a medallion with a female bust with festoons and birds in the
spandrels—one of the most pleasing mosaic designs discovered
in this country. The other pavements found in this part of
the house were of equally ornate character ; and at the extreme
corner, and adjoining the room just described, was a small open
court with an ambulatory, the roof of which apparently was
supported by dwarf columns. The lower portion of this range
of the house was probably the servants' quarters.

Several of the rooms at the head of the upper court had good
mosaic floors, and two had fireplaces. These were typical of
the few fireplaces of the time that have been discovered in this
country. Each had a hearth placed against the wall, consisting
of eight small tiles, with cheeks of tiles on edge, two tiles each
in the one case and a single one in the other. In one or two
instances elsewhere, the hearth was partly recessed in the wall.
Braziers seem to have been in common use in Britain as in Pompeii,
and the fireplaces may be regarded as fixed braziers. The
baths were situated at the lower end of the left corridor, and
were on a large scale for a private house. They contained
four chief rooms, the first to be entered having a rich mosaic
pavement, the second—the cooling-room—a handsome cold bath,
the remaining two being hot rooms with plain mosaic floors.
The ground covered by this extensive Bignor group of buildings
was little short of 600 ft. in length and about 320 ft. in width.

The grandest known example of a Romano-British house was discovered at Woodchester in Gloucestershire, in 1793. Its excavation brought to light two courtyards, the lower about 150 ft.

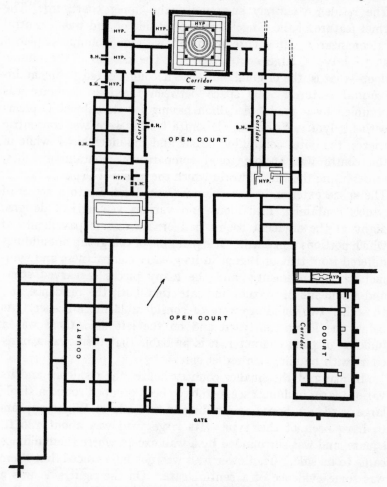

FIG. 27.—Plan of House at Woodchester. (80 ft. to 1 in.)

square, and the upper considerably smaller. The former was bounded on its lower side by a wall with a central gate-house, which, to judge from its remains, was an imposing structure with a large arch between two small ones. On each side of the space was a large isolated block, the one on the right being wholly, or in part, baths, and surrounding a small court, but the use of the other block, which also had an internal court, is uncertain. The residence entirely surrounded the upper courtyard. The chief feature of the range of its upper side or end was a central saloon, nearly 50 ft. square internally, with four columns so placed as to leave a large central space. The design of the mosaic floor—that is, the original one—was accommodated to the architectural features. The space between the four columns was occupied by a grand medallion having for its subject Orpheus with his lyre. Within an elaborate border were two concentric friezes, the outer containing beasts and the inner birds, while in the centre was an octagonal compartment containing fishes, representing the animal world which the music of Orpheus tamed. The space exterior to the columns was divided into a series of panels containing medallions and various geometrical designs. Many of the adjacent rooms had ornate mosaic pavements of which portions remained. The planning of this group of buildings differed from that of Bignor in its greater compactness and symmetrical arrangement ; and the many pieces of carved stone and fragments of statues indicate that both the residence and the other two buildings were of considerable magnificence. As below the lower courtyard and on the left side there was a building of plain character, it is probable that there was a base-court with buildings on either side.

In many of the smaller country houses the residence and its various farm-buildings seem to have been grouped round a single large yard. A house at Brading in the Isle of Wight appears to have been of this type. Its large yard was about 180 ft. square, and was surrounded by a wall except where the buildings came to its side. The lower wall was not fully traced, but there was some evidence of a central gate. On the right side was a barn-like building, similar to, but larger than, the corresponding structure at Spoonley Wood ; but considerable portions of its interior had been divided into rooms by inserted walls, those of the farther end evidently forming a house, while at the lower end were remains of small bath chambers. On the opposite side of the yard was a range of building and shedding. The compact and symmetrical house, with a short corridor or portico between two short wings, occupied the middle of the end of the yard. The right wing contained the smaller division of a large double room with a mosaic pavement, which, like several others in this house, was rich in mythological subjects. A few yards to the right of the house, and attached to the yard wall, was an oblong structure, about 11 ft. wide, containing a large cistern in an alcove, which with little doubt was supplied with water from a spring in the vicinity. This Brading house in its compactness and symmetrical planning represents a by-no-means uncommon variant of the corridor type, and one peculiarly adapted for mansions of medium size. A good example was uncovered near Mansfield Woodhouse, in Nottinghamshire, in the 18th century. It faced, as usual, a large yard, which had on its right side a barn-like building of about the size of the one at Brading, and with evidence that the rooms of its upper end had been inhabited, and that it contained baths at its lower end.

BASILICAL HOUSES

In the foregoing pages several structures have been referred to as barn-like buildings. The one at Spoonley Wood probably was a barn, but the last two examples seem to have been, partly at least, used for human habitation. Some other examples will be given which were undoubted houses, and houses of no mean order. Two buildings excavated at Ickleton in Essex, and at Castlefield near Andover, closely resembled that at Spoonley Wood. The first was associated with a house of the ordinary type, and the second contained the remains of furnaces and hearths. The fallen roof-tiles showed that both had been roofed, but neither yielded evidence of having been used for human habitation.

Fig. 28 is the plan of one of these buildings at Clanville, Hampshire, and is specially interesting as its structural peculiarities were noted by the explorers, and the evidence that it was a house is beyond question. It had two rows of six pillar-bases each. The central space was regarded as an open court, and the pillars as the supports of two porticoes ; but it was noted that the walls of the rooms not only surrounded but covered some of the pillar-bases. Most of the rooms had plain or decorated mosaic floors, and two had hypocausts, while amongst their débris was an abundance of painted plaster and window-glass. The entrance was in the side, where the foundation of a porch was noted. Fig. 29 is the much larger Brading example, which closely resembled that at Mansfield Woodhouse in size. A few of the pillar-bases remained, and the sites of others were indicated by foundations. Many of the internal walls were insertions and

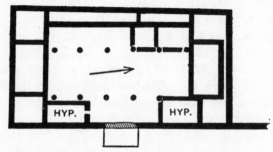

FIG. 28.—House at Clanville.   (40 ft. to 1 in.)

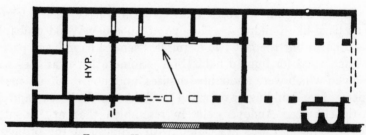

FIG. 29.—House at Brading.   (40 ft. to 1 in.)

had been built over these foundations. The rooms of the west end had concrete floors, painted walls, and glazed windows, and one was heated by a hypocaust. The entrance was in the side, and the lower east corner yielded remains of baths. Baths occupied a similar position at Mansfield Woodhouse. A fine example of one of these buildings, containing some beautiful mosaic pavements, was uncovered at Carisbrook in 1859, and recently another at Petersfield.

These buildings obviously belonged to a different type from

that of the corridor houses. In their main construction they resembled the medieval tithe and monastic barns which probably were a survival of the form. In some of them the rooms at one or both ends appear to have been parts of the original fabric, but many of those within the pillared space were certainly partitioned off subsequently. Our first three examples appear to have been barns, and this calls to mind the statement of Pytheas in the 4th century before our era, that the Britons for lack of sunshine collected their corn and threshed it in large buildings. It is conceivable that the hearths in the Castlefield building were for fires to aid the drying of the corn. But it is equally clear that in our other examples a portion of the interior was used for human habitation, and these demand a little further attention.

The Brading and the Mansfield Woodhouse examples were associated with houses of the ordinary type, to which they appear to have held a subordinate relationship. Major Rooke, who described the latter, suggested that it was the *villa rustica*, where the *villicus* or bailiff lived, the house being the *villa urbana*, the residence of the proprietor. The Clanville and Petersfield examples, on the other hand, were the chief buildings of their respective groups. Each stood on the farther side of a large courtyard with a gateway in the wall of the nearer side, while on the two remaining sides were farm-buildings, and at Petersfield an unusually large bath-building. In these cases, the barn-like building would be the residence of the proprietor, who presumably was a well-to-do farmer.

These basilical houses appear to belong to a primitive type of farmhouse which still survives in Germany, Holland, and elsewhere. Mr. S. O. Addy, in his *Evolution of the English House*, gives several examples, and notably one, a Saxon farmhouse from the German writer, Meitzen, which is singularly to the point. It is described as a large oblong structure (Fig. 30), divided into a nave and aisles, and entered by a large doorway at the lower end. The aisles are divided off into stalls (B) for the horses and cattle, which are foddered from the nave (A), while above in the roof are stored the corn and hay. At the end of the nave is the hearth (D), and on both sides are the cupboard-beds of the master and his family, the farm-hands sleeping on floors above the horses and cattle. To the right and left of the hearth extends a sort of transept (E) ending with windows or glazed doors in the sides of the building, which thus forms two well-lighted wings or recesses for household purposes. Behind the hearth wall are two private rooms (F, H) and a store room (G) ; but these are of comparatively recent introduction in these farm-houses. The smoke of the hearth permeating the whole interior tends to keep insects away and to neutralize the stench from the cattle. This Saxon farmhouse is perhaps exceptional in its large size and symmetrical proportions, but it is unquestionably representative of a widespread and ancient type of building which combined dwelling and farm-offices under a common roof,

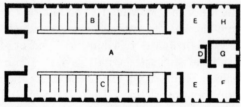

Fig. 30.—Plan of Saxon Farmhouse (after Meitzen)

and the Yorkshire ' coits ' may be regarded as a survival in this country.

The resemblance of this Saxon farmhouse to the Romano-British buildings we have described is apparent at a glance. We have noticed that in some, the rooms at one end appear to be part of the original construction, and these may well have been the original household rooms, the hearth being in the nave in front. It is feasible enough, that with a higher standard of living there would be a desire to gain greater privacy by the addition of new rooms, and these could be easily obtained by partitioning off portions of the main interior. On the other hand, the proprietor and his family might live in an adjacent house, in which case the building, as at Spoonley Wood, would be used for farm pur-poses only—for the beasts in winter, and for the storage of their fodder, also for the storage of grain which could be threshed on the ample ' floor ' of the nave.

The basilical type seems also to have been the source of the Romano-Italian houses. The parallels between the planning of the early Pompeian house before it was modified by Greek influence, and that of the Saxon farmhouse just described, are very close. The *atrium* of the former corresponds with the nave of the latter; the bedrooms with the stalls, and the *alae* with the transeptal extensions beyond the stalls. The *tablinum*, which originally contained the master's bed, and its lateral rooms, have their counterparts at the end of the Saxon house. As the Pompeian houses were built one against the other, the smoke-hole was enlarged into the *compluvium*, to compensate for the loss of side windows ; and the hearth, which was early banished to a special room, the *culina* or kitchen, was represented by the *impluvium*.

The corridor-houses were of a different type of planning altogether, and seem to be the product of a higher stage of culture. A row of rooms opening upon a portico is an ill-adapted structure to shelter man and beast and farm-produce under a common roof. As a human dwelling-place it is consistent, and marks an advance in domestic requirements and comfort. It presupposes that beast and produce had been banished to separate and special buildings. It was certainly not derived from the old Italian type of house. Corridor-houses are found in Gaul and elsewhere on the Continent, but there is no evidence that the type was of Celtic or Germanic origin. It seems rather to be the product of a warm and sunny region, modified with us to suit our colder climate ; and it is not unlikely that it was introduced into Gaul from the Orient by Greek colonists.[1]

[1] For cottages and villages, see *Rom.-Brit. Buildings, etc.,* chap. vi.

CHAPTER V

PUBLIC BUILDINGS AND BATHS

Forums [1]

THE forum may be regarded as the market-place, but it stood for more to the Roman. With its adjuncts, of which the basilica was chief, it was the centre of civic life and movement, combining the functions of market, town hall, law courts, exchange, and a gathering-place where the townsfolk discussed matters of mutual interest, settled points of difference, gossiped and idled—where public notices were displayed, and games were often held and religious festivals celebrated. It was the rendezvous for all classes and for all purposes.

Two forums have been explored in this country with great success, the one at Silchester and the other at Caerwent. They substantially agree in their planning, but the former was the larger and more elaborate structure, and a short description of it will be sufficient. The whole group of buildings—forum proper, with its porticoes and shops, basilica and offices—covered an oblong space about 315 by 278 ft., and was almost entirely surrounded with a portico supported by stone columns. The open square within was 142 by 130 ft., and the basilica formed its west side, the remaining sides having a similar portico to the external one, except where interrupted by the chief entrance on the east side. Between the two porticoes was a range of rooms, probably of two storeys. Most of these seem to have been shops, but some of them were of a different shape and may have been municipal offices, and it is just possible that one near the centre

---

[1] See *Romano-British Buildings and Earthworks* for more detailed information, chap. ix.

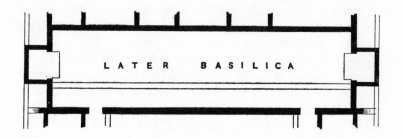

LATER BASILICA

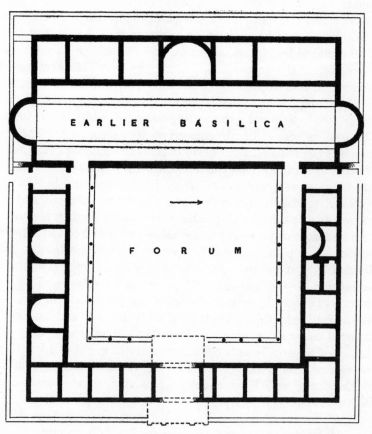

EARLIER BASILICA

FORUM

FIG. 31.—The Forum and Basilica, Silchester. (75 ft. to 1 in.)

of the north side, which had the form of a large apse, was the sanctuary of the city *lares*. The chief entrance was on a grand scale and in the form of a triumphal arch, not less than 45 ft. wide, and, to judge from the fragments of large columns and other carved stones found on the site, must have been architecturally imposing. Besides this, there were two minor entrances, the one on the north and the other on the south, both next the basilica.

The basilica was 233 ft. long and 58 ft. wide. It was originally divided into a nave and aisles by two rows of lofty Corinthian columns ; but subsequently it was partly rebuilt, with a single row dividing the space into a nave and single aisle. In its earlier condition, it had at each end a semicircular tribunal, but these were replaced by rectangular ones, and in each case their raised floors projected into the hall. Along the west side were several apartments and a spacious central apse with a raised floor reached by three steps and probably adorned with a large statue of a female with a mural crown, fragments of which were found. The basilica was evidently entered on its east side, but the wall here is in too reduced a condition to show the remains of doorways or other openings. That the interior of the building had a certain splendour is not only indicated by its architecture, but by the pieces of marble wall-linings found about the tribunals and the fragments of painted wall-plaster generally diffused on the site.

The forum at Caerwent was smaller and it lacked the external portico. Its plan was similar, but simpler. The basilica was divided into nave and aisles by two rows of lofty columns of Corinthian type. The tribunals were rectangular, and one of them is of special interest as the sill of its timber *cancelli* remains. As the wall next the forum is level with the floor and has on its external side two continuous stone steps, it may have been the sleeper of an arcade or a colonnade stretching the full length of the square. This was the usual arrangement in the headquarters of the forts, and it is equally applicable to the basilica at Silchester.

The remains of the basilica at Wroxeter indicate that it was 229 ft. long and 67 ft. wide, and was similarly divided into a nave and aisles by Corinthian columns. The entrance was apparently at one end and a tribunal at the other. Sufficient of the basilica at Cirencester has been excavated to prove that it was of larger dimensions than any of the above, and had the usual nave and two aisles. It had a large semicircular tribunal at one end, and some indications of a porch at the other, and as at Silchester, pieces of marble linings were found. At Chester and Lincoln, the remains of massive structures and colonnades have been exposed, which with little doubt related to the forums and basilicas of those towns.

AMPHITHEATRES [1]

Remains of about a dozen undoubted amphitheatres are known in this country. Those of Dorchester, Caerleon, Richborough, Silchester, and Cirencester are conspicuous and well known ; others, less known, are at Charterhouse on Mendips, Caerwent, Colchester, Maryborough near Penrith, Wroxeter, Aldborough, and elsewhere. With the exception of the Caerwent example, they are in their present condition elliptical depressions surrounded with a bank, the Maumbury Rings at Dorchester being the largest in this country. These amphitheatres are essentially earthworks, their arenas having been excavated, and the soil derived therefrom utilized for the portion of the surrounding bank above the old natural level. It is to this mode of construction they owe their present conspicuousness, that of Caerwent being wholly on the common level was quite unknown until its remains were brought to light by the spade a few years ago. This amphitheatre is exceptional in another respect. It is within the walls of the ancient town, the others mentioned above being outside their respective towns or stations.

The Caerleon amphitheatre, popularly known as King Arthur's Round Table, was sufficiently trenched in 1909, to show that its bank or *cavea* was supported externally by a strong and buttressed wall, and its foot by a thinner wall, the slope for the spectators having a width of 35 ft. The external dimensions are about 274 by 226 ft., and those of the arena about 70 ft. less. Remains of three entrances—on the north, east, and south —were found, and the floor of the arena was indicated by a

<hr />

[1] *Romano-British Buildings and Earthworks*, chap. ix.

thick layer of sand. It is estimated that this amphitheatre would accommodate 4000 people.

The exploration of the Maumbury Rings has been in progress since 1908. The external dimensions are roughly 345 by 333 ft., and it has an entrance at each apex. This great earthwork was utilized for a fort during the Civil War in Charles I.'s time, and in adapting it for the purpose, was considerably altered and disfigured. The excavations proved that the arena was 196 ft. long and about 20 ft. less in width, and was covered with gravel. The spectators' entrance was at the north end, and at the south end were remains of an enclosure opening to the arena and entered at the back by a descending path from a south entrance. This enclosure is supposed to have been the ' den ' in which the beasts were impounded when waiting their turn during the performances.

The Richborough amphitheatre was imperfectly excavated in 1849, when an elliptical wall, enclosing a space 200 ft. by 166 ft., was brought to light, as also the remains of three entrances. The account of the work is meagre, and it is not clear whether this wall represented the inner or the outer ring.

BATHS [1]

The process of the Roman bath was practically identical with that of the Turkish bath among us. Reduced to its barest essentials, the Turkish bath may consist of two rooms, the first a ' cooling-room,' and the second a hot room, provided with a hot-water tank and a seat ; but the intervention of a moderately heated room to which the shampooing and washing processes are relegated, is so advantageous as to be practically a necessity. The cooling-room serves very well as a dressing-room, but a separate apartment may be provided for this. In large public establishments it is usual to have separate shampooing and washing rooms, and two or more sudatory rooms at different temperatures : and besides the necessary plunge-bath, which may be in a special room, there may be a swimming-bath. The equipment must, of course, include a laundry department, and

[1] *Romano-British Buildings and Earthworks*, chap. viii.

various offices for the management and the attendants. But, broadly speaking, the rooms used by the bathers are resolvable into three sets—cool, moderately heated, and very hot.

Vitruvius and other Roman writers, in describing the baths of their times, refer to certain apartments by name. Three of these—the *frigidarium*, *tepidarium*, and *caldarium*—are frequently mentioned ; and as the names etymologically explain their uses, or rather temperatures, they provide a means of bringing the Roman into line with the modern Turkish baths. Galen mentions them respectively as the apartments passed through in rotation, and gives instructions how his patients were to be undressed in the *frigidarium*, to be anointed in the *tepidarium*, and after a stay in the *caldarium*, to be bathed in the plunge-bath of the first apartment upon their return. Other apartments are mentioned by these writers, as the *apodyterium* or *spoliatorium*, the dressing-room ; the *elaeothesium* or *unctuarium*, where the bathers were anointed, or the unguents were kept ; the *lavatorium*, or washing-room ; the *sudatorium*, or sweating-room ; and the *laconicum*, which perhaps is simply an alternative name for the *sudatorium*. It is clear, however, that some of these apartments were not always present, even in large establishments ; also, that the names were not always used in the same sense. Again, the ancient writers differ considerably in the order in which the baths were taken. Perhaps the fashion of bathing changed from time to time, but more likely the order was a matter of personal caprice, and the complex plans of many of the public baths seem arranged to meet this contingency. What is certain is this—the Roman, like the modern Turkish baths, always present a series of apartments from cool to hot.

Several points in the procedure of the Roman bath should here be noticed. As far as we know, soap was not used at all. After perspiration, the body was scraped with the *strigil* [1] to forcibly remove the dirt and dead portions of the cuticle. This was followed by the sponge, and delicate people often dispensed with the *strigil* altogether and used the sponge alone. The place where this scraping process took place would, of course,

[1] Fig. 63.

be one of the hot rooms, sometimes perhaps a special room. At a later stage, when the body was sufficiently cooled, perfumed oil or ointment was rubbed into the skin. These various requisites—strigils, oil, and unguents—were often brought to the public baths by the bathers, especially by the wealthy, who also brought slaves to attend to them. But these could be obtained on the premises, as also the services of attendants ; the poorer bathers, however, scraped and anointed themselves. Physical exercise was a concomitant of the bath. Even domestic baths sometimes had their tennis-court (*sphaeristerium*), as had Pliny's. In most of the public baths there was a spacious court (*palaestra*) with porticoes, exedrae, swimming-bath, etc., and other conveniences for outdoor recreation, ball - playing being a favourite pastime.

Many remains of Roman baths have been discovered in this country. Those at Wroxeter and Silchester were town baths of considerable extent and intricacy ; several in the vicinity of forts were military baths ; but the majority were private baths attached to country houses, and these were, as a rule, of small size, consisting of only the more essential rooms. But in all, the general principle and the method of heating the rooms were the same. A compact little bath-house was excavated at Caerwent in 1855. The two plans (Fig. 32) of this building are at different levels in order to show (1) the rooms used by the bathers and (2) the heating arrangements below. It contained the following sequence of rooms, each opening into the next by a narrow door :—

The first, A, a narrow anteroom, was entered apparently from an open court. On its left, or south side, was a cold-water bath in a large recess, B, with a flagged floor 3 ft. below that of the room, and its sides were of fine concrete painted red. On that next the room was a sill or dwarf wall, 9 ins. high, and within it a step or seat. The drain was in the middle of the south side. The second room, C, lay to the north, and was considerably larger, with a shallow alcove between projecting piers at the farther end. The third, D, was the largest of the series, a simple square room. The fourth, E, was provided with a hot-water bath at its west end. The contiguous walls which

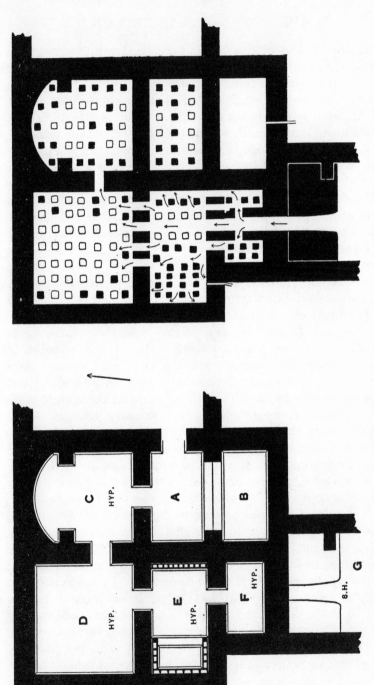

Fig. 32.—Plans of Baths, Caerwent; the first on the floor-level, and the second showing the hypocausts. (10 ft. to 1 in.)

formed three sides of this *alveus* were lined with vertical flue-tiles communicating with the hypocaust below, the opposite wall of the chamber being also similarly lined. The bottom was of a single flag which rested upon the hypocaust pillars, and its sides were of red stucco, with a drain at the south end. The fifth and last room, F, was immediately behind the furnace.

The floors of all these chambers were supported upon roughly squared sandstone pillars, and the intervals between these were spanned with large flagstones, upon which rested the concrete of the floors. This in the first three rooms was overlaid with plain mosaic, the total thickness being about 14 ins. The openings between the rooms were probably covered with rugs or thick curtains, as there were no indications that they had been fitted with wooden doors.

The second plan illustrates the heating of the apartments. The furnace projected into a sunk yard or shed, which would be provided with suitable storage space for the fuel. The aperture was flanked by two strong cheeks or platforms of masonry, 5 ft. high, a usual feature in the furnaces of baths, in order to carry the tank or cauldron in which the water was heated. The hot gases of the fire passed through an arched opening into the hypocausts of the rooms, and the upright wall-flues in room E would induce the necessary draught. It is almost certain that room D, and probably C as well, had also a few wall-flues, to ensure the passage of some of these gases into their hypocausts. The pillared substructure under the ante-room was evidently an arrangement to keep its floor dry, as there was no opening by which these gases could pass into it.

It is evident that there would be a gradation of temperature, that of each successive room from the first one entered being higher than the last, the last being the hottest. C was probably a combined cooling and dressing-room, with a seat in its alcove ; D, the *tepidarium* ; E, the *caldarium* ; and F, a specially hot room or *sudatorium*. This last room, however, was usually omitted in the domestic, and even in larger baths ; and in most instances the *alveus* occupied the space next the furnace.

This Caerwent building is typical, except in its compactness, of the smaller baths in this country. The rooms usually have a linear arrangement, with the entrance at or near one end, and the furnace at the other. Of the military baths, the remains of those at Great Chesters are the most complete. The main block, exclusive of the furnace-house, was 48 ft. long, and was entered from a yard, at one end of which were the latrines. The first room had a flagged floor, a cold-water bath on the left, and a door into another flagged room on the right. Neither room was heated, and the second may very well have been the *apodyterium*. In the side of the anteroom facing the entrance was the door into the *tepidarium*, a small room, and beyond this was the *caldarium*, a spacious room, with a large alcove on either side and a hot-water bath in a large recess at the end. Beyond this was the furnace and its shed. The remains of the military baths at Chesters are more extensive, but less complete. Those of Gellygaer have recently been excavated, and they indicate an irregular building due in part to alterations and extensions. The main structure in its final form was about 87 ft. long, and was remarkable for its large cold-water bath, about 26 by 15 ft., and one of its hot rooms being circular.

The public baths of Calleva underwent so many alterations and extensions that it is difficult to make out its plan for any period. The greatest length that the main building attained was 148 ft. In its original form it was entered from the street under a portico, and this gave access to a peristyled courtyard, which subsequently was enlarged. Next was a spacious *apodyterium*; then a *frigidarium*, with a marble *labrum* in the centre and a cold-water bath at one end; and finally several heated rooms with hot-water *alvei*. All these rooms were at one time or other altered and extended. The public baths of Viroconium were on a larger scale. The plan of the portion which has been excavated is suggestive of a symmetrical building consisting of a central block and east and west wings. The central block seems to have contained a grand entrance-hall with large rooms behind, and beyond these an open court with a large recess on either side (probably *exedrae*), and in the centre the remains of a paved swimming-bath; but all these remains were very indefinite. The excavation of the west wing gave definite results and revealed a series of rooms heated from a furnace-house at the west end.

On the east side of the central block were the remains of other heated rooms which corresponded, as far as they went, with those of the west wing, and strongly suggested an east wing of similar character.   If so, the total length of the range of building, exclusive of furnace-houses, would be 208 ft., and the whole was apparently enclosed in a great peristyled courtyard.   It is probable that the one wing contained men's baths and the other, women's.

CHAPTER VI

RELIGIONS OF ROMAN BRITAIN

The Graeco-Roman and Barbaric Paganisms—Mithraism
and other Eastern Cults—Christianity

AS intimated in the Introduction, the deities and divinities named on altars and tablets, rendered in sculpture, and figured on mosaics in this country, fall into several groups. There were those of the Graeco-Roman pantheon whose worship may be regarded as the official or state religion. There were those bearing barbaric names, mostly Celtic and German, some undoubtedly old British deities, others imported by the soldiery. There were the divine personages of Oriental religions—Mithras, Isis, and the Great Mother of Phrygia—of later introduction. And finally came the religion of Christ.

Of the greater gods of Rome, Jupiter, pre-eminently the patron of the state and its official machinery, is the most frequently named on the altars. His usual formula is I.O.M., ' Jupiter, the best and greatest ' ; and a dedication at Ellenborough, *I.O.M. Capitolino*, specially connects him with his chief seat of worship —the Capitol of Rome—where, associated with Juno and Minerva, he was honoured as the divine head of the state. It is curious that of the Capitoline triad, no trace of the worship of Juno has been found in Britain. There are, however, several inscriptions to Minerva. She is associated with Hercules on an altar at Kirk Haugh in Northumberland ; and at South Shields and Ribchester, tablets have been found recording the restoration of temples to her, and at Chichester, to her and Neptune.

The altars and sculptured representations of Mars are many, and, as might be expected, they have been mostly found among the military remains. The former are usually dedicated to the god, or the holy god, Mars ; otherwise to him in some special capacity, as Mars the Conqueror, Mars the Pacifier, and Mars the Preserver (*Marti Victori—Pacifero—Conservatori*). He is occasionally and appropriately associated with Victory. Although very few altars to Mercury have been found, he was a favourite subject for sculpture, and is invariably shown with his caduceus and often with a purse. The sculptures usually take the form of small panelled reliefs, which were probably placed in the walls of workshops and other buildings devoted to trade and traffic, of which he was the patron. Apollo is usually associated or equated with other deities in Britain. At Ribchester, the dedication of an altar, *Deo Sancto Apollini Apono*, specially connects him with his famous shrine and oracle at Fons Aponi near Padua, which, like our Bath, was much resorted to for its healing waters. Fortuna, the goddess of good luck, was a favourite with the soldiery. More than a dozen altars to her have been found in Britain, on which she is addressed simply as Fortuna, or as Fortuna Conservatorix and Fortuna Redux ; while on one at Chesterholm she appears as Fortuna Populi Romani, the tutelary goddess of the Roman people. There are fewer altars to Victoria, the goddess of victory, but she is a frequent subject in sculpture.

The following deities, to judge from the few remains that relate to them, were sparingly invoked. There are altars to Neptune at Newcastle and Chesterholm ; to Diana at Bath, Newstead, and Caerleon, where also a tablet records the rebuilding of a temple to her ; to Aesculapius at Lanchester and Maryport, while at Binchester he is associated with his daughter Salus, and she alone is the subject of an altar at Caerleon ; and to Bellona, goddess of war, at Old Carlisle, and, according to Spartian, she had a temple at York. The Parcae or Fates have altars at Carlisle and Lincoln ; and the god who brought undertakings to a successful issue, Bonus Eventus, is occasionally associated with Fortuna and other deities.

The tutelary goddesses of Rome and Britain and many genii were invoked. At High Rochester and Maryport are altars to Roma, and on another at the latter place she is styled Roma

Aeterna. Britannia had altars at York (where also is part of a statue of her), Castlehill, and Auchindavy. Originally, a genius was the power which created and maintained a man's life, determined his character, and influenced him for good—something intimately blended with him, yet not himself, and in a sense his guardian spirit. The Genius of the head of the family—the paterfamilias—was ever associated with the Lar and the Penates in the Roman household worship. By a process of extension, nations, societies, cities, and even streets, baths, and places everywhere were deemed to have their genii. Hence we have altars dedicated to the Genius of the Roman people at Stanwix, High Rochester, and elsewhere; to that of Britannia at Chichester; and to that of the Emperor at Chesterholm and High Rochester. Legions, cohorts, *alae*, and centuries, the *praetorium*, and the standards, had their genii, and we have altars to all of them. More still were dedicated, *Genio Loci*, to the Genius of the Place.

Less easy to define is the *numen* of the emperor, which frequently finds a place on our inscriptions, mostly in association with higher divinities. A numen seems originally to have signified any power higher than man; but ultimately the term was confined to the emperors, and perhaps the best English rendering would be the ' divinity ' of the emperor. The soldiers were thus taught to hold the emperor's personality as sacred. Even his authority was deified. Two altars, the one at Walton in Northumberland and the other at Birrens, are dedicated, *Disciplinae Augusti*—to the Discipline of the Emperor. The second altar was found in the *principia*, and it may well have come from the *sacellum*.

Of the rural divinities, the nymphs—the benign beings who dwelled by springs and rivers, in woodlands and meadows, and on hills—were much invoked. On an altar at Risingham is a curiously worded dedication to the nymphs to whom worship is due—*Nymphis verandis*. By a process of metonymy, the water-nymphs are ' Fontes,' on an altar found near Chester, and the field-nymphs ' Campestres,' on one at Castle Hill. Silvanus, the woodland god, beloved of hunters, has several altars; and one at High Rochester is dedicated to the Mountain Deities,

Dis Mountibus; while at Risingham is one to the divine Fosterers or Cultivators of the place, *Dis Cultoribus hujus loci*.

Although the divine beings enumerated above were Roman in name, they were not necessarily *worshipped* as Roman. For instance, several altars, one at Caerleon, are dedicated to the Dolichene Jupiter, *Jovi Dolicheno*, and one at Appleby to Jupiter Serapis, thus equating Jupiter with a famous god, whose chief seat was Doliche in northern Syria, and with the Egyptian Serapis. Further evidence of his worship as Serapis are an inscription recording the erection of a temple to him at York and an altar to the Heliopolitan Jupiter at Carvoran. An altar at Chester to Jupiter Taranus, *I.O.M. Tarano*, may connect him with the German Thor or Thunor; or more probably with Taranucus or Taranucnus, a Gaulish thunder-god, to whom there are several Continental inscriptions. Two altars at Walton in Northumberland, dedicated to Jupiter, are carved with a thunderbolt, the attribute of Jupiter, and a wheel, perhaps thus equating him with a Gaulish sky- or war-god whose attribute was a wheel. This god is apparently the subject of a pottery intaglio recently found at Corbridge, which represents a warrior with a wheel at his feet. We have already noticed that the goddess of the hot springs at Bath was equated with Minerva. The remains of a temple to her have been found in that city, and on or near the site, a beautiful bronze-gilt female head, which, from the circumstance that it appears to have had a helmet, may have represented Minerva, or, strictly speaking, Sul-Minerva.

Several war-gods are equated with Mars in this country. One of these is the Gaulish Belatucadrus, to whom there are more than a dozen altars in the north, on three of which he is addressed as Mars Belatucadrus. There are about the same number to Cocidius, all also in the north. As he is unknown beyond our shores, he may well have been a British god, warlike and haunting the woods, for he is equated with both Mars and Silvanus. Apparently he had an important seat of worship in the neighbourhood of Carlisle, for thereabout the Ravenna chorographer places a Fanocedi, or, as in another manuscript, Fanococidi. At Bath, an altar to Mars Loucetius and Nematona was raised by a native of Treves, in which district, Leucetius, a god of lightning, and his consort Nemetona, were invoked together. In Irish tradition, the latter appears as Nemon, the wife of a war-god, Net ; and somewhere in the south-west of England was Nemetotacis, according to the above chorographer, which may have been named after her. A bronze tablet found at West Coker in Somerset is inscribed to Mars Rigisamus, a Celtic god, ' the most royal.' There is at Glasgow an inscription to Camulus, ' the warlike heaven-god,' who " appears in Gaelic myth as Cumhal, the father of Finn, and in British mythical history as Coel, a duke of Caer Coelvin (known earlier as Camulodunum, and now as Colchester), who seized the crown of Britain, and spent his short reign in a series of battles " (Squire). Although equated on Gaulish inscriptions with Mars, he seems to have been a warlike Jupiter, of whom, perhaps, *Belatucadrus* and *Rigisamus* were epithets. At Chester-le-Street, Carlisle, and Caerwent are inscriptions to Mars Ocelus and Mars Condate, probably also Celtic deities. Condate is an occasional place-name both in Britain and on the Continent. On one of the Caerwent inscriptions Mars Ocelus is equated with the German Lenus. In Hertfordshire, and at York and Old Carlisle, have been found inscriptions, *Marti Toutati* or *Totati*, apparently the fierce Gaulish Toutates referred to by Lucan.

Some remarkable remains of a small temple were discovered on Chapel Hill at Housesteads in 1882–83, and among them were found two altars erected by Frisian Germans, the one dedicated in poor Latin, *Deo Marti Thingso et duabus Alaisiagis Bede et Fimmilene et N. Aug.*, and the other, *Deo Marti et duabus Alaisiagis et N. Aug.*—" To the god Mars Thingsus, the two Alaisiagae, Beda and Fimmelena, and the *numen* of the Emperor." The chief sculptured stone on the site was the head of a doorway, with a central relief of Mars Thingsus, with one hand holding a spear and the other resting upon his shield, while at the feet was a goose or a swan ; and on each side was a nude figure holding a wand or sceptre and a wreath—the two probably representing the two divinities just named. According to Prof. Heinzel of Vienna, Thingsus is Tuis Things, the patron of the national assembly (' thing ') of the Frisians, and he connects the two goddesses with the Bodthing, the general court of justice, and the Fimmel-thing, the movable court.

Grannos, patron of healing-waters, an especial favourite of the Continental Belgae, was invoked as Apollo Grannus at Inveresk. Several places famous for their thermal springs, as Aquae Granni, now Aix-la-Chapelle, Graux, and Grantheim, were named after him. Maponus, another Celtic Apollo, appears on several altars in Britain and the Continent. In Welsh story he appears as Mabon, son of Modron, and a companion of Arthur. The name signifies a child, and Sir John Rhys remarks that the eastern Celts worshipped a juvenile deity, who in Dacia was styled Bonus Puer, and was sometimes identified with Apollo. There are altars at Risingham, Old Penrith, and Netherby to an obscure god, Mogon or Mogons, and on two of them he is specified as of the Cadeni, a tribe of the Vangiones on the Rhine, whose capital was Moguntiacum. A cohort of Vangiones was settled at Risingham, and with little doubt his two altars there were raised by it.

Near Carrawberg was unearthed in 1882–83 the remains of a small temple and a number of altars to a water-goddess, Coventina. On one of the altars she is addressed in barbaric Latin, *Deae Nimfa Coventine*, and she is represented on two sculptured tablets, on the one as reclining on a water-lily, and on the other as attended by two nymphs. She was apparently identified with Minerva, for one of the altars is dedicated to that goddess. As no trace of her worship has been found elsewhere, it is probable that she was a local divinity, and that her name is a latinization of that of the stream at the source of which her shrine stood. The central feature of this temple was a rectangular well which received the water of the spring, and about its floor were many coins and small trinkets, cast in, as Mr. Clayton, the explorer of the remains, suggested, by " love-sick damsels . . . in the hope of obtaining the countenance of the goddess in their views." Similar offerings have been found on the sites of the shrines of several river-goddesses in France ; and the pins which even to-day are dropped into reputed holy wells are a survival of the custom. The Egarmangabis, to whom an altar by a spring near Lanchester was dedicated, was probably a water-goddess ; and the name of a nymph-goddess, Elauna, on an altar at Greta Bridge, is suggestive of a river. Another nymph-goddess, Brigantia, had altars at Chester, London, and several places in the north, on one of which her name is spelled Bergantia ; and at Birrens was found, in 1731, a sculptured relief of a draped female, inscribed to the effect that one Amandus, an architect, dedicated it to Brigantia. This figure, however, is scarcely that of a nymph. It has been regarded as that of the tutelary goddess of the British Brigantes ; but it would equally well represent the goddess of one of the Continental Brigantias, of one of which cities Amandus may have been a native. Perhaps the Brigantia of the altars is the Gaulish Brigindu, who was also reverenced in Ireland, and is still, as St. Brigit.

No divinities of Roman Britain are more interesting and attractive than the ' Matres.' Nearly three dozen altars and inscriptions to them have been found, mostly in the military centres of the north.[1] The ' Mothers ' are typically represented as a triad of seated young women with benign countenances, clad in long robes, and holding baskets of fruit on their laps ; but there are many variants. Sometimes the middle goddess alone has the fruit ; and not seldom the basket is omitted. Occasionally the triad was made up of three single figures. These goddesses were not Roman, nor is there any allusion to them in classical mythology ; nevertheless, their worship was extremely popular, especially among the German and Celtic peoples, and many reminiscences of it lingered far into the Middle Ages. There is no evidence of it in Britain before the conquest ; on the contrary, there are inscriptions which tend to prove that it was introduced by the soldiers. Here and there in the north is an altar to the Transmarine Mothers, *Matribus Tramarinis*, and one at Newcastle reads, *Deabus Matribus Tramarinis Patr(i)is*, which may be rendered, ' To the Mother-goddesses of our fatherland beyond the sea.' Soldiers at Port Carlisle raised an altar to *Our* Mothers ; and at York, to the Mothers of Africa, Italy, and Gaul. However introduced, the worship of these beneficent dispensers of the

[1] For list of remains relating to this cult in Britain, see *Arch. Aelian.*, xv, p. 314.

kindly fruits of the earth, who were ever watchful over the affairs of men, became as popular in this country as on the Continent. There were the Domestic Mothers and the Mothers of the fields, of cities, and of nations. There was a temple to the Mothers of all nations at Walton in Northumberland.

Akin to the Matres were the Sulevae, who were worshipped in Rhineland and elsewhere on the Continent, as well as in Britain. Altars to them have been found at Colchester, Bath, and Cirencester. Those at the second and third places were erected by the same man, Sulinus, a sculptor. The Cirencester altar was found associated with several carved stones which, from their new or unfinished appearance, left little room for doubt that the site was that of the workshop or yard of Sulinus. One of the carvings was a typical Matres group, each figure holding a basket of fruit ; another also shows three seated females, but they are attended by little boys, and the central figure alone has fruit on her lap, and in addition a lamb or kid. It is probable that this group is the Sulevae, who certainly resembled the Matres, and were probably often confused with them.

A notable example of the Romanization of a native cult is furnished by the great shrine of the British Nudd or Lludd at Lydney on the banks of the Severn. The ' silver-handed ' Nudd, benign dispenser of health and wealth, here appears under the latinized form of Nodens or Nudens. He is represented as the classical Sol, drawn in a car by four horses. Zephyrs and tritons, emblematic of his dominion of the winds and the waters, attend him. The whole treatment is Roman ; as also that of the votive tablets with their Latin inscriptions, and the mosaics of the temple.

There yet remain a few inscriptions to barbaric divinities of whom little or nothing is known. An altar at Carvoran is dedicated to Epona, a goddess who is represented on the Continent as riding a mare, or as seated between two foals, and was specially invoked by horsemen and charioteers. Of Anociticus or Antenociticus, to whom two altars have been found on the site of a temple at Benwell, Matunus at Elsden in Northumberland, and Vanauntris at Walton ; and of the goddesses, Ancasta at Bittern, Harimella, Ricagambeda, and Veradecthis at Birrens, and Seltocenia at Ellenborough, little or nothing is known, beyond that they appear to have been Celtic or German deities. Jalonus, altars to whom have been found at Folly, and Overborough, Lancashire, may have been a Spanish god; possibly also Gadunus at Plumpton Wall in Cumberland.

We now turn to the Oriental cults in Britain. Chief of these was Mithraism, the worship of the ancient sun-god of Persia, which, modified by Greek influence, took firm root in Rome in the 1st century, was diffused throughout the west in the 2nd, and was one of the most fashionable of cults in the 3rd. In Graeco-Roman art, Mithras was represented as an Apollo-like deity, clad in Phrygian costume and cap. A conspicuous feature of his shrines were the so-called ' taurine ' sculptures, in which he was shown kneeling on a prostrate bull and plunging a dagger into his neck, the scene being enacted in a cave or grotto. This was the mystic sacrifice—the slaying of the bull, the first created of living things, in order that all other animals might be made out of his blood, a symbol also of a great final sacrifice which was to renew the life of mankind. As accessories in the composition were usually the god's attendants, the Dadophori—Cautes and Cautopites, the one holding a torch upright and the other one reversed; below the bull, a dog and a serpent moving towards the issuing blood as if to drink it; and above the cave, the sun and moon, often personified and drawn in chariots by horses, the one chasing the other away. The two torches appear to represent the summer and the winter solstices, and these, with the sun chasing the moon, symbolize the conflict of light and darkness—of good and evil—in which the god engages, and in which his followers must participate only to become victorious through sacrifice and probation.

An almost complete taurine slab has been found at York, and fragments of another on the site of a Mithraic temple or ' cave ' at Housesteads, where in its perfect condition it occupied a recess at the end of the inner sanctuary. In front of the latter stood another characteristic sculpture between two altars, dedicated to the Invincible Mithras, Lord of the Ages. This stone presented the god at the moment of his mystic birth, within an oval arch or hoop on which were carved the signs of the zodiac. A fine but small taurine slab has been found in London.[1]

The remains of other ' caves ' have been found at Rutchester and Burham in Kent, and an inscription at High Rochester records the erection of one there.   On his inscriptions, his epithets are the ' Invincible ' and the ' Lord of the Ages,' and he is often identified with the sun, as on an altar found at Housesteads—*Deo Soli Invicto Mitrae Seculari*. On another altar from the same mithraeum he is identified with Apollo ; and on yet another he usurps the title of Jupiter—*D.O.M., Invicto Mitrae Saeculari*— ' To the god, best and greatest, the Invincible Mithras, Lord of the Ages.'

Of the worship of the Great Mother, whose chief seat, being Hieropolis in Syria, was commonly known as the Syrian Goddess, there are only few traces in Britain, and the most conspicuous of these are at Carvoran, where a cohort of Hamian archers from Syria or Arabia erected altars to the Syrian and Hamian goddesses. But the most remarkable relic of her worship at Carvoran is a tablet with a long inscription in iambic verse, which Dr. Bruce rendered as follows :—

> "The Virgin in her celestial seat overhangs the Lion,
> Producer of corn,[2] Inventress of sight, Foundress of cities,
> By which gifts it has been our good fortune to know the deities.
> Therefore the same *is* the Mother of the gods, *is* Peace, *is* Virtue, *is* Ceres,
> *Is* the Syrian Goddess poising life and laws in a balance.
> The constellation beheld in the sky hath Syria sent forth
> To Libya to be worshipped, thence have all of us learnt it ;
> Thus hath understood, overspread by thy protecting influence,
> Marcus Caecilius Donatianus, a war-faring
> Tribune *in the office of* prefect, by the bounty of the Emperor."

The Syrian goddess, like Isis, gathered into herself all the chief goddesses of the ancients, and was herself identified with that goddess. Apuleius, in describing an initiation into the mysteries of Isis, makes the Queen of Heaven reveal herself to the devotee

---

[1] *Archaeologia*, lx, p. 46.

[2] Literally, " Bearer of an ear of corn," an allusion to the bright star Spica in the constellation of Virgo, just as we have an allusion to that of Libra in the balance referred to in the fifth line.

thus : " The Phrygians call me the Mother of the gods at Pessinus ; the Athenians, Cecropian Minerva ; I am the Paphian Venus in Cyprus ; Diana Dictynna to the archers of Cretae; the Stygian Proserpine to the Sicilians ; I am the ancient Ceres at Eleusis. To some I am Juno, to others Hecate. Only the Ethiopians and Arians, illumined by the sun's dawning light, and Egypt powerful in her ancient lore, honour me with the ritual proper to me, and call me by my true name, Queen Isis." On the Carvoran tablet, Isis is viewed from the Syrian point of view : " The constellation (Virgo) beheld in the sky, hath Syria sent forth to Libya to be worshipped.   Thence all of us learnt it, etc." [1]

It is probable that a fine statue of a draped female, found at Chesters, may represent the Magna Mater.   Unfortunately the head and arms are missing, and it stands upon a large animal which is also headless, and the legs are broken off.   If this animal is a lion, as has been supposed, the figure is almost certainly that of Cybele, who was early identified with the Syrian goddess ; if an ox, it may represent Isis.   There are, however, no certain traces of the worship of the latter, whose ritual singularly anticipated that of the Catholic Church, in this country ; but we have already noted a temple and altars to Serapis, her brother, with whom she was often associated in worship.

Our knowledge of Christianity in Roman Britain, unlike that of its paganism, is mainly derived from literary sources, the archaeological evidence being singularly meagre.   The only remains which have been certainly identified as a Christian church are at Silchester.   It was a tiny building, smaller than any of the temples found there, smaller indeed than any of the houses ; but as it occupied one of the best positions near the centre of the town, we may conclude that the Christian community was neither poor nor without local influence.   The ' chi-rho ' monogram has been found, associated with pagan subjects, on a mosaic pavement at Frampton in Dorset, cut or scratched in the masonry of a house at Chedworth in Gloucestershire, and

---

[1] Dr. Thomas Hodgson gives a more literal translation of the inscription in *Archaeologia Aeliana*, xxi, 289, and he regards it as virtually an apotheosis of Julia Domna, wife of Severus, a Syrian lady.

engraved on several pewter vessels and objects of personal adornment. A ring bearing a Christian motto has been turned up at Silchester, and out of a large number of tombstones, the inscriptions of only two or three have a Christian cast. These represent the only definite witnesses to the presence of Christianity out of the vast number of relics of the Roman era that have been found in this country, and it would seem that, so far as archaeological evidence goes, the heavy atmosphere of paganism hung over our land from first to last.

Yet if we credit the statements of early writers, there was a vigorous Christianity in this island, planted by the apostles themselves, contributing hundreds of martyrs under the Diocletian persecution, and in the 4th century the dominant religion, fully organized, and represented by its bishops in the great ecclesiastical councils of that century. The evidence for the apostolic foundation of the Romano-British church, however, is vague and contradictory, and it is based upon the statements of writers of a later and uncritical age. However and whenever introduced, we stand upon surer ground from the beginning of the 3rd century onwards. Tertullian, writing about that time, states that parts of Britain were already subject to Christ ; and in the 4th century, Athanasius, Hilary of Poitiers, Chrysostom, and Jerome, all refer in high terms to the faith and discipline of the British Church. The lists of the clergy who were present at the ecclesiastical councils of Arles, Sardica, and Ariminium in the same century, include British bishops, and those who attended the first are specified as the bishops of London, York, and Caerleon, or perhaps Lincoln. But perhaps the best evidence that Christianity had taken firm root in Roman Britain, was the existence of a native church in the 5th and 6th centuries in those parts of the island which were not affected by the English conquest. It is impossible to regard this church as otherwise than a survival of Romano-British Christianity.

But how is the witness of history to be reconciled with the comparative silence of archaeology ? As yet no satisfactory answer is forthcoming. It may have been—but there is no evidence for it—that the Romano-British Christians belonged exclusively to the poorer classes of society, and that their churches were constructed of timber and wattle, and so have perished entirely. Or, that in what is now England, the Faith survived the English conquest to a greater extent than is commonly supposed, and that many of our existing churches of most ancient foundation had a Roman origin. St. Martin's at Canterbury, according to Bede, " was built whilst the Romans were still in the island," and the churches of Reculver, Dover Castle, and Lyminge have been instanced as Roman churches, but all that can be said of them is that they are partly built of Roman materials. Too little is known of Romano-British Christianity to render it at all certain whether the basilica-type was as rigidly adhered to as on the Continent. In both Silchester and Caerwent, buildings have been found which might very well have served for churches.

The absence of churches in the rural districts is less difficult. With a small population and only a portion of it Christian, it would rarely happen that there would be a sufficient number of Christian families in any one district to maintain a church. The Christian proprietor of a villa probably had his domestic chapel, a large room in his house, where he, his family and dependants assembled for worship. If wealthy enough, he had a chaplain ; otherwise he would depend upon the visits of a missionary-priest. In the natural order of development, the room in the house would give place to the separate church, and the villa would be recognized as its parish ; but perhaps this stage was rarely reached in rural Roman Britain.

CHAPTER VII

RELIGIOUS BUILDINGS AND ALTARS

Temples [1]

THE remains of only a few Roman buildings in this country have been satisfactorily identified as temples, and these, with one exception, the remains of a small temple found at Bath in 1790, have failed to throw definite light upon their superstructures. This temple stood at the north-west corner of the Roman baths, but unfortunately no plan is extant. Sufficient of the sculptured details, however, are preserved to indicate that the façade was about 25 ft. wide, thoroughly Roman in character, with fluted columns of Corinthian type, a richly sculptured cornice, and a rather lofty pediment. The tympanum had for its central feature a medallion supported by two victories, a frequent device in Roman art. On the medallion was a Gorgon's head, with wings and serpents intertwined with the hair as usual, but curiously with moustache and beard as well—possibly the vagary of the sculptor. The rest of the field appears to have been filled in with military trophies, and amongst these was an owl, which, with the Gorgon's head (both attributes of Minerva), leaves little doubt that the temple was dedicated to Sul-Minerva.

The remains of four temples have been found at Silchester. Two of these were in a walled enclosure just within the east gate, and they were square structures, the larger 73 ft. and the smaller 50 ft., each enclosing a square *cella*. The entrances were probably on their eastern sides, which were only partly explored. The concrete floor of each was raised on a solid substructure repre-

---

[1] For more detailed particulars, see *Rom.-Brit. Buildings and Earthworks*, chap. x.

senting the characteristic *podium* of a Roman temple. The outer wall probably supported a colonnade, and the pieces of moulded plaster and marble linings, found about both sites, showed that these buildings were of an ornate description. A smaller temple near the centre of the town differed in being oblong, 36 ft. 6 ins. long and 35 ft. wide. It had a raised concrete floor and a wide doorway at the east end, with a corresponding one into the *cella*, and within the latter at the opposite end were the foundations of a shrine. Fragments of columns found near probably belonged to this temple, which, to judge from a piece of inscription, was dedicated to Mars. The remaining temple was polygonal, with sixteen sides, 65 ft. in diameter, and with a large *cella* of the same shape. The whole structure was reduced to below its floor-level, but it is probable that it had a mosaic pavement. No fragments of columns or other architectural details were found, and little else can be said of it, beyond that the polygonal form was favourable for a peristyle, as by it the need for a curved cornice would be avoided.

Remains of other buildings of similar type to the last have been found in this country. One at Weycock, near Maidstone, was octagonal with an inner chamber of the same shape. Another at West Mersea, in Essex, was circular, 65 ft. in diameter, and resembled a cogged wheel, having twelve buttress-like projections, which probably supported the columns of a peristyle, and six internal walls radiating spoke-wise from a small central hexagonal cell. The site is described as somewhat raised, and roofing-tiles lay scattered about.

The remaining temples that have been found in this country were rectangular. The temple of Coventina, at Carrawburgh, referred to on page 106, was 46 ft. long and 44 ft. wide, and the *cella* was represented by a massively constructed cistern 8 ft. 6 ins. by 7 ft. 9 ins., and 7 ft. deep, which received the water of the spring. The whole structure was reduced to below the level, raised floor. Within the past century worked stones and the shaft of a column lay on the site, indicating apparently that this temple was a substantial stone structure with a peristyle. The remarkable assemblage of altars, coins, and other objects found in the cistern has already been described.

The remains of two temples of apparently a different type have been found at Caerwent and at Lydney in Gloucestershire. The former was 45 ft. long and 42 ft. wide, with three buttresses on each side, and a square *cella* which had an apse at its north end, the entrance, of which no trace remained, being at the south end. This temple was about 52 ft. from the north side of the main thoroughfare of Venta Silurum and stood in an open space. Along the street-side were the remains of a narrow building about 64 ft. long with a plain mosaic pavement and an apse at its east end. The entrance to the precincts was in the south side

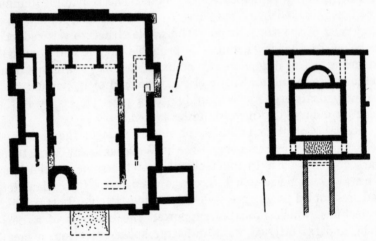

FIG. 33.—Plans of Temples at Lydney Park and Caerwent. (40 ft. to 1 in)

of this structure ; and from the opposite side extended a walled walk leading to the temple.

The temple at Lydney was not only remarkable in itself, but was one of a remarkable group of buildings on the summit of a knoll overlooking the Severn, and within the lines of an intrenchment of earlier date. The temple itself stood within an open space bounded on the east by a spacious quadrangular house and on the north by a long narrow range of rooms, while away to the north-east was an extensive and intricate bath-building. As already noticed on page 108, it was dedicated to Nodens or Nudens, latinised forms of the British god Nudd or

Lludd. The whole group indicates a sacred site of great importance, as its extent and rich mosaic pavements betoken ; and
although the buildings were of the Roman era, there is little
doubt that the worship of Nudd here dates from an earlier age.
So far as is known, there was no large Romano-British population
in the vicinity, so it seems likely that the house was a *hospitium*
for the accommodation of visitors to the shrine, many of whom,
to judge from the votive tablets, came to be cured of diseases.
The temple was 88 ft. long and 62 ft. wide, with the entrance
at the south end as at Caerwent. It differed, however, in having
two chapel-like enclosures on each side within projecting recesses
of the external wall, and in the *cella* having three internal recesses
at the north end. The south end of the *cella* had disappeared,
but on the left side of the site of its entrance was a small apsidal
structure of unknown use. The floors were of rich mosaic. At
the south-east corner of the building was a room which may have
been the sacristan's abode.

In the foregoing examples of temples we can distinguish
several types. The temple of Sul-Minerva appears to have been
of the ordinary Roman form. Of similar character, probably,
were the third Silchester example and the temple of Coventina,
except that in their central isolated *cellae* they were less Roman.
More remote still were the Caerwent and Lydney examples,
which could hardly have had peristyles. These, however, all
agreed in being oblong structures, a form which suggests a longitudinal roof with pedimented ends, and which we may distinguish as the 'longitudinal type.' The polygonal and circular
structures belong to another or 'central type,' of which the
temple of Vesta at Rome is a familiar example. In these, the
front and the back would not be distinguishable so far as their
main architectural features went, and the roof would probably
be conical. The two *square* temples at Silchester may perhaps
also be classed with these.

The worship of Mithras, as already stated, was firmly planted
in Britain, but the only undoubted remains of a temple have
been found at Housesteads. This *mithraeum* was constructed
in an excavation in the side of a hill at a spot where a spring
issues—an essential in the worship of this god. Of the west end,

which would contain the entrance-vestibule, little remained. The middle portion or body of the structure was 16 ft. wide and about twice that in length. It had a central passage or 'nave,' between two narrow platforms or 'aisles,' at least 2 ft. high, upon which the votaries knelt during the celebration of the mysteries, and near its west end was a sunk tank to receive the water of the spring. The inner cell or sanctuary, which contained the remarkable sculptures and altars mentioned on page 109, was discovered and destroyed many years previously. A curious subterranean chamber of Roman age, discovered at Burham in Kent in 1894, was almost certainly a Mithraic 'cave,' although no remains of altars or other objects to indicate that it had a religious use were found. It was constructed of chalk blocks in a sand-bank, and was 39 ft. 6 ins. by 19 ft. 6 ins. internally, and covered with a barrel vault. At the west end was a passage-entrance which had apparently a zigzag turn in it to prevent the interior of the chamber being seen from without, and at the east end were three round-headed niches in the wall.

The existence of other temples is known from inscriptions, but in only two or three instances are there any remains, and these are scanty and indeterminate. There were temples to Jupiter at Bewcastle and Dorchester, to Mars at Carvoran, to Apollo at Lincoln and Moresby, to Diana at Caerleon, to Neptune and Minerva at Chichester, to Serapis at York, to the Matres at Benwell and Castlesteads, to Roma at Chester, and to Mithras or Sol at Birdoswald, Rutchester, and High Rochester. In some other places, inscriptions record the erection or restoration of temples without naming the gods to whom they were dedicated.

SHRINES [1]

In Italy, every house seems to have had its shrine, where the Lares, the beneficent guardians of the household, the Penates, the protectors of the stores and storehouse, and the Genius, the tutelary divinity of the master of the house, were worshipped daily and to whom sacrifices were offered on special occasions. The first and the last were specially associated and usually

[1] *Rom.-Brit. Buildings and Earthworks*, chap. x.

grouped together, and were shown as little figures or as paintings. In Pompeii they were usually enshrined in a small niche in the atrium, kitchen, or dining-room, with an altar or shelf below for offerings. On each side of the latter was nearly always depicted in paint two serpents, which, whatever their origin, came to be regarded as symbolic of the master and mistress, that of the former being distinguished by a crest. In the larger houses, the niche was elaborated into the façade of a small temple, or it took the form of one attached to the wall, or standing free, sometimes in the garden. More rarely, the *aedicula* was enclosed in a chapel (*lararium*), which might be a special room in the house or a detached building.

The evidence for this domestic worship in Britain is very slight ; but if the Pompeian custom of mural shrines prevailed here, this is not surprising, as the walls of the houses are almost invariably reduced to too low a level. Small rooms, often with rich mosaic floors, have been identified as *lararia* ; and in one of these at Silchester were the foundations of a small isolated structure which may very well have been the podium of an *aedicula*. In the courtyard of a large house there, were the foundations of a similar structure which may have been an open-air *aedicula*. There is no reason to doubt that the small figures of divinities in terra-cotta and bronze seen in most of our collections belonged to domestic shrines ; and possibly also the small reliefs of the Mothers, whose worship may have taken the place of that of the Italian household divinities.

The evidence for public shrines is perhaps a little stronger. Just as the Roman houses had their divinities, so had the streets and cities theirs—Lares Compitales and Lares Praesides; and besides these, there were other public shrines. The Pompeian street shrines were as varied as the domestic, and in a general way resembled them. Occasionally, however, the public shrines were of a more elaborate description. In several instances the shrine was within a little street-side room open in front, with a niche for the divinities and altars for their worship, within. It has been supposed that the large female figure which stood in front of the central apse of the basilica at Silchester represented the genius of the town, and that the apse was the municipal shrine.   Perhaps the figure was simply a personification of Calleva or of the *civitas* of the Atrebates.   The position and form of the city sanctuary at Pompeii suggests that a large shallow apse on the north side of the forum may have been the corresponding structure.   In a similar position in the forum at Caerwent is a mass of masonry which looks like the podium of a small temple.   The remains of a street-side apsidal room between two smaller rooms at Silchester may relate to a public shrine.   At Caerwent have been found the remains of possibly another public shrine.   They indicated a square room, open in front, but with a kerbing containing mortice-holes as if for a wooden fence or screen. Within was a small platform and upon it a rudely sculptured head, the one suggestive of the podium of an *aedicula* and the other of a divinity that belonged to it.   Altogether these remains recall the arrangement of some of the street-side shrines of Pompeii.

Of the military shrines—those of the forts—sufficient has already been said on pages 55-6.   The *nymphaea* represent another class.   A small isolated building close by the remains of the Romano-British house at Chedworth, Gloucestershire, seems with little doubt to be one of these.   It is rectangular externally, with an open front, two low side walls with internal pilasters, and an apsidal back, the internal dimensions being about 19 ft. in width and 25 ft. in depth.   In the centre of the floor is a sunk octagonal basin, which received the water of an adjacent spring.   The original arrangement, as disclosed by a lower floor, was rather different, and a small altar buried in the débris between the two floors goes far to prove the sacred character of the site.   Apart from this, the little edifice with its picturesque surroundings must have been a pleasant retreat, the silence broken by the musical plash of the water and the song of the birds, all conducive to meditation.

CHURCHES [1]

The only undoubted remains of a Christian church as yet known in this country were uncovered at Silchester in 1892,

---

[1] For further details, see *Rom.-Brit. Buildings and Earthworks*, chap. x.

but as unfortunately they were very scanty, little remaining above the floor-level, the plan, Fig. 34, is necessarily imperfect. The church was a small structure, only 42 ft. long and 27 ft.

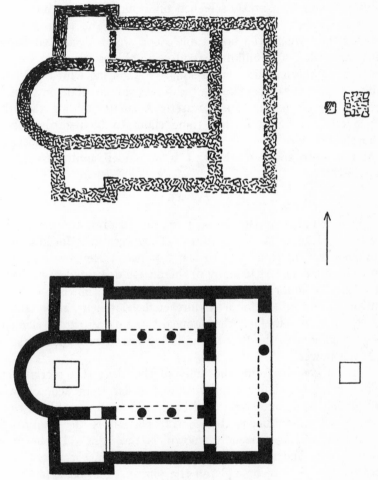

FIG. 34.—Plan of Church, Silchester, and conjectural restoration.   (15 ft. to 1 in.)

wide ; nevertheless, the plan exhibits all the chief features of a typical early Christian basilica. Its orientation, as in many early Italian churches, was the reverse of the present custom,

the chancel being to the west.   It was entered through an internal
porch or narthex, at the east end, and was divided into a nave
and two aisles by arcades of which the sleeper-walls remain.
Two transepts—the *prothesis* and *diaconicum* of early Christian
writers—were apparently screened off from the aisles, but open
to the western prolongation of the nave.   The floor was of
mosaic, and where the holy table stood was a decorated panel
of finer work.   The building stood in an oblong space, in which,
in front of the narthex, was a square foundation which presumably supported the *cantharus*, and at its side a small pit, which
probably received the waste water.   A small building recently
discovered at Caerwent has some claim to be regarded as a
church.   It has a western apse and two transeptal spaces ;
but the main space to the east is undivided, and there is no
narthex.

ALTARS

Few remains of the Roman era in Britain are more distinctively Roman than the altars.   They were introduced by the
conquerors, and from first to last retained a Roman character,
in spite of the fact that many of them were dedicated to barbaric
deities.   Their forms were already matured at the time of their
introduction, and so far from further development, they tended
to degenerate.   In fact, they appeal to us as an exotic element
—they came with the Romans and they ceased with the break-up
of their power.

In its general form, the body of the altar is a rectangular
block of stone, higher than wide, and wider than deep, with a
projecting head or capital and base, and these are usually enriched with mouldings.   Its central portion is the *truncus* of
Vitruvius, but now usually known as the ' die.'   If the altar
is inscribed, the inscription is on its front, but occasionally it
begins on the head or ends on the plinth.   The back is almost
invariably plain, showing that the altar was normally placed
against a wall ; in rare instances, however, the mouldings of
capital and base are continued across the back, and, rarer still,
the back is ornamented.   The upper member of the capital is
usually thickened into an abacus, often attaining a height equal-

ling or even surpassing that of the plinth. Broadly speaking, the altar never loses its pedestal form. No matter how rudely it may be fashioned, there is a capital and a base, even if only indicated by groovings.

The upper surface of the head is sometimes flat, but it usually has a cavity to receive the offering, circular or square. It may be simply hollowed out of the top, or it may have an elevated rim ; more often, however, it is in the summit of a central rising —conical, dome-shaped, or of some other form. The cavity is the *focus* or 'hearth,' the place of the fire which consumed the offering. But in our altars it is too small for a fire for such a purpose ; moreover its interior rarely shows any perceptible effects of burning. When circular, it has frequently a central boss, recalling the pushed-up centre often observed in the *paterae* of the period; and in several instances—one at Birrens—the raised rim has two handles. It would seem, therefore, that the sculptors regarded the circular cavities as representing *paterae* to receive libations ; and that fire, if used, had degenerated to the small proportions of a merely representative rite.

Another feature of the summit, which is almost always present in the larger altars, is two lateral cylindrical rolls, one on either side of the focus. Their meaning is obscure. They have been supposed to represent two bundles of sticks for the fire, but their ornamentation never suggests such an origin. They were known as *pulvini*, cushions, and, long before the conquest of Britain, were a usual feature of altars and of altar-like tombs, their ends being treated as spirals developed from the upper surface of the structure. Earlier still, they appeared as rectangular ridges or kerbs.

It is mainly in the treatment of these summit-features that the altars differ. As already stated, the focus may be simply sunk in a tabular surface, or it may be raised. *Pulvini* may be present or absent, and if present, they may be in full relief or be more or less absorbed in the head, and to such a degree as to be scarcely recognizable. The altars without *pulvini* are mostly small ones, with flat tops. Fig. 35, A, on the other hand, is a large one of the type from High Rochester and dedicated to Roma. A similar altar of equally good design from Cor-

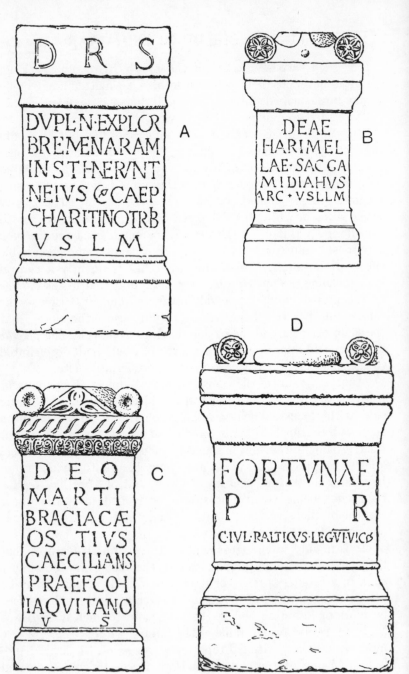

FIG. 35.—Altars. A, High Rochester; B, Birrens; C, Haddon Hall; D, Chesterholm. (1/12)

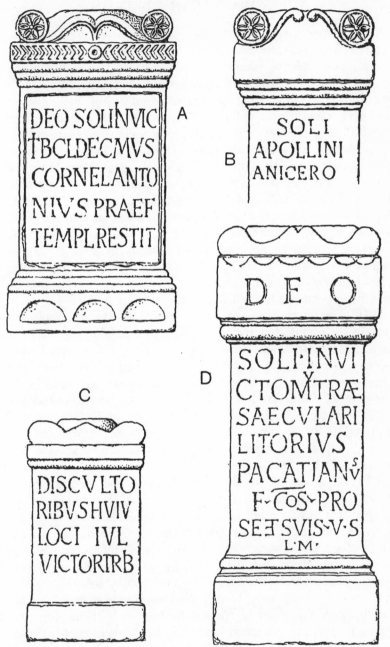

FIG. 36.—Altars. A and B, Rutcheste ; C, Risingham ; D, Housesteads. ($\frac{1}{12}$)

125

bridge is now in the British Museum ; but, speaking generally, altars of this form are not notable for good workmanship.

We now pass to altars with *pulvini*. In the earlier altars these were rolls flowing out of and, so to speak, resting on their flat tops, the ends being treated as volutes, but such *pulvini* are very rare in this country. In Fig. 37, D, an altar from High Rochester, they are indicated by volutes, but are buried in the head. In a fine but time-worn Chester altar to Fortuna, Aesculapius and Salus, in the British Museum, they have the ancient form, but terminate in human masks instead of volutes. In our altars the pulvini are almost always of a cylindrical form ; but as the attachment of such a form to a flat surface is narrow and weak, various methods of securing a firmer hold were devised. In the fine altar to Fortuna from Chesterholm (Fig. 35, D) the sculptor has provided the requisite support by leaving two claw-like brackets on the outer side of each. Between the *pulvini* will be noticed the beaded rim of the circular focus.

This treatment, however, is exceptional, the necessary support usually being effected by so raising and enlarging the focus as to coalesce with or die into these features. The exposed front of the ' focus-mount ' invites some decorative treatment, and this usually takes the form of a small pediment, well seen in the altar to Mars at Haddon Hall (Fig. 35, C). Scrolly pediments, as in Fig. 36, A and B, altars to the Sun at Rutchester, and Fig. 35, B, to Harimella at Birrens, are not uncommon. In late altars, the pediment is often lofty, and it may survive as a panel, as in Fig. 37, C.

In the altar to Jupiter from Old Carlisle (A, Fig. 37) we have another and not uncommon treatment. Here the pediment, if the term is now admissible, fills the whole space between the pulvini, and little of the curvature of these is exposed. They have, so to speak, so far sunk into the head, that if their ends were not expressed as discs they would hardly be recognized as *pulvini*. In the large altar to the Sun-god from Housesteads (Fig. 36, D), for instance, they may be regarded as simply portions of the scrolly pedestal ; and in the small altar from Risingham (Fig. 36, C) they are flattened and are less reminiscent of their origin. Contrariwise, they may be wholly absorbed in the head and be only represented by medallions, as in the crude and uninscribed altar (Fig. 37, B) from Rutchester. They are subject to other vagaries. For instance, the sculptor of the large altar Minerva at High Rochester (Fig. 38, A) has doubled their number and a central medallion almost suggests a fifth. Occasionally there are short transverse *pulvini* between the normal ones ; and a most elaborate altar at Maryport[1] has three on either side, stacked one above the other. In the altar to Jupiter, also at Maryport (Fig. 38, B), we have an extreme departure from the traditional form, and except for its dedication and focus it would hardly be taken for an altar at all.

Every part of an altar received decorative treatment, but some parts less than others. The front of the die, for instance, being appropriated to the inscription, is rarely ornamented. Occasionally it is panelled by a moulded or cabled border, as in Fig. 36, A. One of the altars to Mithras at Rutchester[2] has the word ' Deo ' of its inscription within a wreath, and the name of the dedicator on a standard or banner below, the whole being between two incised palm branches. A beautiful altar to Neptune at Newcastle[3] has the name of the god within an ansate panel on the head, the rest of the short inscription being continued on the panelled front of the die and divided vertically by a trident and dolphin, emblems of the god. Occasionally the figure of the god to whom an altar is dedicated takes the place of an inscription, and five small altars in the British Museum from Kings Stanley in Gloucestershire are good examples. Less frequently the front is sculptured with an appropriate subject other than a god, as that of a man in a paludamentum in the act of sacrificing, on a fine altar at Carlisle.[4] The sides of the die are more often ornamented, and the favourite devices are sacrificial implements, as the axe and the knife used in slaying and cutting up the victim, and the *urceus* or jug and *patera*, the one to hold the wine and the other to receive the portion for a libation ; and to these is occasionally added an ox or its head to represent the victim. And combined with, or instead of, these, the emblems or figures of gods are occasionally introduced. The Chester altar,

---

[1] Bruce, *Roman Wall*, p. 410. [2] *Roman Wall*, p. 127.
[3] Black Gate Museum, Newcastle. [4] *Roman Wall*, p. 296.

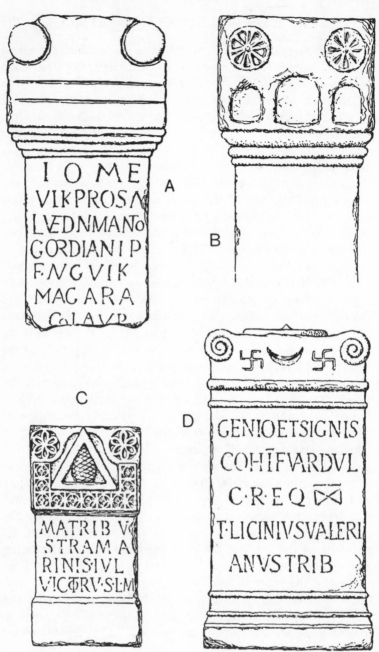

FIG. 37.—Altars. A, Old Carlisle ; B, Rutchester ; C, Risingham ;
D High Rochester. ($\frac{1}{12}$)

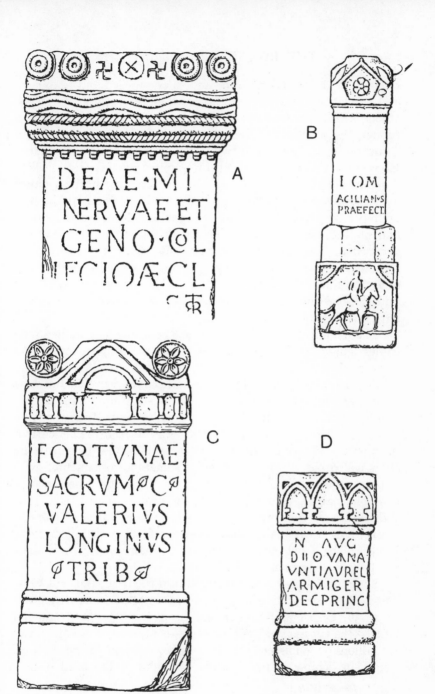

FIG. 38.—Altars. A, High Rochester ; B, Maryport ; C, Risingham ; D, Walton House. ($\frac{1}{12}$)

referred to above, has its front and sides panelled and festooned, and the latter are sculptured with an unusual array of objects, among which may be distinguished a jug, *patera*, and knife, a rudder, the attribute of Fortune, the staff of Aesculapius, and a cornucopiae.   The sides of two large altars to Jupiter at Walton House [1] bear the thunderbolt for Jupiter and a wheel, which possibly equates the Jupiter of these altars with the Gaulish ' wheel-god.'   On an altar to the Genius Loci, found at Chester, are represented, on the one side, the genius holding a cornucopiae, and on the other, acanthus leaves arising from a vase.   The decoration, however, like the acanthus leaves just referred to, sometimes has no apparent symbolism, as in the case of a fine altar to Minerva at Birrens,[2] the sides of the die and the front and sides of the abacus and plinth of which have panels filled with an arabesques of ivy.

The mouldings and the abacus are occasionally enriched with cables, guillochs, foliage, rosettes, or geometrical patterns.   An altar at Birrens has its abacus and plinth panelled and containing dolphins.[3]   The plinth of another raised to Cocidius near Lanercost,[4] by the Twentieth Legion, is sculptured with a boar amidst foliage—a subject which equally befits the woodland god and the legion whose symbol was a boar.   The curious Maryport altar (Fig. 38, B) has a well-carved horseman on its panelled base.   The pediment is sometimes ornamented with a boss, rosetted medallion, foliage, bust, or some device of a symbolic nature, as a vase, ewer, crescent, swastica, etc.   The *pulvini* are often encircled with a belt or band and are otherwise plain, but occasionally they are enriched with overlapping leaves.   The front ends are usually ornamented with bosses, rosettes, or concentric circles.

Sometimes the abacus is merged into the head, thus enlarging the field for decorative display, as in an altar from Risingham (Fig. 36, C).   The front of the head has a sunk triangular panel—the survival of the pediment—containing a fir-cone ; two medallions, reminiscent of the *pulvini* ;   and a geometrical diaper in ' chip-carving ' ;   while the sides of the head display

[1] *Roman Wall*, p. 278.   [2] *Proc. Soc. Ant. Scot.* xxx, p. 153.
[3] *Ib.* p. 153.   [4] *Roman Wall*, p. 268.

similar carving.   An altar to Egarmangabis found at Lanchester [1] in 1893 is remarkable for its rich display of ' chip ' and other carved work which covers every available space except the back and the front of the die.

Occasionally the head is treated architecturally, as an altar at Walton House (Fig. 38, D), which presents a simple arcade of three arches singularly anticipative of Norman or Early English work.   An altar to Fortune at Risingham (Fig. 38, C) has its abacus ornamented with a colonnade of balluster-shaped columns supporting a flat architrave, the middle intercolumniation having a semicircular arch.   The head of another altar to Fortune, from the same place, has a similar but more elaborate treatment.   More elaborate still is the head of an altar dedicated to the Discipline of the Emperor at Birrens.[2]   Here, instead of the colonnade, is a broad band of ' chip-carving,' and the central arched recess is certainly intended to represent an alcove with a semi-dome.   The arch is supported by two balluster-shaped shafts, and between these are two panels in mitred frames, possibly to indicate that the alcove-wall is encrusted with marbles, but more likely they represent low wooden doors or gates.   The altar was found in the well of the headquarters, and this, together with its dedication to the Discipline of the Emperor, suggests that it originally stood in or by the *sacellum* where the genius, the emperor, and the standards were reverenced.   In this case the recess may well have represented a *sacellum*, and its introduction would have an appropriate significance.   With these altars may be classed an uninscribed one at Chesterholm.[3]   The angles of the die are capped with square pilasters with foliate capitals, and the mouldings of the capital and base are simple and elegant. On the one side is a wreath and a palm-branch, and on the other apparently a club.   The central arched recess of the head is lofty, supported by two small columns, and contains the figure of a warrior.   On each side of the recess is a single intercolumniation containing a scallop-shell ;   and on each side of the head is a similar shell with a festoon below it.

The inscriptions, like Roman inscriptions generally, are

[1] *Brit. Arch. Assoc.* l, p. 105.   [2] *Proc. Soc. Ant. Scot.* xxx, p. 131.
[3] *Roman Wall*, p. 216.

terse, and the words are often clipped or are reduced to initials only, as in the formula, V.S.L.M., with which they usually end, and which may be extended thus—*Votum solvit libens merito*, " He fulfils his vow, willingly, dutifully." [1]   Similarly, I.O.M. stands for *Jovi optimo maximo*, " To Jupiter, the best, and greatest " ; D.D. for *donum dedit*, literally, " He gave the gift " ; and P. may mean *posuit*. Words that may reasonably be inferred are frequently omitted altogether. The inscription ordinarily names (1) the god or gods to whom the altar was dedicated, and (2) the person or persons who raised it; and to the latter is often added the reason or motive of the act.

For brevity, the inscription on the altar to Neptune at Newcastle can hardly be surpassed—

NEPTVNO LE		*(Neptuno. Legio*
VI	VI	*Sex, Victrix*
P	P	*Pia Fidelis)*

" To Neptune—the Sixth Legion, ' Victorious, Pious, Faithful.' " The next is the inscription of an altar raised by a soldier of the same legion at Chesterholm (Fig. 35, D)—

FORTVNA	*(Fortunae*
P R	*Populi Romani.*
CIVL RALTICVS LEG VI VIC	*Caius Julius Ralticus, Legionis VI Victricis.)*

" To Fortune of the Roman People. Caius Julius Ralticus of the Sixth Legion, ' The Victorious ' (has raised this altar)." The next, from Housesteads,[2] gives not only the name but the condition of the dedicator—

DEO	*(Deo*
SILVANO	*Silvano*
COCIDIO	*Cocidio*
QV FLORIVS	*Quintus Florius*
MATERNIVS	*Maternius,*
PRAEF COH	*Praefectus Cohortis*
I TVNG	*Primi Tungrorum*
V S L M.	*V.S.L.M.)*

---

[1] Sometimes reduced to V.S., which may be rendered, " He pays or paid his vow " ; or even to L.M., the V.S. being understood.

[2] *Roman Wall*, p. 193.

" To the god Silvanus Cocidius. Quintus Florius Maternius, Prefect of the First Cohort of Tungrians (placed this). He fulfilled his vow, willingly, dutifully."

Several inscriptions giving the circumstances of the erection of an altar will now be given. One at York [1] was on the occasion of the erection of a temple—

DEO SANCTO	(*Deo Sancto*
SERAPI	*Serapi*
TEMPLVM A SO	*Templum a so-*
LO FECIT	*lo fecit,*
CL HIERONY	*Claudius Hierony-*
MIANVS LEG	*mianus, Legatus*
LEG VI VIC.	*Legionis VI Victricis.*)

" To the holy god Serapis. Claudius Hieronymianus, Legate of the Sixth Legion, ' The Victorious ' erected the temple from the ground." The inscription of the altar already referred to at Carvoran (Fig. 36, A) similarly commemorates the restoration of a temple of Mithras. Another at Carvoran was the outcome of a vision, perhaps in a dream—

FORTVN AVG	(*Fortunae Augustae.*
PRO SALVTE L AELI	*Pro Salute Lucii Aelii*
CAESARIS EX VISV	*Caesaris, ex Visu,*
T FLA SECVNDVS	*T(itus ?) Flavius Secundus*
PRAEF COH I HAM	*Praefectus Cohortis I Ham-*
IORVM SAGITTAR	*iorum Sagittariorum*
V S L M	*V.S.L.M.*)

" To Fortune the August. This altar was raised for the safety (or welfare) of Caesar Lucius Aelius, by Titus Flavius Secundus, Prefect of the First Cohort of Hamian Archers, having been directed to do so in a vision. He payed his vow, etc." This inscription is also interesting, as its date can be fixed within the narrow limits of two years, Lucius Aelius, the adopted son of Hadrian, being created Caesar in 136 and dying in 138. Sometimes the names of the consuls are given, and these supply the actual year. The Carvoran inscription also illustrates that an altar might be raised by one person for the benefit of another. It is not unusual for the dedicator to include his family—PRO SE

[1] In Museum.

ET SVIS, or, as on an Housesteads altar, his son—PRO SE ET PROCVLO FIL (for himself and his son Proculus).

The notable capture of a wild boar, which had long terrified the countryside, led to the erection of an altar near Stanhope,[1] appropriately to Silvanus. The inscription is long, but the abbreviated words are few—

```
         SILVANO INVICTO SAC
        C TETIVS VETVRIVS MICIA
        NVS PRAEF ALAE SEBOSIA
        NAE OB APRVM EXIMIAE
        FORMAE CAPTVM QVEM
           MVLTI ANTECESSO
           RES EIVS PRAEDARI
        NON POTVERVNT V S L M.
```

Its purport is as follows—" Sacred to Silvanus the Invincible. Caius Tetius Veturius Micianus, Prefect of the Sebosian Ala (erected this), in consequence of the capture of a wild boar of extraordinary size, which many of his predecessors had not been able to destroy. He fulfilled his vow, etc." It certainly has a ring of self-advertisement !

One would have thought that the religious conditions of Britain were too complex to have left room for intolerance or persecution, but an altar at Bath records such an outburst, exceptional though it may have been. Its inscription may be rendered, " This holy place, wrecked by insolent hands, has been cleansed and dedicated anew to the excellence and *numen* of the Emperor, by Gaius Severius Emeritus (Centurian ?)."

Occasionally the name of the god is not given, and in these cases we may assume that the altar was associated with an image or some other inscription which identified it with some deity, or that the dedication was an open one leaving it to the user to address what god he pleased. This applies equally to the large number of uninscribed altars. Several examples of altars inscribed to more than one deity have come before the reader's notice. The remarkable Maryport altar, described on page 127, was dedicated by the tribune of a cohort hailing from the province of Mauritania Caesarum, to no less than four deities—the local Genius, Fortune, Eternal Rome, and Good Fate ; and a certain Frumentus of

[1] *Roman Wall*, p. 393.

Birrens was either so sceptical of the individual infallibility of the gods, or so catholic in his faith, that he addressed himself to all gods and goddesses ! In a few instances the name of the dedicator is omitted, and in a few others it is placed first ; but, notwithstanding the general rule that the name of the god is first, the chief concern of most of the altar-inscriptions is the dedicator.

CHAPTER VIII

SEPULCHRAL REMAINS

DIVERSITY OF FUNERAL CUSTOMS—CREMATION AND INHUMA-
TION—TOMBSTONES AND THEIR INSCRIPTIONS

O F the fixed remains of the Roman era in Britain, those which relate to the burial of the dead are the most numerous. Our archaeological literature teems with notices of their discovery, and as these casually meet the eyes of the readers, they give rise to an impression of bewildering diversity. It is only by the comparison of a large number of them that the diversity, although great, is seen to have a limit. But why the diversity at all? This suggests a number of interesting questions. How far are the differences contemporary —how far successive? To what extent are they due to local conditions, to the diverse religious beliefs of the time, and to foreign influences? Are the modes of burial substantially a legacy of the customs of the pre-Roman natives, or a Roman importation? It is probable that all of these contributed to the complex, but it is hardly possible at present to assign their relative shares in bringing about the result.

Diversity of funerary customs, however, long preceded the Romans in the west. During the two or three centuries before the conquest, both cremation and simple inhumation were in vogue in England, the latter preponderating in the north and the former in the south. In Yorkshire, many skeletons of this period, laid in a contracted attitude or at full length, in cists, wooden coffins, or simply in graves, have been found, and some of them were remarkable for the wealth of associated objects. Of the many urn-fields in the south-eastern counties, one at

Aylesbury [1] was notable. The cremated remains, all in earthen vessels, were in circular holes, unmarked by mounds ; and with most were associated other vessels, several being bronze ewers and tankards, and these, as also the smaller objects, were of Late-Celtic type. In another urn-field, near Haslemere in Surrey,[2] the cineraries were generally accompanied with accessory vessels ; but the pottery was of later type and assignable to the period of Roman influence immediately before the conquest. In both burial-grounds, many of the graves were arranged in ' family circles.'

The interments of Roman Britain are also of both kinds, burnt and unburnt, but the former predominate. They occur singly or in small groups near the houses of the time, and in large aggregates outside the town walls, clustering especially about the roads leading from the gates, as at Rome and Pompeii. The chief burial-ground at Colchester extended for about a mile on each side of the road which issued from the west gate. The cemeteries of York were also of great extent, and considerable numbers of interments have been found outside the walls of Viroconium, Verulamium, and Bath. Contrary to the early Roman laws which prohibited sepulture in towns, burials took place within the limits of Roman London and Caerwent, but apparently only few. The graves were mostly ' flat,' that is, they were not covered with mounds ; but tumuli are known, and some of large size, as, for instance, one of a group of seven, known as the Bartlow Hills, at Ashdon in Kent, and explored with remarkable results, was 147 ft. in diameter and 47 ft. high. The custom of placing various objects, chiefly vessels of pottery and glass, with the dead, was as general as in previous times. Inscribed tombstones were common, but their absence or fewness in districts where suitable stone was not obtainable, renders it probable that wooden memorials were also used.

There is little doubt that in the earlier part of the era cremation was the prevailing, if not the sole, custom in this country. It was so in Italy ; but by the beginning of the 5th century it was so completely a thing of the past, that Macrobius could learn nothing about it except from books. There is a consensus

[1] *Archaeologia*, lii, p. 315.   [2] *Proc. Soc. Ant.* xxi, p. 217.

of opinion that it was supplanted by inhumation in Britain by the middle of the 4th century.

This is somewhat confirmed by the fact that in a group of burials, the interments are occasionally of one kind only. The larger and earlier burial-ground at Colchester, and that by the side of the Watling Street at Wroxeter, contained only burnt remains ; and similar burial-grounds have been found at Swanmore in the Isle of Wight,[1] near Dover, by the side of the Roman road to Canterbury,[2] and at Witham in Essex and Larkfield near Maidstone.[3]   On the other hand, two hundred graves opened in the Isle of Portland about 1850,[4] three hundred half-a-mile east of Irchester, Northamptonshire, in 1873,[5] more than seventy on the north side of Great Chesterford, Essex,[6] and eleven at Chatham Lines in 1897,[7] yielded only unburnt interments.

In most aggregates of graves, there is a large preponderance of the one or the other, and sometimes their positions indicate their sequence.   The excavation of a small burial-ground at Litlington, Royston, in 1821,[8] was specially interesting, as it proved that the burnt interments it contained were, with one exception, older than the unburnt.   It was a rectangular walled space about 390 ft. long, and the burials were arranged in parallel rows.   These originally consisted of burnt remains in urns, some of which were afterwards displaced and scattered, when the graves were dug for the unburnt corpses. The exception referred to, was a skeleton *below* an urn of burnt bones.   That the enclosed space had been used for a long period was proved by the coins, and it is clear that during this interval cremation was supplanted by inhumation, but not suddenly, the skeleton followed by an urned interment implying an overlap.

This Litlington enclosure is interesting in other respects. Within two of the corners, the ground was burnt and covered with wood-ashes, and there is little doubt that the funeral piles were erected on these spots.   Similar *ustrina* have been observed

[1] *Brit. Arch. Assoc.* xxiii, p. 213.   [2] *Arch. Jour.* xvi, p. 297.
[3] *Proc. Soc. Ant.* 2, xvii, p. 94.   [4] *Arch. Jour.* x, p. 60.
[5] *Vict. Hist.* Northamp. i, 183.   [6] *Arch. Jour.* xvii, p. 117.
[7] *Proc. Soc. Ant.* 2, xviii, p. 39.   [8] *Archaeologia*, xxvi, p. 368.

in other burial-grounds. But it was not unusual for the body to be burned over the grave. At Wroxeter, for instance, two or three interments were in large square pits, the sides and floors of which were excessively burnt and blackened with charcoal.[1] It is probable that we have at Litlington a villa burial-ground, as traces of apparently a large rural house of the time were noticed in the vicinity.

A smaller walled cemetery was examined at Lockham near Maidstone, in 1842.[2] The entrance appeared to be on the north-east side, where also were the remains of funeral fires. Six undisturbed interments were found, consisting of burnt bones in glass and earthenware vessels, with which were associated other vessels, several of bronze, and four iron lamps. Two of these interments were in built cists or vaults and two in large *amphorae* with the necks removed. The enclosure also contained the remains of a rectangular tomb-house, 14 ft. by 12 ft. 6 ins., and of another, circular, and 11 ft. 6 ins. in diameter. The latter was of peculiar interest. Above a plinth of pink cement was a stuccoed dado 2 ft. high, decorated in colours ; and to judge from the vague description, the scheme consisted of small reddish-brown squares separated by broad bands of pale yellow on which were parallel groovings in red. Above this, the wall was painted green and ornamented with engaged columns and pilasters (presumably alternating) in red, each with a square blue base. The height of the structure and how treated above are matters of conjecture. No mention is made of a doorway, but as the north-east side was excessively ruined, it may have been on that side, and this applies equally to the rectangular tomb-house. Both had been rifled, but as a portion of a skeleton was found in the former, and the interior of the latter was large enough to contain a sarcophagus or coffin, we may conclude that the interments were unburnt.

At Holwood Hill, Kent,[3] near the remains of apparently a large house, were found a small rectangular tomb-house with an entrance in the west side, and containing a stone sarcophagus or coffin, two other coffins in graves, and a circular buttressed

---

[1] *Uriconium*, p. 346.   [2] *Arch. Cantiana*, lxii, p. 76.
[3] *Archaeologia*, xxi, p. 336.

building, 30 ft. in diameter, with an entrance on the east. This structure had been painted red externally, and with various colours on the inner side. The interior had been rifled, but a single trench disclosed broken pottery and charcoal. Possibly this mausoleum contained burnt interments, but those of the coffins would certainly be unburnt. Similar large circular buildings have been noticed at Chedworth and at Wiggenhall in Sussex.

<h3>BURNT INTERMENTS</h3>

The general rule in the case of cremation was to place the burnt bones collected from the site of the pile or *rogus* in an earthen vessel. Vessels of various shapes and sizes were used for the purpose ; but globose jars or *ollae* of the forms of C 5, 9, and 11, Fig. 45, were so customary that these are popularly known as cinerary urns. They, however, were common domestic utensils of the time, and so far as is known no pottery was specially made for funerary purposes in this country. The vessels occasionally had lids, as H 11, Fig. 50 ; more frequently a shallow saucer or dish, a piece of flat stone, or a tile, served as a cover. Less frequently glass vessels were used, especially the large square or cylindrical handled bottles, Fig. 52, A, C ; and less frequently still the burnt bones were sealed up in cylindrical leaden receptacles or *ossuaria*, of which there are good examples in the British and York Museums.

As a rule, the cinerary with its contents was simply placed in a hole in the ground about 18 ins. or 2 ft. deep, with or without accessories, and was then buried. But frequently some sort of additional protection was devised. Occasionally the hole or grave was converted into a small vault by covering it with a large tile or stone. Or a cist was constructed in it of four tiles on their edges for the sides, and a fifth for the cover, of which several have been found at Colchester.[1] Or the receptacle was of masonry, as at Lockham. A more carefully made *loculus* was hewn out of a cubical block of stone with a flat stone for its cover, as one found at Carlisle,[2] within which was a square glass *ampulla* containing the human ashes, with an earthenware

---

[1] *Brit. Arch. Assoc.* v, p. 134.   [2] *Arch. Journ.* xxi, p. 88.

lamp in its mouth and small vessel by its side. A large cylindrical example from Harpenden, Hertfordshire, now in the British Museum,[1] rested upon, and was covered by, two oblong blocks of stone 5 ft. long, and contained a glass cinerary with four other vessels around it. Other examples of cylindrical *loculi* have been found, with circular slabs for their covers ; and one at Cirencester [2] had for its cover a cylindrical block of the same size as the lower one, instead of a slab. Large *amphorae* with the necks broken off were occasionally used for the same purpose as at Holwood Hill, and others have been found at Colchester,[3] Lincoln, London, Hemel Hempstead, Stratford-Bow, and Hoo St. Werburgh.[4] Cists of a tent-like form constructed of roofing-tiles have been found at York and elsewhere. In these, two rows of the flat tiles (*tegulae*) were inclined against one another, roof-wise, the ridge being capped with the half-round tiles (*imbrices*), while a flat tile closed in each end. In one at York only burnt bones were found ; in another were several vessels, one containing burnt bones, all resting on a tiled floor.[5]

The reader has already learned something of the objects— the ' grave-goods '—associated with cremated interments. No-where can these be better studied than in the Joslin Collection in the Colchester Museum. The ' finds ' from each grave are grouped together. There are 123 groups, and nearly all relate to burnt interments. In the majority, the cineraries are earthen *ollae* ; in several, small *amphorae* ; and in one, a basin. Two are glass vessels—a two-handled jar with lid and a hexagonal bottle ; one a cylindrical ' ossuary ' of lead ; and another, a wooden toilet or dressing-box with bronze fittings and lock. With the exception of several cists of tiles, the cineraries and their accessories were simply buried in the earth.

The accessories are extremely varied. Vessels of pottery are the most numerous ; then follow in descending order, bracelets or bangles, necklaces and beads, glass vessels consisting mostly of the little bottles known as lachrymatories, lamps, brooches,

[1] *Arch. Journ.* ii, p. 251.   [2] *Brit. Arch. Assoc.* iv, p. 70.   [3] *Ib.* ii, p. 275.
[4] *Arch. Journ.* ii, p. 255 ; *Archaeologia*, xii, p. 108 ; xxvii, pp. 412, 434.
[5] *Archaeologia*, ii, p. 177 ; *Arch. Jour.* xxv, p. 294. Several have been recently found at Newstead.

pins, dice and counters used in games, finger- and hair-rings, coins, dressing-boxes, mirrors, tweezers and nail-cleaners, charms or amulets, spindle-whorls, spear-heads, a buckle, clay figure of a bird, piece of bronze chain, nails of sandal, bronze *ligula*, and a few other single objects. These were mostly placed at the side of, or around, the cineraries, as in the Aylesford and Haslemere graves; but in more than a dozen burials, some were in the cineraries with the burnt bones, and these were mostly articles relating to personal attire and adornment which had passed through the fire with their owners.

Excluding the saucers and other shallow vessels used as covers for the cineraries, about 270 vessels of pottery are associated with 92 cremated interments in the collection, representing an average of nearly 3 to each, but the actual numbers range from 1 to 14, the prevailing numbers, however, being 2, 3, and 4. These vessels are of all shapes and wares, but are mostly of the smaller sizes. Of the glass vessels, 33 out of a total of about 40 are the so-called ' tear-bottles ' which probably contained balsams or aromatic unguents, and ten at least of them are described as ' fused,' indicating that they had passed through the fire. All the lamps are of earthenware, but their distribution is uneven, the 28 examples being associated with 17 interments, one of these having 6. All the objects relating to games, consisting of square dice and a larger number of ' counters ' were found in one cinerary, and had been burnt. It will be noticed that most of the remaining objects related to the toilet. The sex and age of the dead are often indicated by the accompaniments. With women were buried bracelets, mirrors, dressing-boxes, and the like; and with infants, *tetinae* or feeding-bottles and small odds and ends which may have been their cherished playthings.

The Joslin Collection is so well representative of the generality of the cremated burials of the era, that further examples, with the exception of the remarkable burial-mounds at Ashdon in Essex, are unnecessary. Of these, six were explored between 1832 and 1840,[1] and each was found to cover a single cremated interment, deposited in a receptacle or tomb, and surrounded with a wealth of grave-goods. Under the largest mound were the remains of a

---

[1] *Archaeologia*, xxv, p. 1 ; xxvi, pp. 300, 462 ; xxviii, p. 1 ; xxix, p. 1.

wooden chest or tomb, 4 ft. 2 ins. by 3 ft. 8 ins., and 2 ft. high, containing the cinerary, a square-handled bottle of green glass, and the following objects : a bronze jug or ewer (Fig. 54, D), inlaid with silver and lying in a bronze *patera* ; a richly enamelled globular bronze *situla* ; a bronze lamp ; two bronze bath strigils ; a folding seat resembling a camp-stool of iron, with bronze ornaments and indications of a leather top ; a narrow-necked glass flask stopped with some bituminous substance and containing a partly congealed oil floating on a sweet liquid with an apple-like odour ; another smaller glass flask which had been stopped in a similar manner ; a small square glass *amphora* containing decomposed vegetable matter ; a tall square glass-handled bottle ; and a small earthen vessel. Just outside the chest was a large earthen *amphora* containing earth, ashes, and fragments of burnt bones, apparently the final gatherings from the site of the funeral pile.

The other mounds were of smaller size, but their contents, although less elaborate, were similar. Four of the receptacles were of wood, and the remaining one was strongly constructed of tiles and closed in by larger tiles in overstepping courses. In four of these, the burnt bones were in glass vessels, and in one they formed a central heap. With three of the interments, were bronze ewers and *paterae* associated together as in the largest tumulus ; and with all were glass and earthen vessels. Among the remaining accessories were four iron hanging lamps as at Lockham, the metal mountings and other remains of three dressing-boxes, a small wooden tankard with bronze fittings,[1] a small decayed basket, and a sponge. One of the glass flasks contained a fatty substance, and another traces of a liquid. In one of the wooden cists, the bronze vessels had been covered with a linen cloth, and the floor strewn with branches of box.

A similar association of a bronze ewer and *patera* has been observed in some other cremated interments, notably in one near Canterbury and in others at Medbourn in Leicestershire and Shefford in Bedfordshire. These vessels recall the ewer and *patera* so often carved on the altars (p. 127), and this suggests that they served a like purpose in the funeral ceremonies. We

[1] The handles of similar tankards have been found at Caerwent and Newstead.

know from Roman writers that it was customary to pour or sprinkle wine on the pile and on the remains after the fire ; and it may well have been that the utensils used for the purpose were often deposited in the tomb. Bronze vessels, it is true, are rarely found associated with the dead, but ordinary glass and earthen vessels may have been more generally used. It was also customary to scatter perfumes and odoriferous gums and spices on the pile, and it is by no means improbable that these were brought to it in the so-called ' tear-bottles ' and other small vessels so frequently found in the graves. Two of the five Bartlow Hills lamps retained remains of charred wicks showing that they had been placed in the tombs, lighted—another ancient and widespread custom, probably of Oriental origin, but apparently far from universal in this country. The three glass bottles containing vegetable liquids or their traces, apparently a mixture of honey and oil in one case, and a vessel containing fowls' bones, are of special interest, as very few deposits of like nature have been found elsewhere. Almost invariably the vessels, mostly of pottery, associated with Roman interments, whether burnt or unburnt, have supplied no clue whether they were placed in the tombs empty or otherwise. We know that it was a general practice almost everywhere in an early stage of culture to place foods and other things useful in life with the dead, either with a view of propitiating their ghosts or in some way of satisfying their wants. In our Roman era, the meaning of the custom may have been so far lost sight of that it was only represented by empty vessels as a rule. Food-stuffs under ordinary conditions would rapidly disappear by the ordinary processes of decay, but the exceptional instances cited above go far to show that the ancient usage was still in vogue. On the other hand, many objects of personal use, as brooches, rings, bracelets, and the like, were parts of the attire in which the deceased was burnt, and in the case of unburnt burials in which he or she was interred. Others again, as dressing-cases and their contents, mirrors, and children's toys, we may conceive to be treasured trinkets, deposited in the grave from no other motive than a loving regard for the dead. The branches of box in one of the Bartlow Hills tombs may also indicate a general custom, as leaves of the same plant have been found in a Chesterford burial, and the remains of foliage in several others.

UNBURNT INTERMENTS

Where Roman influence was strong, the dead body, when buried unburnt, was almost invariably laid at full length in the grave. To what extent the prehistoric custom of burying it in a contracted or flexed attitude passed into Roman times is uncertain. Lieut.-General Pitt-Rivers exhumed many contracted and extended skeletons about the sites of the Romano-British villages at Woodcutts, Rotherley, and Woodyates in Wiltshire,[1] but as these villages were of pre-Roman origin it may well be that some of the burials were older than the conquest. Still, it is noteworthy that the few objects which were undoubtedly Roman, or had a Roman *facies*, were mostly associated with the extended skeletons. Seven or eight of the extended skeletons had hobnails about their feet, showing that they had been buried in their shoes or sandals, and presumably in their clothes as well. In the graves of about as many there were iron nails in positions to imply that they belonged to wooden coffins of which no other traces remained.[2] Vessels of pottery were few. With five of the seventeen Woodyates burials there were Roman coins, and three of these were found by the heads of the skeletons, leading the General to consider that, in accordance with a well-known Roman custom, each had been placed in the mouth of the deceased as a fee for Charon to ferry him across the Styx. Coins in similar positions have been found in graves elsewhere in this country, showing that the custom was observed; but, however common in Italy, it does not seem to have been general with us. The heads of the skeletons of these three villages pointed in various directions, some to the north, but more generally the extended skeletons lay in directions roughly east and west, with the heads mostly in the latter direction, and this appears to have been the prevailing orientation in Roman Britain.

---

[1] *Excavations*, i, p. 33 ; ii, p. 190 ; iii, p. 204.
[2] Of eleven interments at Chatham, most yielded the large nails of wooden coffins, and five of the skeletons had hob-nails at the feet. *Arch. Cantiana*, xxiii, p. 14.

Wooden coffins or chests were certainly in common use during the Roman era, as the frequent presence in the graves of not only nails, but of iron or bronze bindings, hinges, and other mountings, prove, but very few remain. A good example of a rectangular coffin was found at Stanley Grange, Derbyshire,[1] in 1903. It was constructed of oak boards which appeared to have been pegged together, as there were no nails or other metal details. The skeleton was extended at full length with the head to the east-north-east, and on its right side was a small hexagonal bottle of glass. Occasionally a wooden coffin was enclosed in a cist constructed of flag-stones or tiles, and examples of both have been found at York.

Coffins hewn out of a single block of stone were much used, especially where suitable stone was at hand, Bath stone being especially adapted for the purpose. These coffins are usually wedge-shaped; sometimes they approximate to the modern form, and rarely are rectangular. Occasionally they were rounded within at the head or the foot. They appear to have always had covers, flat, rounded, or slightly coped, and of a single piece or several. They were usually roughly hewn into shape and were intended to be buried; but occasionally they were carefully finished, with or without inscriptions, and more or less decorated, and these were certainly not buried.

A good example of the latter sort was found in the Green, Westminster Abbey, in 1869.[2] It was 7 ft. long, 2 ft. 5 ins. wide at the head, and 2 ft. at the foot, and 18 ins. high, and it had a coped cover. One side and the cover alone were ornamented, the former having an inscription to the deceased, and the latter a cross of a common type of the 11th or 12th century in relief. Apparently it originally occupied a recess, the cover and front alone being exposed to view. The Christian emblem indicates that it was re-used at the time it was carved. This was no uncommon practice, and Bede[3] records an instance. When the remains of St. Etheldreda, abbess of Ely, were translated to the new church in the 7th century, they were placed

---

[1] *Derbyshire Arch. Jour.* xxvi, p. 227.   See also *Arch. Jour.* vi, p. 109; xii, p. 197 ; *Brit. Arch. Jour.* 1858, p. 336.

[2] *Arch. Jour.* xxvii, p. 103.   [3] *Hist. Eccl.* bk. iv, xix.

in a marble coffin most beautifully wrought, which was found outside an abandoned city called Grantecester. This ' abandoned city ' was Roman, and there is no doubt that the coffin was from its cemetery.

Marble coffins, although frequent in Italy and Gaul, must have been rare in this country, for apparently there is no example in our collections. Still, several highly ornamented ones in stone are known, the finest, perhaps, being one in the British Museum from Haydon Square, London.[1] It would be better described as a coffer or sarcophagus than a coffin, for it is rectangular, with a coped cover. On the front is a large panel filled with a wavy godrooned pattern, with a central medallion containing the profile-bust of a boy in low relief, and on each end a basket of fruit, while the slopes of the cover have a handsome foliated design. The cover was originally fastened down by an iron strap or clamp at each end. This sarcophagus contained a leaden coffin in which were found the remains of a boy. As the back is quite plain, it evidently stood against a wall, perhaps the back of a small tomb-house, as those at Holwood and Lockham. Remains of these structures have also been found at York and elsewhere.

Lead coffins have been frequently found, but comparatively few have escaped the melting-pot. They were wedge-shaped or rectangular, and were usually made of a single sheet of lead with the corners so cut out that when the sides and ends were beaten up, the cut edges either met or the one could be doubled over the other, the joints being fused or soldered. The covers overlapped the sides and were often made in the same manner. They were occasionally plain, but more often decorated. The decoration was simple and characteristic, consisting of straight beaded lines in relief, arranged in bold zigzags, saltires, or other rectangular figures, and the intervals often contained simple devices, of which the scallop was the most frequent. The ornamentation was effected by stamps which were pressed into the sand-bed on which the lead sheet was cast. There are fine examples in the Colchester and York Museums. A rectangular one found at Bexhill in 1871 had, in addition to the ordinary

[1] *Arch. Jour.* x, p. 255; Price, *Roman Antiquities*, Mansion House, plate iv.

ornamentation, small reliefs of a lion, ewer, and Medusa's head repeated several times ; and another found in the Kent Road, London, had figures of Minerva in its compartments. There are several instances of these coffins being enclosed in shells of stone or wood, and probably the latter was customary. Lead coffins are more frequent in the east and south-east than in the west.[1]

A remarkable burial-mound known as Eastlow Hill, containing a skeleton in a leaden coffin, was opened at Rougham in Kent, in 1844. The coffin, enclosed in a wooden shell, was in a tomb built in the form of a small house, 12 ft. long and 6 ft. 6 ins. wide, of masonry with a tiled roof, upon a concrete platform. The only object associated with the skeleton was a small coin near the head ; but a small chamber at one end of the ' house ' contained broken glass and other vessels.[2]

There was a curious custom both here and on the Continent, of covering the corpse in the coffin with liquefied lime, or, according to other statements, plaster of Paris. The result is that the hardened material often retains a perfect impression of the body and its clothing, and actual portions of the latter are sometimes preserved. There are several examples of these calcareous fillings in the York Museum. One covered the body of a lady and her child, and the garment in which she was buried was of a velvety texture ornamented with crimson or purple stripes. Another indicates that the corpse was entirely covered with a coarse canvas. In another example, the body had been habited, the legs crossed, and the feet shod ; and, upon the limy matrix being removed, the following objects were found above the left shoulder—a portion of a gold ring and two jet rings, two gold ear-rings, two bracelets, several bronze rings, and two bead necklaces. In another example, a young lady had been entirely enveloped in a coarse cloth, and deposited in a leaden coffin enclosed within a stone one, her head apparently resting on a pillow ; the most interesting feature is that the calcareous environment preserved her coiffure intact. Her auburn hair

[1] *Arch. Jour.* x, pp. 61, 255 ; xii, pp. 78, 283 ; xvii, p. 99 ; xx, p. 99. *Brit. Arch. Jour.* ii, p. 297 ; xx, pp. 88, 200. *Collect. Antiq.* iv, p. 173. *Archaeologia*, xvii, p. 333 ; xxxi, p. 308.

[2] *Arch. Journ.* lvii, p. 97.

had been slightly twisted and coiled at the back of the head in the circular fashion in vogue during the Constantine period, and secured by two jet pins.[1]

TOMBSTONES

The tombstones, like the Roman altars, are ' good, bad, and indifferent.' Some found in the vicinity of the military centres are, we can well imagine, the products of men who were better soldiers than stone-cutters ; others, notably at London and Colchester, were certainly made by skilled masons. Like the altars, too, they exhibit no Late-Celtic traits in their ornamentation. With few exceptions, they are, like our headstones, slabs of stone bearing on their fronts the epitaphs. The simplest are rectangular slabs, sometimes quite plain, but more often panelled in front ; and the panel may be rectangular, or have a gabled head, in which case the head may be converted into a pediment by a horizontal line of moulding across its foot. There is a good London tombstone of the latter type in the British Museum in which the tympanum is ornamented with a trident and two dolphins, each external spandrel having a roundel. Another found at Great Chesters has the pediment of an unusual ogee outline and containing a two-handled vase.

More often the summit of the slab is *shaped* to the pediment, and most of the finest tombstones are of this type. In these a definite architectural effect was often obtained by flanking the front with two pilasters. In another British Museum example, the pilasters are panelled and ornamented with floral scrolls, and have quasi-Corinthian capitals, the tympanum being filled with foliage. The pilasters are sometimes fluted, and occasionally they simulate engaged columns. The pediment is sometimes flanked with ornaments, and these are usually lions, as in tombstones at Wroxeter and Benwell, the latter having a curious rayed human head in the tympanum.

In the most elaborate tombstones, the panel or in lieu thereof a shallow round-headed niche or alcove contains a sculptured subject, the inscription being at the foot. There are several

[1] *Arch. Aelian.* viii, 127.

types of these sculptured stones. In the most frequent, the
deceased is represented standing at full length. There is a
notable example in the Colchester Museum (Fig. 39),[1] in which
the deceased, a centurion of the Twentieth Legion, Marcus
Favonius, is represented in military dress with his left hand on
his sword and holding in his right the insignia of his office, a
staff. This tombstone is specially interesting because it was
found fallen over the lead essuary which contained the ashes.
Another fine example of the type was found at South Shields.
It presents the deceased, a woman, seated, and apparently
knitting, in an alcove, which is flanked with two panelled pilasters
supporting an elaborate pediment (Fig. 39). Of much simpler
character is the tombstone of a boy aged five years, found at
Old Penrith. The figure of the deceased has a whip in one hand
and in the other what seems to be a toy, and it occupies a deeply
sunk panel. Occasionally there are two figures, as those of a
centurion and his wife at Chester. A tombstone at York has
four figures, those of a soldier, his wife, and his infant son and
daughter.

Another type of these sculptured monuments presents a
horseman riding over a fallen barbarian and often in the act of
spearing him—a device of Greek origin and presumably confined
to the graves of soldiers. There are several examples in the
Chester Museum, and others have been found at Hexham, Wroxeter,
Bath, Cirencester (Fig. 40), and elsewhere. A third type,
known as that of the ' sepulchral banquet,' is of great antiquity
and has an Eastern origin, and probably it originated in ancestor
worship. The deceased is represented as reclining on a couch,
with a small tripod table in front, and holding a goblet in the
right hand ; and there is usually a juvenile attendant before
or behind the couch. There are several examples at Chester,
others at Corbridge, York (Fig. 40), South Shields, and elsewhere.

Sufficient has been said to give the reader a general idea of
the funeral monuments of the era. The exceptions in this country
are few. There are a few instances of memorials in the form of
a pillar or stele. One in the Guildhall Museum is a hexagonal
pedestal inscribed to a lady, Claudia Martina, and it was probably

[1] *Brit. Arch. Assoc.* xxvi, pp. 26, 240.

FIG. 39. TOMBSTONES AT COLCHESTER AND SOUTH SHIELDS

surmounted with her statue, as a female head of stone was found with it. Others are mural tablets which were probably affixed to tomb-houses, and we have already described several carved and inscribed stone coffins which were evidently intended to be exposed, and thus to serve as the memorials of the dead. The sculptured subjects, instead of conforming to the three types given above, occasionally depict scenes from mythology or from daily life.

The epitaph generally records (1) the name of the deceased mostly with some brief particulars as to his or her station or condition ; (2) the age at death, and, in the case of a soldier, the length of his service ; and (3) the person or persons who raised the monument. It is usually prefaced with D.M., *Dis manibus*, ' To the gods of the shades,' but probably it came to have no definite meaning and is best rendered, ' To the memory of.' It sometimes ends, especially in the earlier monuments, with H.S.E., *Hic situs est*, ' He or she lies here.' The name of the deceased is usually in the nominative, and when not so in the dative. More particulars, as a rule, are given of the soldier than the civilian. The length of his service is nearly always stated, and often his legion or cohort, his birthplace, and ' tribe,' and if an officer, his rank. The age is expressed by an abbreviation of *vixit annos*, as VIX. AN. XXIV, ' He lived twenty-four years,' or of *annorum*, as AN. XXXI., ' Thirty-one years (of age) ' ; and the soldier's service by an abbreviation of *stipendiorum*, as STIP. XIII, ' He served thirteen (years).' If the heir erected the monument the formula is H.F.C., *Heres faciendum curavit*, ' His heir caused this to be made ' ; if a father did this—PATER F. C. The same may be expressed by F. for *fecit* or P. for *posuit*—thus VACIA SOROR˙ F., ' The sister made this ' ; CAEC. MVSICVS LIB. EIVS P., ' Her freedman, Caecilius Musicus, placed this.'

The following examples will give the reader ,a general idea of the epitaphs of the era :—

At Chester—D. M. P. RVSTIO FABIA CRESCEN. BRIX. MIL. LEG. XX. V. V. AN. XXX STIP. X GROMA HERES FAC. C. " In memory of P. Rustius Crescens of the Fabian tribe from Brixia, a soldier of the Twentieth Legion, ' The Valerian and Victorious,' aged thirty years and served ten. Groma, his heir, had this (stone) made." (Brixia, now Brescia, in Italy.)

Cirencester—RVFVS SITA EQVES CHO. VI TRACVM ANN. XL STIP. XXII HEREDES EXS TEST. F. CVRAVE. H. S. E. " Rufus Sita, horseman of the Sixth Cohort of Thracians, lived forty years and served twenty-two. His heirs, in accordance to his will, had this erected. He is laid here " (Fig. 40).

Great Chesters—DIS M. PERVICAE FILIA F. " In memory of Pervica. Her daughter erected this."

Silchester—MEMORIAE FL. VICTORINAE T. TAM. VICTOR CONIVNX POSVIT. " In memory. To Flavia Victorina, Titus Tamphilus (?) Victor, her husband, placed this."

York—D M SIMPLICIAE FLORENTINE ANIME INNOCENTISSIME QVE VIXIT MENSES DECEM FILICIVS SIMPLEX PATER FECIT LEG VI V. " To the divine shades. To Simplicia Florentina, a most innocent thing, who lived ten months. Filicius Simplex of the Sixth Legion, ' The Victorious,' the father, erected this."

Chesters—D.M.S. FABIE HONORATE FABIVS HONORATIVS TRIBVN. COH. I VANGION. ET AVRELIA EGLICIANE FECERVNT FILIE DVLCISSIMME. " Sacred to the gods of the shades. To Fabia Honorata, Fabius Hono-ratius, tribune of the First Cohort of Vangiones, and Aurelia Egleciane, raised this to their daughter most sweet."

Housesteads—D.M. ANICIO INGENVO MEDICO ORDI COH. PRIMAE TVNGR. VIX. AN. XXV. " To the memory of Anicius Ingenuus, physician in ordinary to the First Cohort of Tungrians, lived twenty-five years."

FIG. 40. TOMBSTONES AT CIRENCESTER AND YORK

CHAPTER IX

POTTERY

<small>Characteristics—Manufacture and Decoration—Classi-fication—Potters' Kilns</small>

POTSHERDS are found on almost every Roman site and often in great abundance. It was an old opinion that the potter's wheel was a Roman introduction into this island, hence that 'thrown' pottery, unless imported, was no older than the Roman era ; but it is now known that the natives used the wheel for two centuries or more before the conquest, and produced vessels of refined fabrique and artistic form. This Late-Celtic pottery, formerly classed as Roman, is found on Roman sites in the south of England, and there is little doubt that its manufacture survived the conquest unchanged. The term 'Roman pottery' is convenient and permissible, so long as it is understood to signify the ceramic products from whatever source, that were ordinarily used in Roman Britain.

This pottery, whether of home manufacture or imported, shows a marked advance in technique, and this was probably due to Roman influence ; but this influence is less discernible in the forms and decoration. The work of the provincial potters has all the appearance of being substantially an indigenous development, and if it had a southern origin its prototypes must be sought in Italian and Greek forms before the advent of Rome as a world-power.

A notable exception, however, is the lustrous red pottery—the so-called 'Samian,' known on the Continent as 'terra sigil-lata'—which is found in considerable abundance in this country. It was not made here, and to the late Mr. C. Roach Smith stands the credit of first demonstrating that it was imported from the Continent. Subsequently, Dr. Dragendorff in Germany and M. Déchelette in France proved that it was manufactured in the valleys of the Loire and the Rhine from early in the 1st century to about the middle of the 3rd. From these centres it was dispersed throughout the empire, but especially in the western provinces and Italy. The fabric, however, was not indigenous to Gaul. Wares of the same kind had long been made in Italy, and notably in and around Arretium, the modern Arezzo. It is significant that the manufacture declined in Italy in the same century that it appeared in Gaul, thus rendering it probable that the Italian potters migrated thither. This affords an explanation of the exotic character of this pottery on Gaulish soil; and it was the presence of this provincial redglaze which influenced the art of the local potters, whose imitations are known as 'pseudo-Samian.' The earlier examples of the ware resembled those of Italy, but gradually new forms arose and some of the older died out ; the decoration, too, changed, but not to such a degree as to disguise its parentage.

It is almost impossible to convey by verbal description an adequate impression of the pottery of the era. This is best obtained by an inspection of a good collection, as that of the Colchester, Guildhall, Reading, or York Museum. The following are some of its broader distinguishing features : There is an absence of white bodies which are so marked a feature in modern ceramic productions. The nearest approach is creamy-buff ; but there is a preference for colours ranging from bright red, through tones of dusky maroons and browns to black, for the finer wares. There is an absence of painted subjects so characteristic of the Greek pottery, and of polychrome decoration so familiar to us. Painted work is comparatively rare, and is confined to simple stripes and scrolls, bold in effect, but often crudely executed. The prevailing decoration is in relief and generally displays considerable skill and artistic merit. Comparatively few have bright surfaces, and these, as a rule, are better described as lustrous or glossy, than as glazed. The material is earthenware : none has the hard and vitreous texture of our stoneware and porcelain. The forms vary exceedingly.

There are jugs, bowls and basins, shallow vessels of various shapes which only approximate to our saucers, plates, and dishes in their shallowness or their flatness, and others of shapes not represented in the ordinary vessels we use. On the other hand, we look in vain for forms resembling our tea- and coffee-pots, sauce-boats, and teacups. Less artistic than the Greek, the pottery nevertheless displays a gracefulness of curve not seen in the medieval, and not ordinarily in the modern. The vessels for the commonest purposes have an artistic feeling which contrasts with the severely utilitarian appearance of our culinary earthenware.

The methods of manufacture were simple. Although hand-made pottery was used—examples have been found at Silchester —it was exceptional. Broadly speaking, the wares were shaped on the wheel, but it is probable that the finest were finished on the lathe. The redglaze with raised figure and other subjects was, after leaving the thrower, pressed into moulds, and after re-moval, the feet were added, and lastly their interiors, the feet, and the external plain surfaces and beadings were finished on the wheel or the lathe ; but moulding seems to have been rarely practised in this country.[1] The colour of the pottery depended largely upon the clay used, but the potters were adepts at heightening or masking the natural colour. This was generally effected by a superficial wash or engobe, a process well known to the medieval and the modern potters. A vessel of dingy red clay, dipped, when in the ' green ' state, in a thin mixture of fine pipe-clay and water, received a film which upon firing assumed a delicate cream colour. By the addition of yellow or red ochre, or of varying mixtures of the two, to the ' slip,' the resultant tint ranged from yellow-buff to salmon or pink. But for the finer wares there was a decided preference for a full red, and for various tones of deep warm browns and dusky maroons on the one hand, and for greys ending in black on the other. Some of these were certainly produced by the addition of mineral colouring agents to the engobe ; but the darkest shades, and

---

[1] Portions of three different moulds for bowls (Form 37) were found at Pul-borough, Sussex, in 1909, and several other examples have been found in this country.

especially the greys and black, are due to the presence of carbon, sometimes as a superficial film, but more often it permeates the body as well. How the carbon was introduced is uncertain, and will be referred to later.

If by glaze is understood a translucent glass perceptibly distinct from the body although merging into it—as the glaze of modern porcelain—it is rarely seen on the pottery of the Roman era. Now and again fragments are found bearing a greenish-yellow glaze resembling that commonly seen on medieval wares, and apparently produced by the same method, that is, by dusting powdered galena (native sulphide of lead) over the clay pieces before firing. The glossiness of the redglaze more resembles that of the 18th-century saltglaze than a true glaze, that is, it appears to represent the surface of the pottery itself. Analyses have proved that the superficial portions of this ware are richer in soda than the interior, and it is not unlikely that the glossiness was the result of a chemical reaction between this alkali and the body-clay. Some of the finer black wares have a similar glossiness. Generally speaking, the dark brown and liver-coloured engobes have a faint waxy lustre, but not infrequently the finest dark wares have a bright metalloid surface, and even a slight iridescence. Occasionally vessels of fine texture have a smooth surface evidently produced by friction. These may be described as polished wares, and it is not unlikely that they were rendered bright by the application of wax.

The decoration of the pottery, however elaborate, is always in good taste : it never oversteps its proper province, or is so pronounced as to detract from the form. As already stated, the finest and most characteristic decoration is in relief. There were several methods by which it was produced, but first in importance is moulded work (Fig. 43, Nos. 1, 13, 17). The moulds, in which the decorated redglaze vessels were pressed, were of fine porous earthenware, unglazed, in order that much of the moisture of the clay pressed into them should be rapidly absorbed, and thus induce shrinkage and allow of the vessel being withdrawn. The mould was made on the wheel, and probably its interior was shaped by an iron ' profile ' ; then, while it was still moist, the decorative details were impressed from stamps of earthenware,

FIG. 41. ROMAN POTTERY, COLCHESTER MUSEUM

metal, gypsum, and other materials. The bands of egg-and-tongue and other patterns were probably impressed from roulettes or wheel-like instruments, applied, in the case of the horizontal ones, while the mould was revolving. A comparatively small stock of these stamps admitted of innumerable combinations of decorative elements. Another method by which raised ornamentation was produced is occasionally seen on the finest redglaze (Fig. 44, Nos. 21, 34). The decorative details were made separately, each consisting of a piece of clay pressed into a metal intaglio and then applied to the surface of the vessel—a method in which Wedgwood among the moderns excelled; but it is usually combined with ' barbotine ' decoration.

This barbotine or ' slip ' decoration (Fig. 46, Nos. 5, 6, 8 ; Fig. 49, No. 5) is characteristic of the finer dark wares of Gaul and Britain, on which it is seen at its best. It was effected by the same or a similar process to that of the 17th-century potters, that is by trailing slip or thin clay upon the surface from a small vessel with a quill spout. The work had to be done rapidly, and its success depended upon an artistic instinct combined with unhesitating movement, both which qualities the Roman potters possessed in high degree. It was peculiarly adapted for scrolly designs, and the scrolls by the same movement of the hand could be made to terminate in disc-like or leaf-like expansions. These designs, simple as they are, are remarkably graceful and pleasing. But the clever decorators frequently essayed with equal success the task of delineating hounds chasing deer, and even human figures, as the gladiators engaged in combat on a large vase at Colchester (Fig. 41). A simple decoration consisting of lines of raised dots or studs arranged in oblong or lozenge-shaped patches (Fig. 45, Nos. 2, 7) is frequently met with, and it appears to have been produced by a comb-like tool alternately dipped in slip and applied to the side of the vessel. In barbotine work, the decoration was either of the same or of a different colour from that of the ground. In the latter, the trails were cream coloured, pale yellow, or red, which thus contrasted with the dark engobed surface of the vessel. In the former they were not necessarily of the same clay as the body, as in these cases the engobe was applied after the decoration.

Other varieties of raised decoration are occasionally seen. One may be described as finger-pressed work. In this the vessel, or some portion of it, appears to have been coated with a thick slip, which by the pressure of the finger was forced up into ridges. By this means various curvilinear diapers were obtained, of which the scale (Fig. 46, No. 2) and an irregular 'crocodile-skin' pattern are noteworthy. Vertical bands or 'pillars' of scale pattern were manipulated by the same process on strips of applied clay. In 'frilled' work the thrower gave the vessel one or more thin flange-like beads, and these were then waved by the alternate up and down pressure of the finger or some tool (Fig. 50, No. 7). In 'indented' work, the sides of the vessel were gently pressed in to produce a series of shallow flutings or other hollows, as in Fig. 42. 'Rough-cast' work was effected by coating the portions of the vessel to be so treated, with a thin slip, and then scattering over it coarsely powdered clay or pottery.

Sunk decoration may be conveniently divided into incised and impressed, but neither is a conspicuous feature of the pottery of the time. The common grey and black globular jars and dishes often exhibit a simple trellis made by a pointed tool, but so lightly so that the lines are less visible as grooves than as burnished strokes (Fig. 45, Nos. 4, 5, 9). An incised pattern is occasionally seen which consists of a band of concentric semicircles from which depend series of parallel lines stroked in with a comb-like tool—a pattern apparently suggested by the 'festoon-and-tassel' (Fig. 47, No. 2). Impressed work is a common feature of the 'pseudo-Samian' ware—a fine ware with a thin red engobe somewhat imitating, or perhaps it would be more correct to say, inspired by the redglaze. The stamps were apparently of wood, cut into the forms of simple rosettes, circles, notched segments of circles, and so forth. Both incised and impressed work was, however, more frequently accomplished on the wheel. The comb held against the revolving vessel gave rise to a band of parallel lines, and if moved up and down, to a wavy band of the same—a simple decoration often seen on the commonest wares. The hatched bands and surfaces frequent on all varieties of the pottery, and commonly known as 'engine-turning,' were evidently impressed from notched wheels or roulettes (Fig. 46, Nos. 4, 12,

FIG. 42. ROMAN POTTERY, COLCHESTER MUSEUM

13). Sometimes a definite pattern — as the egg-and-tongue— was cut on the edge of the roulette, and bands of this character occasionally occur on the ' pseudo-Samian ' referred to above. There is another and rare variety of sunk decoration, confined to redglaze, which may be called ' cut-work,' for it was certainly effected by gouges and V-shaped chisels. The cut-out portions normally take the form of vesica-shaped hollows, which are arranged to form stellate and other patterns. It is curious that the potters of the period did not avail themselves of sgraffiato decoration, that is the cutting through an engobe, in order to show a pattern in the colour of the body.

Painted decoration, as already stated, represents the least developed side of the potter's art of the period. It may be described as ' clay-painting,' and it differs from true barbotine, in the use of a thinner slip and its application with a brush. The patterns are similar, and it is not always easy to distinguish between trailed and painted work. Common pale buff wares, probably of Broseley clay, are often relieved with thin washes of red, but they rarely take the form of definite patterns. Marbled work may be conveniently referred to here. It is excessively rare, and was almost certainly imported. It appears to have been effected in the same manner as the marblings of the old Staffordshire potters, that is, by the partial blending of slips of several colours on the surface of the vessel.

The uses and ancient names of the different vessels are a difficult branch of inquiry. One thing, however, is clear : the vessels were essentially made for use. The distinction between ' useful ' and ' ornamental ' wares is modern, and came into prominence under Wedgwood and his contemporaries, who adopted classical models for their ornamental products. There is no evidence that the Gaulish and British potters copied antique Greek, Etruscan, or Oriental pottery to meet an antiquarian taste, or introduced novelties for purely display purposes. On the contrary, their shapes were those in vogue in their own day. Roman writers occasionally refer to various pottery vessels by name, and now and again mention their uses. There were vessels for the storage of wine and other comestibles—for culinary purposes—for the table ; and others appropriate for religious rites and to hold the ashes of the dead.   The large vessels for the transport and storage of wine, oils, figs, and other liquids and solids, were according to their shapes and sizes designated *dolia, amphorae, cadi,* etc.   There were *urnae* for carrying water ; *urcei, ampullae,* and *lagenae,* which corresponded with our jugs ; *poculi,* or cups, of which there were various forms with special names, some borrowed from the Greeks ; *patinae, patellae,* and *catinae,* probably dish and saucer-shaped vessels mostly for the table ; *ollae* and *pelves* for culinary and other household purposes ; and other names of uncertain application.   The attempts to identify the vessels to which these names applied are only partially successful ; and so far as the pottery found on our sites is concerned, the task seems hopeless, for these Roman writers lived at different periods and referred mostly to the wares of Italy, whereas those of Gaul and Britain were of local origin or were modified by local influences.

No satisfactory classification of the pottery of the Roman era has yet been, or at present can be, devised.   Any system that makes one feature to the exclusion of others, as the material or rather its colour, or the ornamentation, or even the form, important as this is, the basis of classification, is necessarily an artificial one.   The ideal system would be one based upon the sources of manufacture, whether individual factories or regions where wares of distinctive character were made.   But at present this is only possible in a limited degree.   The Gaulish redglaze stands well defined from all other wares.   Less definitely, the fine and mostly dark wares, characterized by the prevalency of the forms shown in Fig. 46 and of barbotine decoration, may be treated as another group ; and as these were extensively made in the Nen valley in the vicinity of Castor, ' Castor ' or ' Durobrivian ' has almost come to be a general term for this kind of pottery wherever made.   The red ' pseudo-Samian ' ware represents another well-marked group and probably of Continental origin.   We may similarly detach a few more groups, but there will remain a large irresolvable residue made anywhere where suitable clay abounded.

It would facilitate the study of the pottery if a definite terminology for the forms of the vessels could be adopted ; but this would be difficult to accomplish, for with few exceptions form merges into form in a tantalizing fashion. Dragendorff[1] did useful service by publishing the chief forms of the redglaze and giving a number to each, and his list has been extended by Dechelette[2] and Walters,[3] and no doubt will yet be added to as new forms are discovered. He arranged his forms in a systematic manner before giving them their numbers. His first 14 examples are Italian, some of which are also provincial, the remaining 41 being Gaulish and German. In each series, they are arranged in the same order, beginning with dish-like vessels and ending with craters and tall vases; the sequence, however, ceases with the appended forms of Déchelette (23 in 1904), and with further additions the general numbering will become more arbitrary. It is obvious that if his system is extended to the pottery generally, the numbers would soon run into hundreds and it would be impossible to carry in the mind the forms they relate to.

As the pages of pottery figured in outline will give a better idea of the forms than written description; it is only necessary to supplement them with comments. The figures are from actual examples mostly in museums, and they include all the ordinary forms with a few of the rarer. As the interiors of the shallow vessels were exposed to view, consequently were carefully finished, one-half of their figures present their sections and internal profiles.

A. REDGLAZE ('TERRA SIGILLATA' OR 'SAMIAN' WARE)
(Figs. 43 and 44)

This ware as found in Britain is derived from three chief centres: La Graufesenque, the *Condatomagus* of the Ruteni, in the south of France; Lezoux in the Auvergne in central France; and Rheinzabern, the ancient *Tabernae Rhenanae*, near Speyer on the Rhine,—but most of it is from the second. The manufacture of pottery at La Graufesenque was already old when the Romans appeared on the scene; but under their influence the Rutenian potters produced a fabric closely resembling the Arretine, between A.D. 50 and 100. At Lezoux, redglaze was made about as early,

---

[1] *Bonner Jahrbuecher,* xcvi, xcix.
[2] *Les vases ceramiques ornés de la Gaule Romaine.*
[3] *Catalogue of Roman Pottery,* Brit. Mus.

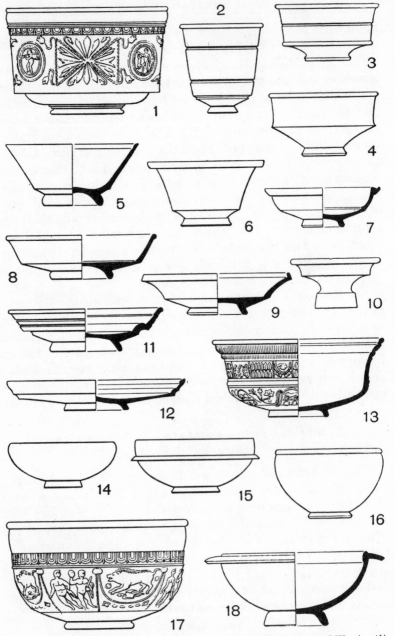

FIG. 43.—A. Examples of Roman Redglaze (*Terra Sigillata* or 'Samian' Ware). (¼)

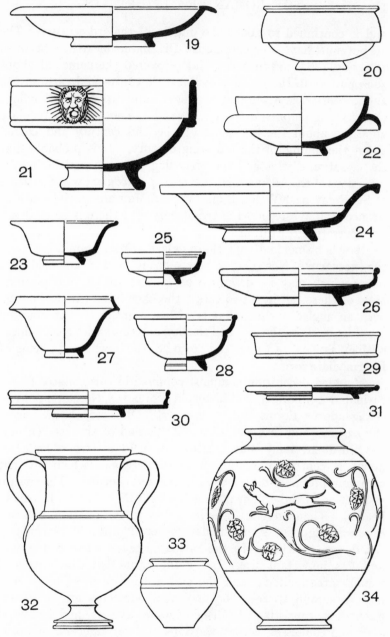

FIG. 44.—A. Examples of Roman Redglaze (*Terra Sigillata* or 'Samian' Ware). ($\frac{1}{4}$)

and it continued to about the middle of the 3rd century. The output must have been enormous—Dr. Plique unearthed, between 1879 and 1885, 188 furnaces, and recovered the names of about 3000 potters in the vicinity of the little town—and early in the 2nd century, the Arvernian products were exported throughout the western empire and even beyond. The Rhenish redglaze appeared about the beginning of the 2nd century and ceased about the middle of the following century. It is probable that the cessation of this and the preceding industry was due to the incursions of the Allemanni in A.D. 256–9. Redglaze was also made at St. Remy near Vichy, Banassac, and Montans in the south of France, and Westerndorf near Salzberg, but there is no evidence of exportation to Britain.

It will be noticed that the redglaze vessels figured are, with the exception of Nos. 32–3–4, bowls, basins, and various shallower forms which may be described as saucers, dishes, and platters. Most of these fall into two series, those, as Nos. 1 to 12 and 25, with an angled outline, that is with a more or less pronounced shoulder between the foot and the lip ; and those with a curvilinear outline, as Nos. 14 to 24, and 26 to 28, the bowl No. 13 being of intermediate form.

Moulded decoration is almost confined in this country to the carinated, cylindrical, and hemispherical bowls, Nos. 13, 1, and 17 [Dragendorf's Forms, 29, 30, and 37]. Of these, the first were the earliest, and disappeared about the end of the 1st century, the third surviving and holding the field in strong force for about a century or more, while the second, which are not common, probably disappeared in the 2nd century. The general disposition of the ornamentation varies little. The lip is usually beaded. Then after an interval below it, is a narrow band of egg-and-tongue or some similar pattern ; and this surmounts the decorated frieze. In the carinated bowls there is a second and less important frieze below the carination which itself is usually ornamented ; and the earlier hemispherical bowls also have a second frieze. The decorative elements are extremely diversified, consisting of foliage, flowers, diapers, and figures of gods and goddesses, heroes, warriors, athletes, dancers, sphinxes, centaurs, mermaids, birds, beasts, fishes, etc. ; and their combinations are equally diversified—on one frieze there may be a continuous scroll of foliage ; on another a continuous hunting scene ; on a third, figures in medallions or compartments, with intervening diapers, and so forth.

Moulded decoration also occurs on redglaze that imitates metallic vessels, especially *patellae* and small bowls with two flat ear-like handles, but examples are rarely found in this country, and if decorated, the decoration is confined to the handles.

Reliefs in applique, usually combined with barbotine, apparently survived moulding. They are confined to globular jars or *ollae* as Nos. 33 and 34, and other tall vessels as No. 32, that could not well have been moulded. The reliefs in applique are mostly mythological beings, personifications, and busts, the foliage and other subordinate details of the decorative scheme being largely in barbotine. Examples of this decoration are rare in this country ; but a simple ornamentation of conventional ivy-leaves in barbotine—perhaps sometimes moulded—on the convex flanges of bowls and saucers of the forms of Nos. 18, 19, and 22, is common, and long preceded applique.

Of the plain vessels of the first series named above, Nos. 5 and 8 [Forms 33 and 31] are frequently found and were made to the close of the redglaze period. Nos. 3 and 4 [8] and 11 and 12 [16 and 15] are rare and probably early, and may be considered as the prototypes of the former. Nos. 2 [64] and 10, both in the Guildhall Museum, are rarer still. In the curvilinear series are two prevailing forms, the hemispherical and the campanulate, of which Nos. 16 and 24 may be taken as types. Of the former, small bowls with convex flanges, as Nos. 18 and 22 [35 and 38] are the most frequent, and the second had a long innings ; the rest are rather scarce, especially No. 20 [81]. The campanulate form, as in Nos. 23 [7], 24, and 27 [7], is also rare and undoubtedly early. The little basin, No. 28 [27], is freely found, and seems to have been made almost to the close of the provincial redglaze period. The curious *mortarium* with the lion-head spout, No. 21 [45], is a decidedly late form. The platters, Nos. 29 and 30 [22 and 17], are survivals of Italian prototypes, and No. 31, in the Colchester Museum, is most unusual. Nos. 32 [53] and 34 [72] are both uncommon, and have already been referred to.

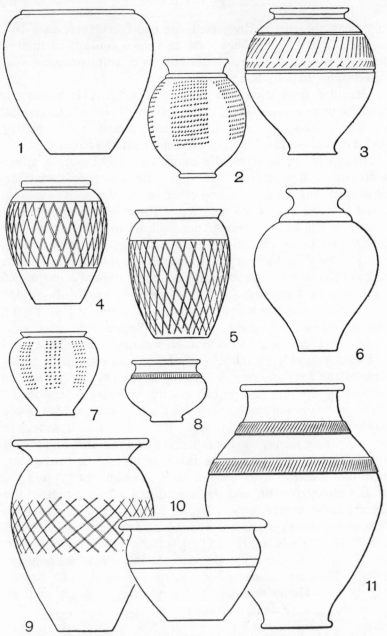

FIG. 45.—B. Examples of *Ollae* or Jars in other Fabrics than Redglaze. (¼)

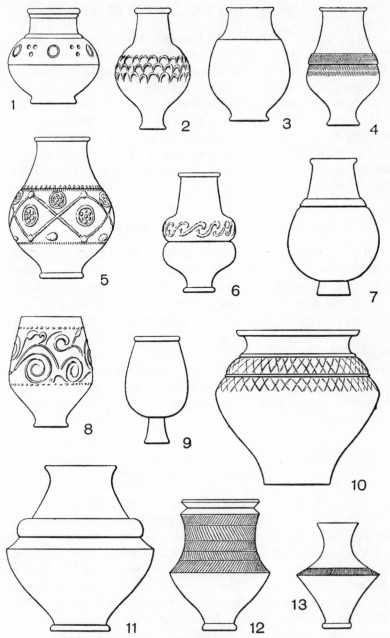

FIG. 46.—C. Examples of *Olla*-like Vessels, or Cups, in other Fabrics than Redglaze. ($\frac{1}{4}$)

167

In a general way, the earlier redglaze is thinner, harder, brighter and redder than the later.   Much of it is stamped with the makers' names, usually within the vessel on the bottom, but occasionally on the side externally.   As a rule the name is in a sunk oblong label, but occasionally, especially in the German fabrics, this is in the form of a foot, a circle, or a half-moon.   It is either in the nominative, with or without F or FE for *fecit*, or in the genitive, with O or OF for *officina* or M for *manu*.   The names are mostly Gaulish, and the lettering often exhibits Gaulish peculiarities.

B. *OLLAE* OR JARS OF OTHER FABRICS THAN REDGLAZE (Fig. 45)

The examples figured chiefly differ in their lips, and broadly speaking the small beaded and cornice-like lips of Nos. 3, 4, and 5 are early, while the curved lips of Nos. 6, 8, and 10 occurred throughout the Romano-British period.   No. 9 with its faint trellis pattern is a very common form in coarse black and grey wares, and was much used as a cooking-pot.   The little ' poppy-head ' vase, No. 2, as also No. 7, are in fine engobed ware, and No. 8, from London, has a bright plumbago-like surface.   The cordoned bands of this and Nos. 6 and 11 are perhaps Late-Celtic legacies.   No. 10 may be considered as a passage-form from the jar to the bowl.

C. OLLA-LIKE VESSELS, OR CUPS, OF OTHER FABRICS THAN REDGLAZE (FIG. 46)

Nos. 2 to 9, also 13, are in the thin engobed ware usually identified as Castor and Upchurch ; but similar vessels were made on the Rhine and in northern Gaul.   The convivial inscriptions which they occasionally bear—as BIBE, BIBE VINAS, VINVM TIBI DVLCIS, etc.—indicate their use.   No. 2, from Colchester, exhibits the scale pattern (page 158) ; and Nos. 5, 6, and 8, barbotine decoration, light on a dark ground in the first two, and in the last, covered with the engobe.   No. 1, from London, is in fine red ware, ornamented with annulated bosses alternating with concave roundels.   Nos. 10 and 11, carinated and cordoned jars from

Colchester and Silchester, have Late-Celtic affinities. No. 12, from Silchester, and ornamented with engine-turning, is most unusual ; while the strongly carinated little cup, No. 13, is not uncommon.

D. BOWLS AND BOWL-LIKE VESSELS OF OTHER FABRICS THAN REDGLAZE (Fig. 47)

Bowls with flat flanged lips as Nos. 1 and 6, of which many were found at Gellygaer, are of common red and black wares, and are an early type. No. 2 is of distinctive form, fabric and ornamentation, probably of Continental origin, and referred to on page 158. Nos. 3 and 4 are pleasing shapes, the one from Silchester and the other from Colchester ; and No. 5, from the centurion's grave at Colchester, is delicately turned in a hard brownish ware. No. 9, in the Maidstone Museum, has marked Late-Celtic features. Nos. 7, 8, 10, 12, and 14 are imitations of redglaze ('pseudo-Samian'), from Colchester and Caerwent. No. 11 is a passage-form between the bowl and the olla. The pan-shaped bowl, No. 13, is common enough in black ware, and No. 13, from London, is of fine texture with a jet-like surface.

E. AND F. SHALLOW VESSELS (SAUCERS AND DISHES) AND AM-PHORAE OF OTHER FABRICS THAN REDGLAZE (Fig. 48)

Shallow vessels like Nos. 1 to 6 may be designated saucers or dishes according to whether they have foot-rings or flat bases. No. 1, from Gellygaer, is of coarse red ware, and Nos. 2 and 3, from Colchester and Silchester, are of fine texture with a surface-film of intense black. They all have a central 'kick,' and with little doubt are early. No. 4 is a common form in ordinary black ware, and No. 5 is less frequent, and in both red and black wares.

Fragments of large *amphorae* are constantly found on our Roman sites. These ponderous vessels of coarse buff or red clay were from 20 to 30 ins. in height, and No. 8 is a prevailing form, but they were often taller in proportion to their girth. The makers' names are often stamped on the handles, and indicate

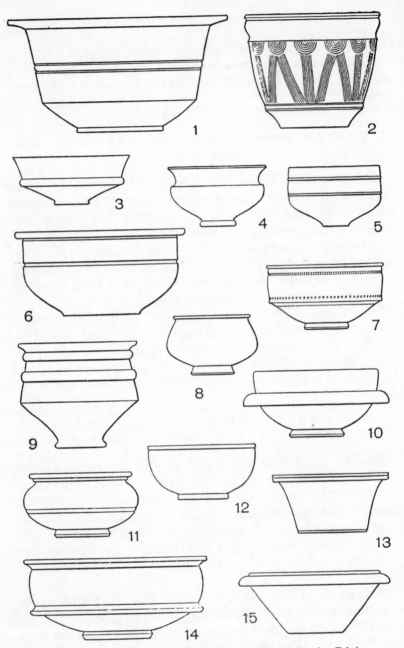

FIG. 47.—D. Examples of Bowls and Bowl-like Vessels in other Fabrics than Redglaze. (¼)

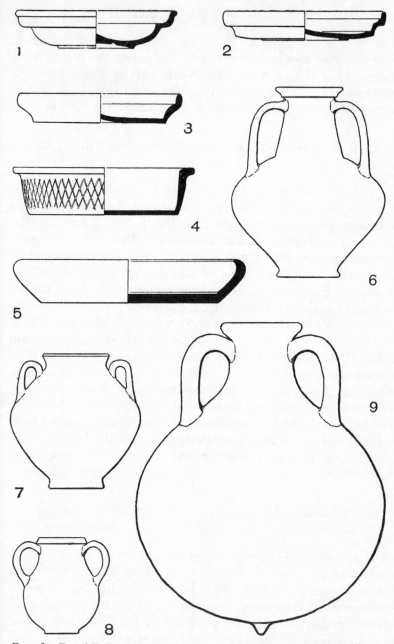

Fig. 48.—E. and F. Shallow Vessels (Saucers and Dishes) and *Amphorae* in other Fabrics than Redglaze. (¼)

171

that they were derived, as a rule, from southern countries. Probably they owe their presence in this country to having been imported full of wine or oil. Small *amphorae*, as Nos. 6, 7, and 9, are much less common, and many, as the second, may be described as two-handled jars, the handles of these being often mere eyelets.

G. JUGS (*AMPULLAE*) OF OTHER FABRICS THAN REDGLAZE
(Fig. 49)

Jugs vary but little. If to the flask No. 1 a handle is added, it will represent the prevailing shape, except that the neck often approximates to a cylindrical form, as in Nos. 7 and 8. The handles are round or flattish in section. The lip is frequently cornice-like, as in Nos. 4, 7, and 10, and it is comparatively seldom that there is a spout. Jugs of this description are commonly in plain buff and red wares, and the better sort have an engobe or wash of a brighter colour. No. 4, a pale buff jug from Silchester, is remarkable for its squatness; and No. 6, a London example, is decidedly unusual. No. 5 is a highly finished example with slip scrolls, from Colchester. No. 8 has its spreading lip, nipped to form a spout, and No. 11 is an unusual form in the Maidstone Museum. No. 5 is a curious fine red vessel from Colchester, examples of which have been found in London and elsewhere. The front of the neck is ornamented with a mask impressed from a mould and on the back is a flat strip—apparently legacies of an earlier form with a mask-spout and a handle, but now quite functionless.

H. MISCELLANEOUS VESSELS OF OTHER FABRICS THAN REDGLAZE
(Fig. 50)

Nos. 1 and 2, both from Caerwent, are two types of handled beakers or cups, which are usually in common black ware, but are by no means plentiful. Gen. Pitt-Rivers found both types at Rushmore and Rotherley, some of his examples having small eyelet handles.[1] Nos. 3 and 8 (Guildhall and Silchester) belong to a large class of diminutive vases, usually in fine red or buff

[1] Vol. i, pp. 103 and 113; vol. ii, p. 153.

wares, which probably served a variety of purposes—to hold
unguents, cosmetics, and the like, and as children's playthings,
dice-boxes, etc. Nos. 4 and 5 are probably of Continental origin.
The one, from a Colchester interment, is painted with light scrolls
on a red engobe, and the other, a Bath example, has trailed scrolls
covered with a blackish engobe. The tall vase, No. 6, from
Silchester, is of fine red ware with light slip decoration. The
'frilled' tazza, No. 7, occurs in various 'coarse' wares and is not
uncommon. The remaining illustrations are examples of covered
vessels and indicate the usual shapes of the lids. No. 9 is of fine
engobed pottery ornamented with 'engine-turning,' attributed
to Castor, and decidedly rare ; Nos. 10 and 11, two common
grey cineraries from Colchester ; and No. 12, a lid from
Gellygaer.

I. EARTHENWARE MORTARS (*MORTARIA*, *PELVES ?*) OF ALL FABRICS
(Fig. 51)

The mortar was a highly specialized vessel, pan-shaped, with a
concave interior studded with fragments of quartz or iron-slag
pressed into the surface while soft, and with a strong overhanging
rim and spout. It was used for triturating, mashing or mixing
substances, especially foods, the hard fragments aiding the
process and preserving the surface from abrasion. From the
absence of pestles, it may be inferred that these were of wood.
The rims vary considerably. Three types may be distinguished—
the roll and bead (Fig. 51, A to D); the 'hammer-head' (H and
I) ; and the vertical (J and K). The latter two appear to be derived
from the first, which almost certainly was the earliest, and E, F,
and G may be regarded as passage-forms between it and the
second. Vertical rims are characteristic of the redglaze mortars
(Fig. 44, No. 21) and its imitations, all the other forms being
in ordinary red and buff wares.

The strong projecting rim led the writer to suggest many years
ago,[1] that the vessel was not ordinarily used *resting* on a table—
its small bottom would render it unsteady in this position—but
that it was inserted into a round hole large enough to receive the

[1] *Derbysh. Arch. Soc.* xl, plate vii.

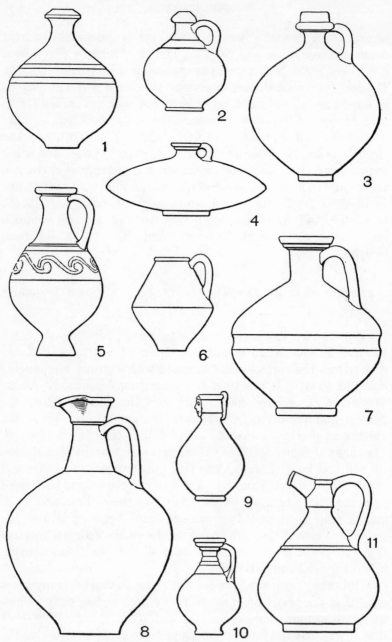

FIG. 49.—G. Examples of Jugs (*Ampullae*) in other Fabrics than Redglaze. (¼)

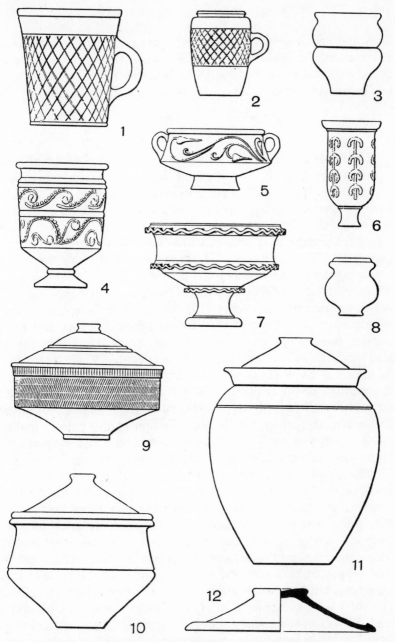

FIG. 50.—H. Miscellaneous Vessels in other Fabrics than Redglaze. ($\frac{1}{4}$)

175

body and yet to allow the rim to rest upon its edge, as indicated in the section, Fig. 51. The fact that, while the internal surface and the rim are carefully finished, the exterior of the body is often left in a rough condition, goes far to confirm this conjecture.

POTTERS' KILNS

The remains of a considerable number of these kilns have been found in this country. They varied in shape, size, and construction, but all appear to have been on the same principle. They were subterranean structures with their summits level with the surface or slightly protruding. The simpler were circular, from 3 to 4 ft. or more in diameter, with a tunnel-like furnace on the floor-level. This, however, did not open directly into the oven which contained the vessels to be fired, but into a space below it with a perforated roof or diaphragm to allow the hot gases of the fire to ascend into the oven. It is evident that these small kilns were packed with the wares to be fired from the top, and this implies an opening large enough for the purpose. The opening also served as a chimney, but, unless restricted, it would be wasteful of heat. No doubt there was a simple contrivance for reducing it according to the requirements of the draught, or for closing it altogether. Some of the Continental kilns appear to have had a lateral opening for the introduction of the pottery and a small chimney or smoke-vent in the vaulted roof, and some of our larger examples may have had a similar arrangement.

The simpler kilns were lined with clay mixed with chaff or grass, and often with broken pottery or tiles, to mitigate the contraction under the action of fire. The perforated bottom or diaphragm was of denser clay, or of tiles specially made for the purpose—wedge-shaped, the wide ends resting on a set-off or ledge around the interior, and the points meeting in the centre and supported by a pier usually projecting from the back of the structure, but sometimes isolated. In the more elaborate kilns, the sides were constructed of curved bricks cemented with clay, and the roof of the furnace was often arched. Many kilns of this type have been found in the neighbourhood of Castor, and a group of four arranged crosswise and apparently fed from a common

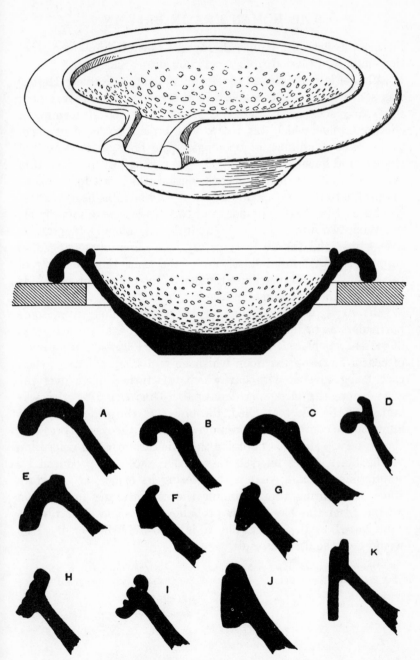

FIG. 51.—I. Mortars (*Mortaria, Pelves*?) in all Earthenware Fabrics.   (All ⅓)

furnace-pit, near St. Paul's, in 1677.[1] Two of simple construction similarly radiated from a common pit at Silchester.[2]

A larger kiln of different construction, found at Radlett, Herts,[3] was somewhat oval in shape. In the centre was an oval pier, the space between it and the surrounding set-off forming a continuous flue, which was arched with broken bricks so arranged as to leave a number of openings. The floor above was " of clinkers and burnt clay laid loosely, over which was placed a thin layer of sand "—a mode of construction which would render it permeable to the heat of the furnace. Of five kilns near Lexden, Colchester,[4] four were circular, and two of these were remarkable in having two furnaces each. The fifth was oblong, 5 ft. 4 ins. by 4 ft. 4 ins., and the under-structure was admirably arranged to support the perforated floor and at the same time to allow of the heat being well distributed under it, there being on each side of the flue three rectangular recesses.

Mr. Artis, in his account of the Castor kilns, gives some particulars as to the packing. It would seem that as each layer of vessels was placed, the packer's assistant followed with a layer of coarse hay or grass upon which he laid small pellets of clay, each being covered with hay which was turned down over the edge before the next was deposited. Thus tier after tier was laid until the kiln was filled, the object of the pellets being to allow of the contents being removed without the risk of breaking the pottery. He was of opinion that the carbonaceous coloration of the black ware, referred to on page 156, was produced by smothering the kiln, that is, by closing its orifice, at a certain stage of the firing, thus confining the carbonaceous fumes from arising from the hay. It is probable that some such process contributed to the effect, but it is doubtful whether it alone would give the desired result.

[1] Illustrations of Roman London, p. 79.   [2] Archaeologia, lxii, p. 328.
[3] Proc. Soc. Ant. 2, xvii, p. 261.   [4] Collectanea, Antiqua, i, p. 1.

CHAPTER X

GLASS, METAL, AND STONE UTENSILS

GLASS

ALMOST invariably broken glass is found on our Roman sites, but never in the profusion of the potsherds. We need not infer from this that glass was scarce or costly. To-day, a domestic rubbish-heap discloses more broken earthenware and porcelain than glass, and this in both cases is due to the latter material being, from its brittleness and inability to withstand sudden changes of temperature, of more limited use than the former. The general diffusion of Roman glass warrants a belief that it was both well known and in regular use in the homes of the era, but perfect vessels are rarely found on their sites. The majority of these in our museums have been obtained from graves, where many of them were used as cineraries and others as accessories, their careful burial having conduced to their preservation.

The combined action of the moisture and carbonic acid of the soil has often rendered the surface of the glass more or less opaque. If the action has been slight, a beautiful iridescent lustre may result, beloved of connoisseurs, but masking the original brilliancy of the surface; if severe, the surface may be in a scaling condition. In most large collections, some of the glass is in an unchanged condition, and well indicates the high attainments of the glass-makers of the era, both in their material and their technical processes.

How high these attainments reached, is well seen in the ' onyx ' glass, of which the Portland vase in the British Museum is a familiar example, with cameo-like figures which are unrivalled

in glass-carving ; in the ' millefiori ' or fused-mosaic glass, sometimes resembling a richly coloured coralline marble, and sometimes a brecciated marble ; and in the ' diatretum,' distinguished
for its deeply undercut ornamentation. But glass-wares of the
costliness and high finish of these need not detain us further, for
although not uncommon in Italy, the finding of fragments in
this country is of excessively rare occurrence. They indicate that
the glass-workers had command of a wide range of colours, but
they seem not to have attained to a pure transparent red. They
certainly used copper, iron, manganese and antimony in their
production, and probably also cobalt for some of the rich deep
blues.

The vessels ordinarily met with here are of a useful kind,
consisting of bottles of a variety of forms and sizes, ewers, jars,
cups, beakers, and saucers, mostly with a bluish-green tinge and
highly transparent. In the finer qualities the tinge is slighter,
but absolutely colourless glass is rare. If the tinge is not green,
it is a faint saffron or honey-colour, but nearly always with a
suspicion of green. Vessels, however, in what may be properly
called coloured glass, are by no means uncommon, deep blue and
green, and various yellow tones ranging from amber to a rich
brown, being the most frequent.

In the forms and decorations of the vessels, the Roman glass-
worker went his own way, and his products rarely simulated those
of the potter and the metal-worker. As might be expected, he
turned out wares of various grades—strong, plain, and cheap for
common and rough purposes, and highly refined, which had a
delicacy of form and finish that can hardly be excelled. Most
of the glass vessels of Roman Britain were simply blown, and they
indicate a high proficiency in the use of the blow-iron. The little
cup with its widespread and turned-down rim (Fig. 53, B),
from Caerwent, is a simple and not unpleasing example. It is
thin and wellshaped, and its foot is a ring of glass deftly attached
to the base. The cylindrical handled bottle (A), from Boughton
Monchelsea, Kent, is a small specimen of a common form, fragments of which are found on most Roman sites. These vessels
are of common greenish glass, and are mostly from about 8 ins. to
1 ft. in height. They invariably have wide handles, strong and

FIG. 52.—Examples of Roman Glass Vessels. (¼)

181

sturdy, reeded externally, and attached to the shoulder by a spreading base. This reeding is characteristic of the handles of the time, and the claw-like feet of the reeds, well seen also in our examples, C, D, E, F, give a sense of firmness of grip. The last three, from burials at Sittingbourne, Colchester, and Faversham respectively, are decanter-like bottles. The spiral string of glass round the neck of the first gives it an admirable finish. Vessels of the shape of the second have been more frequently found than the other two, but without the smaller handle. The trail of glass, frilled by the dexterous use of the pincers, below these handles, is not uncommon. The third is remarkable for the vertical pillars round the body.

In C we have a moulded square variant of A of equally common occurrence, with a precisely similar handle. Similar hexagonal, and more rarely octagonal, bottles are also met with, occasionally with two handles. The bodies of these bottles were moulded, and their bottoms often have simple devices, as panels, interlaced triangles, concentric circles, etc., in raised lines, and sometimes letters, probably initials of the makers' names.[1] A small jug from Colchester, in the British Museum, was shaped by being blown into a mould or cage of wire network, the impression of which shows on the glass.

H is a beaker-like cup of the finest workmanship, and ornamented with grooved bands, from one of the Bartlow Hills tombs. Fragments of similar cups, but not necessarily of quite the same shape, have been found on many of our Roman sites. A piece of one was turned up at Gellygaer with the edge of the spreading lip ground and polished, and the narrow horizontal groovings cut on the lathe.

The godrooned or 'pillared' bowl, I, was not uncommon. These bowls were often in coloured glass—deep blue, full green, amber, or mulberry; but fragments have been found in London and Silchester of several colours mingled together after the fashion of the coloured clays of the old Staffordshire 'agate' ware. They were evidently moulded. The writer examined some pieces of these bowls in the Caerleon Museum, and found that the inner surface and the outer above the pillars had been ground and

[1] As AP within a circle at Great Chesterford, *Arch. Jour.* xvii, p. 126.

polished, apparently on the lathe, from which, it would seem, that whatever the process of moulding may have been, it left the inner surface in a rough or uneven condition.

Moulded cylindrical cups of greenish glass, exhibiting chariot races and gladiatorial combats in relief, and arranged in tiers with appropriate inscriptions, have been sparingly found.   The portion of one found at Hartlip presents a charioteer in a *biga* on the point of reaching the *metae*, and on the tier below two gladiators. A perfect cup of the kind from Colchester in the British Museum has a chariot race in two tiers, with an inscription above to the effect that Crescens beats Hierax, Olympias, and Antilocus.[1]

The beaker-like cup G, from a grave at Barnwell, Cambridge-shire, and now in the British Museum, has a singularly modern appearance.   It is of rather thick glass with a faint greenish honey tinge, and its ornamentation consists of oval depressions, cut out on the lapidary's wheel.   Pieces of precisely similar cups have been found at London, Caerwent, Gellygaer, Birrens, Ardoch, Wilderspool, and probably elsewhere, as such pieces may be easily mistaken for modern cut glass.   The little cup J, in the Guildhall collection, presents another type of decoration rarely met with.   It is of thin yellowish blown glass, with applied ' nail-head ' ornamentation.

The little blown glass bottles, commonly known as lachry-matories or *unguentaria*, were not confined to funerary purposes, but were in general use for holding perfumes, unguents, and served all the purposes of small bottles with us.   It was mentioned on page 140, that large bottles of the forms of A and C were often used to hold the ashes of the dead ; less often these were placed in large globular glass jars.   The one shown in Fig. 52 is a simple example, about 9 ins. in diameter, from a burial in Lockham Wood, and now in the Maidstone Museum.   More usually they had two handles and occasionally glass lids, and a good example, with the leaden cist in which it was found in Warwick Square, London, is in the British Museum.   It is not unlikely that these vessels were specially made for funerary purposes.

Very little is known of the sources of manufacture of Roman glass-ware in Britain.   In 1859, Mr. Roach Smith knew of

[1] See also, *Brit. Arch. Assoc.* v, p. 371.

no vestige of Roman glass furnaces in this island ; nor did Mr. Thomas Wright, sixteen years later, but he suggested that water-rolled lumps of coloured glass found on the beach near Brighton were derived from the site of Roman glass-works which had long been encroached upon by the sea. Even as late as 1907, Mr. Edward Dillon, in his book on glass, could only suggest that if anywhere in England, traces of such works might be expected between the Medway and the Isle of Thanet. Mr. Thomas May, however, has been able to make a strong case for the manufacture of glass at Wilderspool near Warrington in Roman times. During his excavations he uncovered the remains of five workshops containing peculiar ovens. These were singly or in pairs in dense clay platforms, hardened by fire. Some were oval, from about 2 ft. 6 ins. to 5 ft. long, having at one end a flue or stoke-hole reached from a hearth, and at the opposite end or in the side, another flue, blocked at the end in several instances with a flag-stone. Others were simple rounded cavities with a stoke-hole. Mr. May considered that the former were annealing ovens or ' lires,' and that the latter had contained melting-pots. In the vicinity of these structures, he found several lumps of crude glass, glass-scum, calcined flint, a lump of chalk, and pieces of broken glass—all more or less confirmatory of the manufacture of glass ; also a stone slab with a shallow recess, 12 by 8 ins., which he regarded as a mould for window-glass.[1]

To what extent glass was made in Roman Britain is at present unknown. The glass vessels found in this country resemble those of Roman Gaul, where the manufacture obtained a foothold as early as Pliny's time, and flourished greatly, to judge from the known sites of glass-works and the wealth of specimens in the French museums. Our Roman glassware closely resembles that of northern Gaul, and it has long been noticed that the parts of England nearest Gaul—Kent, London, and Essex—have been most prolific in this ware. The glass may have been largely imported from Gaul, or Gaulish glass-workers may have settled in these contiguous parts of England. Either would explain the relative plentifulness, and perhaps both contributed to it.

[1] *Warrington's Roman Remains*, pp. 37, 82.

FIG. 53. ROMAN GLASS-WARE, MAIDSTONE MUSEUM

METAL

The metallic vessels of Roman Britain that have survived are of bronze, pewter, and silver, the first being the most numerous, and the last the rarest ; but as a class these vessels are among the rarer 'finds' of the era. It must not be inferred from this that they were correspondingly rare during that era. One vessel of metal would outlast many of pottery and glass, and, when worn out, its metallic value would save it from the rubbish heap. Most of the examples in our collections have been deposited with the dead or purposely hidden.

Whether beaten or cast, these vessels indicate, as a class, a perfect mastery of the metal-worker over his materials. Their curves are graceful and precise, and, when ornamented, the ornamentation is usually finely and carefully executed. Occasionally they exhibit engraved decoration ; less so, enamelled.

Of the bronze vessels, two forms are noteworthy—the *ampulla* or jug, and a pan with a straight horizontal handle known as the *patera*, also as the *patina* or *patella*. Both in form and decoration, these exhibit little provincial influence. Precisely similar vessels have been abundantly found in Pompeii, and its region was an important centre of the manufacture, exporting its products to Britain and even beyond the limits of the empire. There is no evidence that vessels of the kind were made in Britain ; but it is almost certain that some were made in Gaul, either by Italian artisans or by natives who copied Italian forms.

Four examples of jugs are shown in Fig. 54, A, B, C, D. The first was associated with the *patera*, D, in a grave near Canterbury.[1] It so closely resembles some Pompeian examples that there is little doubt it came from the same source. The next two are good examples of the plainer wares of the kind, the one from Tewkesbury and the other from Winchester, both in the British Museum. The last is from one of the Bartlow Hills tombs,[2] in which it was associated with a similar *patera* to the one just referred to, and is decorated with a band of niello

[1] *Proc. Soc. Ant.* 2, xviii, p. 279.   [2] *Archaeologia*, xxvi, p. 33.

below the neck. The plainer jugs are usually without spouts, as in the two examples given ; and in the more elaborate, the spout is sometimes produced by an angled indentation on each side, thus giving the mouth a pleasing trefoiled shape. Two jugs of this form were obtained from the Bartlow Hills and another from a grave at Sittingbourne. Almost invariably the handle terminates below in a human or an animal's head, or a small medallion. In our Bartlow Hills example it is an ox's skull.

Two forms of the *patera* can be distinguished—a shallow one with the bottom usually bossed up in the centre, and the handle cylindrical and ending in an animal's head ; and a deep one with a flat bottom and a wide flat handle. F is a typical example of the first, from the grave near Canterbury. Two of the Bartlow Hills *paterae* resembled it, but the third[1] differed in the ornamentation of the handle, which, instead of being fluted or reeded, had a *cippus*, masks, basket of fruit, and other objects mostly of some religious significance. Another found near South Shields had an inscription to Apollo round the boss, and there is a silver example found in Gracechurch Street, in the British Museum.

The second form is of more frequent occurrence, and G is an example from Herringfleet,[2] which is representative of. a large number. The sides convexly taper to the flat bottom, and the handle terminates in a disc with a central hole, the curves of its concave sides flowing into those of the mouth and disc. The disc is relieved with concentric corrugations, and the bowl with a bead below the lip. Beyond these, ornamentation rarely goes further, but in the present example the upper surface of the handle has a conventional *thyrsus*, and, what is rare, the maker's name, Quatinus.

Five vessels of this form, graduated in size, have been found at Castle Howard, and two of the handles are stamped P. CIPI POLIB. and C. CIPI POLVIBI. Another in Wigtownshire bears the same maker's name. The Cipii appear to have been a firm in or near Herculaneum, and their products have been found as far away as France, Austria, Switzerland, Germany, and

---

[1] *Archaeologia*, xxviii, p. 2.   [2] *Proc. Soc. Ant.* 2, xvi, p. 237.

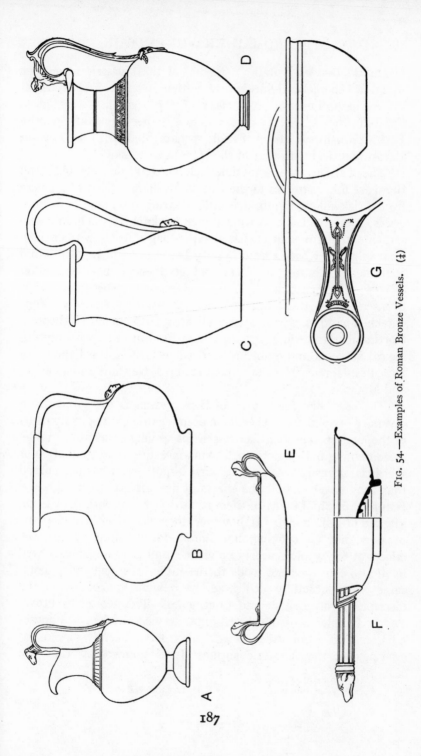

FIG. 54.—Examples of Roman Bronze Vessels. ($\frac{1}{4}$)

Denmark, besides Britain. ' Nests ' of these vessels have been found at Abergele, Helmsdale in Sutherlandshire, and Irchester in Northamptonshire. A variant of the form has a recurved lip, and often a slightly recurved foot. One found at Swinton Park, Yorkshire,[1] had a handle ornamented with a *Thyrsus* almost identical with that of the Herringfleet ' skillet.'

The handles are sometimes elaborately ornamented, and there are fine examples in the British Museum. That of a *patera* from Prickwillow, Cambridgeshire,[2] bearing the name of Bodvo-genus, is adorned with a winged genius, dolphins, shell, and sea-serpents, the grip being enchased with foliage filled in with enamel. That of a silver *patera* from County Durham,[3] which when found contained a number of silver and gold finger-rings and other articles, is enriched with scrolly and refined arabesques, and it is inscribed to the Mother Goddesses—MATR FAB DVBIT. Four detached handles, part of a large silver hoard found at Capheaton, Northumberland,[4] in 1747, are ornamented in relief with mytho-logical subjects and emblems, and these include the Labours of Hercules, Mercury, Bacchus and a moenad, Neptune and a nereid, and Minerva.

The uses, like the names, of these vessels is the subject of a diversity of opinions. They have been regarded as the equivalents of the modern saucepans, as vessels for serving stews at the table, as combining both functions, as wine-measures, and as libation or sacrificial utensils. Against the first hypothesis it has been urged that they never exhibit the effects of fire, also that the high and beautiful finish of many of them is not consistent with their being kitchen utensils at all. If, however, they were held over charcoal braziers, not for cooking, but simply for warming viands, the effects of fire would scarcely be visible, and they might very well have also conveyed the foods to the table. On the other hand, some were certainly dedicated to religious purposes, as the inscriptions on British and Continental silver examples prove. Poorer temples probably had bronze services, and in the house-hold, metallic and other vessels may have been reserved for offerings at the domestic shrine. It is noteworthy that the

[1] *Arch. Jour.* vi, p. 47.   [2] *Archaeologia*, xxviii, p. 436.
[3] *Arch. Jour.* viii, p. 35.   [4] *Archaeologia*, xv, p. 393.

paterae figured on the altars resemble those of our first division, and are nearly always associated with ewers, just as they were in the Bartlow Hills.   The *patera* appears to have been a saucer-like vessel for liquids only, and derived from the Greek *phiale*, both being used for libations.   The central boss or *omphalos* of the latter provided a small hollow underneath for a finger to be caught in when the vessel was held.   The Romans or Etruscans added the handle, and the *omphalos* survived as an ornamental feature.   The *patina* and its diminutive, *patella*, appear to have been used for solid or semi-solid foods, either in cooking or for serving up at the table ;   and perhaps these terms should be confined to the vessels of our second division.

Shallow bowls of thin bronze ranging from about 8 to 14 ins. in diameter, with or without two loop-handles, were in regular use, and fine examples may be seen in the British and York Museums.   They are excellently made and usually quite plain, but the handles are often slightly ornamented.   Fig. 54, E, is a peculiarly graceful example found in one of the Bartlow Hills.[1] As it was associated, like the *paterae* in two of the other tombs of these ' hills,' with a bronze ewer, it presumably had a similar ritual use.   A silver bowl with a flanged lip, highly ornamented on the upper surface, was found at Corbridge in 1736.

Bronze colanders or strainers have occasionally been found, but rarely perfect in consequence of their thinness.   They are hemispherical, with or without handles, and the holes are usually arranged in patterns.   One with a wide flanged rim was associated with a bronze *patina* at Kyngadle [2] in Carmarthenshire, now in the Welsh Museum, and a similar one, but lacking its flange, was found at Ribchester.   An Ickleton [3] example had a long, flat, horizontal handle, the grip having incurved sides, and precisely similar strainers have been found at Pompeii.

Flat-bottomed trays, described also as plates or salvers, have been sparingly found.   There is a small example in the Guildhall, with a flat, engrailed rim, the shoulder and edge being neatly finished with a bead.   Globular bronze camp-kettles have been

---

[1] *Archaeologia*, xxix, p. 3.   [2] *Arch. Camb.* 6, i. p. 21.
[3] *Brit. Arch. Assoc.* iv, p. 376.

found at Newstead. Bronze lamps will be referred to in Chapter XII.

Bronze vessels were sometimes adorned with champlevé enamel. These were cast with sinkings to receive the enamel. A remarkably fine example was obtained from the Bartlow Hills. It was a small globular *situla*,[1] with moulded foot, recurved lip, and a movable handle attached by rings arising from acanthus leaves on the sides of the vessel. The enamelled decoration consisted of belts of foliage and simple geometrical patterns, in translucent blue, opaque red, and green, and the exposed bronze had been gilded. Several small bowls or cups with similar decoration have been found, and notably one near Marlborough [2] with a line of inscription below the lip, ABALLAVA VXELLODVM G AMBOGLAN S BANNA · A. MAIS—names of Roman places in the neighbourhood of Carlisle. Possibly it was made for some society connected with these places. In the British Museum are two cups of similar character, the one from Brougham near Standon, and the other from Harwood, Northumberland. These enamelled vessels appear to have emanated from a common source, and probably British.

As already stated, pewter is less frequent than bronze. A large table service of this alloy, carefully secreted by burial, was discovered at Icklingham, Suffolk, in 1840, and about forty pieces of it are now in the British Museum. In the same museum are thirty-two pieces of another service found similarly buried at Appleshaw, Hampshire,[3] in 1897, and another hoard found near Ely in 1858.[4] A Roman well at Brislington, Bristol,[5] yielded seven pewter jugs in 1899, and other examples have been found at Caerwent, Colchester, London, and elsewhere. Pewter is more susceptible to chemical change by contact with the soil than bronze, and the Roman examples are usually in a friable condition, with a peculiar pearly sheen. The proportions of tin and lead in the Roman examples vary, and as a rule the percentage of the latter is greater than in the English alloy.

The most characteristic vessels in Roman pewter are large

---

[1] *Archaeologia*, xxvi, plate xxxv. [2] *Arch. Jour.* xiv, 282.
[3] *Archaeologia*, lvi, p. 7. [4] *Arch. Jour.* xxxii, p. 330.
[5] *Vict. Hist.* Somerset, i, p. 305.

circular platters or *lances*.   There are ten from the Appleshaw, eleven from the Icklingham, and six from the Ely hoards, in the British Museum.   Occasionally they were square instead of circular.   Of the other Appleshaw forms, five are hemispherical bowls from 4 to 6 ins. in diameter, and three others have a curved flange below the lip—a form frequent in the redglaze pottery (Fig. 44, No. 22).   Several cups reproduce familiar forms in Castor, New Forest, and kindred wares (Fig. 46, No. 3).   The rest of the hoard consists of two jugs, several saucers, a curious chalice, and an oval dish with a flat handle at one end and ornamented with a fish in the centre.   The decoration of the Roman pewter, which is almost confined to the *lances*, is very distinctive, consisting of incised lines filled with black bituminous inlays.   The prevailing designs present a framework of interlacing bands, in the interspaces of which are small ornaments, and the central feature is often a large rosette—a scheme of decoration which recalls that of many mosaic pavements and has a distinct Byzantine feeling.   On one of the Appleshaw saucers is shown the ' chi-rho ' symbol, and it also occurs on a Roman cake of pewter found in the Thames at Battersea.[1]

It is noteworthy that as a class the pewter forms and decoration have little in common with those of bronze.   The old English pewterer regarded his material as a substitute for silver, and took the simpler silver forms for his models.   This is true to some extent of the Roman pewterer, but he certainly did not copy bronze vessels.   Many of the Appleshaw vessels were copies of the current table-ware in pottery, and the *lances* were probably from silver models.   The decoration and especially the Christian symbol are suggestive that the use of pewter came in late in Roman Britain ;   and this is further suggested by the fact that pewter at Minton was associated with coins ranging from A.D. 360 to 410, and a hoard of 1500 coins from Constantine to Gratian in Cambridgeshire was deposited in a pewter jar.[2]

[1] *Proc. Soc. Ant.* 2, ii, p. 235.   [2] *Ibid.* 2, xii, p. 56.

STONE

The most important stone utensil was the revolving quern
(*mola versatilis*), entire stones or fragments of which are constantly found on Romano-British domestic sites. Although
invented only two or three centuries before our era, it was already
established in Britain, and probably had displaced the older
saddle-quern (*mola trusatilis*) in the southern parts of the island,
at the time of the Roman conquest. The typical quern of
Roman Britain differed from its predecessor in being larger and
flatter. The grinding-face of the nether stone was still convex
(that of the upper stone being correspondingly concave), and this
form was due to a mistaken notion that it aided the discharge of
the meal. Externally, it was circular with a more or less convex
summit. The 'eye' of the upper stone was more or less dished
above to serve as a hopper, and frequently its funnel-shaped
hollow had a raised rim. The prevailing size was 15 ins. in
diameter, but specimens 2 or 3 ins. smaller or larger are occasionally found. The grinding-faces were often transversely grooved
to facilitate the flow of the meal.

The lower stone had the necessary central hole for the wooden
or iron pin on which the upper stone revolved. In the simpler
and presumably earlier querns, the rynd or block which contained
the socket for the pin was of wood. This was sufficiently
narrow that when driven into the 'eye' it left a space on either
side for the passage of the grain. In the more elaborate querns
the rynd was of iron with two or more arms, the ends of which
fitted into grooves on the under surface of the stone. The
wooden handle was usually flat and horizontal, and was driven
into a wedge-shaped sinking in the upper surface, and only rarely
into a lateral socket. In a few instances, querns have retained
their handles, a notable example being one found at Silchester.[1]

Most of the examples found in this country are of native
stones—the old red sandstone and conglomerate and millstone-
grit being commonly used for the purpose. But the favourite
material was the volcanic rock quarried at Andernach on the

[1] *Archaeologia*, lvi, p. 240.

Rhine, which has been extensively worked into mill-stones from Roman times downwards, and querns made from it were imported into this country in large numbers.

Stone mortars of two forms, the tall and the shallow, were used in Roman Britain. The former resembled in the depth of their cavities the old-fashioned brass mortars of the apothecary and the kitchen, and externally they had, as a rule, the tapering form of a modern flower-pot. Their shape and thickness indicate that they were used for pounding rather than for mixing substances. These mortars are rather rare. One a foot high has been found at Camelon, and fragments of three others at Bar Hill.[1] Another of different type, with a semicircular lug on one side of its rim, was dug up at Wroxeter.

The cavity of the shallow form usually approximated to that of a saucer, but with sides curving upwards ; but not seldom the sides were abruptly vertical and the bottom concave or even flat. Almost invariably the rims had two or more lateral rectangular projections or lugs, obviously to support the vessel when set in a cavity in a table or bench. These mortars were of all sizes from about 6 to 18 ins. in diameter, and were of various kinds of stone, the smaller being sometimes of marble. They were apparently used for triturating powders, grinding and mixing colours, mashing fruits and foods, and other kindred purposes. As, in the case of the earthenware mortars, pestles have not been found, we may infer that they were of wood.

Stone was also used for a variety of other utensils and implements, as large weights, spindle-whorls, quoits, whetstones, troughs, mullers, heavy mauls, pounders, net-sinkers, and loom-weights. At Wroxeter, London, Rushmore, and Bar Hill have been found small rectangular palettes of marble, slate, and other fine stone, which were probably used for mixing colours or unguents.[2]

[1] *Proc. Soc. Ant. Scot.* xxxv, p. 414 ; *Roman Forts on Bar Hill*, p. 89.
[2] *Uriconium*, p. 177 ; Pitt-Rivers, *Excavations*, i, p. 67 ; *Roman Forts on Bar Hill*, p. 90.

CHAPTER XI

IRON IMPLEMENTS AND APPLIANCES

HOARDS—ARTISANS' AND HUSBANDMEN'S TOOLS—DOMESTIC
APPLIANCES—CUTLERY, &c.

THE products of the Romano-British ironsmith were severely
utilitarian and rarely exhibit ornamentation. In this he differed
from his medieval and modern successors, as also from his contemporary bronze-smith. It would seem that the capability of
iron for ornamental work was practically unknown or disregarded,
nevertheless it was used for an immense number of purposes.
The iron used was wrought, not cast; the only known example of
the latter is a statuette found in a slag-heap of the era at
Beauport near Hastings.[1]

Three noteworthy hoards of iron—one found at Great Chesterford [2] in 1855, and two at Silchester in 1890 and 1900 [3]—will give
the reader an insight into the ironmongery of the era.[4] The first
two were in rubbish-pits and the last in a well, and each apparently consisted of a smith's tools and stock-in-trade. The
latter comprised tools and other articles, finished and unfinished,
such as were used by carpenters, farriers, shoemakers, husbandmen and others, domestic appliances, and all sorts of oddments
that are best described as ' scrap '—unconsidered pieces of iron
collected by the possessors or received in exchange for goods
supplied and services rendered. In the aggregate the total
number of items in these hoards was nearly three hundred, and
included the following :—22 hammers of various shapes and

---

[1] *Proc. Soc. Ant.* 2, xiv, p. 359.   [2] *Arch. Jour.* xiii, p. 1.
[3] *Archaeologia*, lii, p. 742 ; liv, p. 139 ; lvii, p. 246.
[4] Liger, *La Ferronerie* is a useful book of reference.

sizes, 10 axes, 3 adzes, 3 tongs of different types, 9 socketed chisels, 5 socketed gouges, 3 files or rasps, 1 plane, 1 centre-bit, 1 saw, 1 farrier's tool of a type known as the ' boutoir ' in France, 2 dividers or compasses, 4 paring-knives, 2 heavy anvils and an anvil bed, 3 shoemakers' anvils, 2 nail-makers' tools, 2 sates, 1 drift, 1 wringer or hand-lever, 1 shears, 1 turf-cutter, 10 plough coulters, 12 scythes, 17 mowers' anvils, 2 forks (?), 8 large bars of uncertain use, 1 axle-tree (?), 10 felloe-bands, 2 or 3 axle-boxes (?), 1 small wheel, several shoes for staves or poles, several knives and choppers, 1 large gridiron, 1 square girder, 5 or 6 padlocks and 3 keys for the same, 1 lamp, 1 millstone rynd, 8 shackles, 2 horse-shoes and a ' hipposandal,' several bucket-handles and hoops, 3 lengths of chain and a curious object with chains attached to it, 1 large ring, 7 hinges, and 4 holdfasts, the residue consisting of hooks, pieces of straps, bands, and other fragments.

The heavier hammers of the era, as Fig. 55, A, resemble our sledge-hammers, and B, a frequent lighter form, has its ' cross-paned ' end blunt as in our joiners' hammers. Both examples are from Silchester, and the former is probably a smith's hammer and the latter a carpenter's. Hammers of the latter form with the ' cross-paned ' end sharp were probably masons' walling-hammers. The shaft-holes are often small, and Sir John Evans conjectured that compound hafts with iron ends were used for these. He also observed instances in which the face of the hammer was ' steeled ' by a plate of steel welded to it.[1] The Silchester example, C, is an unusual combination of hammer and light pick, and is probably a mason's tool. D, also from Silchester, combines hammer and adze, and resembles a tool used by modern wheelwrights and coopers.

The two Silchester axes, F and G, represent the ordinary Roman forms. The former approximates to the present American felling axe, and the latter to the Kent axe. These axes vary considerably in size and weight, and doubtless served all the industrial purposes of their modern successors. Other shapes are rarely found. One at Lydney resembles some of the Saxon battle-axes in its crescentic form and long cutting-edge. One in the Guildhall, H, with a spike behind, is certainly a butcher's

[1] *Archaeologia*, liv, p. 145.

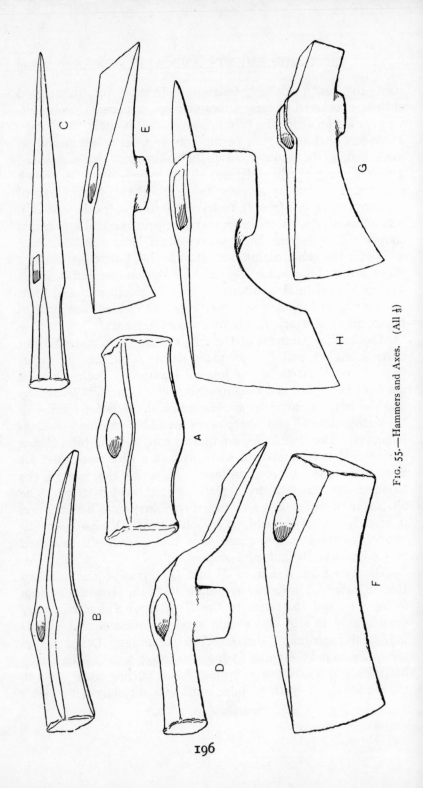

Fig. 55.—Hammers and Axes. (All ⅓)

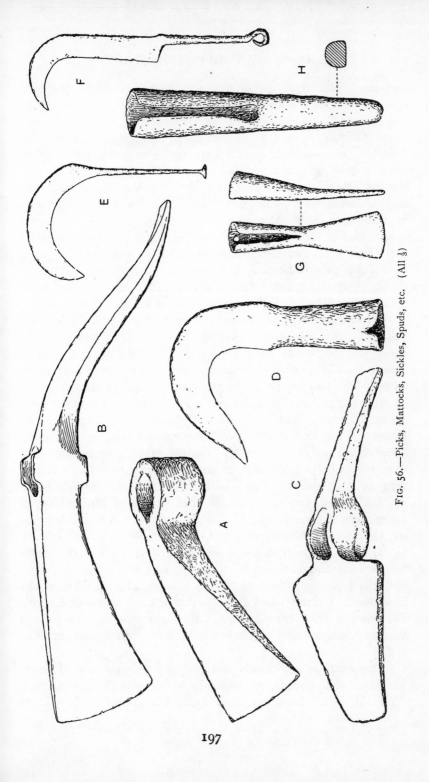

FIG. 56.—Picks, Mattocks, Sickles, Spuds, etc. (All ⅓)

197

pole-axe. The tool, E, from Lakenheath, Suffolk, may be described as an axe-adze, and is not uncommon. The adzes of the era are in general similar to the modern, and Fig. 56, A, from Ardoch, is a typical example. Occasionally they are wider, or are gouge-shaped, a form specially useful for shaping the staves of tubs and barrels. It is hardly possible to draw a line between adzes, hoes, and mattocks. Both axes and mattocks are combined with picks, but neither quite resemble the pick-axes and pick-mattocks of to-day. Examples of the former have been found at Newstead, B, and of the latter at Aldborough, C, and elsewhere. An implement smaller than the last, but with two sharp prongs behind, has been found at Lydney, Rough Castle, and Caerwent. The Roman pick, pure and simple, seems to have had a single arm like the medieval.

Of smiths' tongs of the simpler sort, Fig. 57, A, is a good example from Silchester. A large variety with the points of the grip turned up at right angles, and the one again turned so as to overlap the other, has been found at Silchester and New-stead. The pincers, B, in the Guildhall, would be indispensable to both carpenters and farriers. Files and rasps have been sparingly found, and D is a small Guildhall example of the latter. A larger flat rasp, with a cranked tang and coarsely serrated on one face, obtained from the first Silchester hoard, is seemingly a carpenter's tool, as also a similar rasp with a straight tang at Aldborough. Drills with tapering square or flat butts are fairly common, and indicate that braces or kindred appliances were in general use, but as no example has come down to us, they were probably of wood, like our old-fashioned braces. G, H, and I—a rimer, a gouge-bit, and apparently a large centre-bit—are certainly carpenters' tools, the first two in the Guildhall and the last from Chesterford. F is a metal drill, also in the Guildhall. J is described as a shoemaker's awl in Roach Smith's *Illustrations of Roman London.* It has a wooden handle and bronze ferrule; and a similar tool has been found at Bar Hill.

Five examples of chisels and gouges are shown, and of these, M, from Housesteads, is probably a mason's chisel, the rest, K, L, N, O, all from Silchester, being carpenters' tools. These

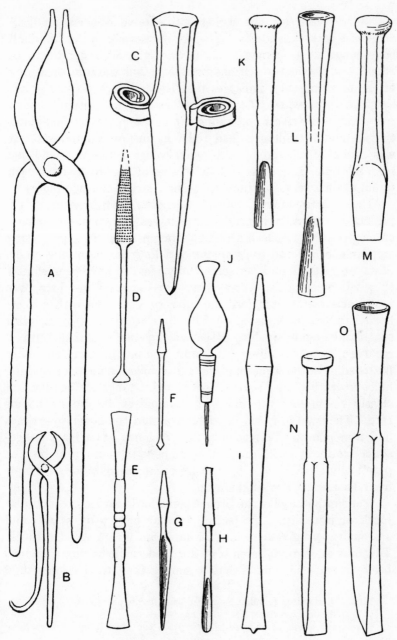

FIG. 57.—Pincers, Drills, Chisels, Gouges, etc.   (All ⅓)

199

are of two varieties, the socketed to receive wooden handles,[1] and those with expanded solid heads, but several in the Guildhall have tangs. The plane associated with the Silchester hoard of 1890 [2] was of wood which has perished ; but the iron sheathing of the face and sides indicates that it was a jack-plane 13¼ ins. long and 2¼ ins. wide. The blade still remains in position between two transverse rivets extending from side-plate to side-plate, that behind threading a lead roller against which it rests. It was probably secured by a wooden wedge between it and the rivet in front. The remains of two planes of similar size have been found at Caerwent, but they apparently lacked the side-plates.

The ' paring-knives ' of the Silchester hoards seem to represent the modern joiners' bench-knives. Each has a convex cutting-edge, 8 or 9 ins. long, and a straight back with a projecting stop at one end and the remains of a long handle at the other. Saws are rarely found perfect. Many seem to have been similar to small billet saws. A tapering hand-saw, 20 ins. long, was found at Great Chesterford, and a very small one with a deer-horn handle, at Newstead. The iron tool, Fig. 57, E, with spatula-like ends, is one of several in the Guildhall, and is regarded as a modelling tool, and another has one end only flattened. In the same museum are a hollow punch for making holes in leather, and several trowels with tangs for handles, all closely resembling the modern. Compasses are by no means rare. They were of iron or of bronze, and the latter sometimes had iron points. Occasionally the rivet has a slot for a wedge-shaped cotter by which the joint could be so tightened as to become practically rigid. Fig. 68, H, is an ornamented bronze example from Tingewick, Buckinghamshire.

The smith's anvil of the Great Chesterford hoard is a rectangular block of iron with a projecting tabular face, 7 by 5 ins., and a stout tapering tang below for insertion into a wooden block. The Silchester anvil resembles the modern in having a conical beak at one end, and it has a similar tang to the foregoing.[3]

---

[1] One of four chisels found at Newstead has a haft of deer-horn.

[2] Figured in *Archaeologia*, liv, 151.

[3] These two anvils are figured in *Arch. Jour.* xiii, plate i; and *Archaeologia*, liv, p. 142.

Although modern in appearance, it is of a form that goes back to the Bronze Age.[1] A small anvil similar to those used by goldsmiths was found at Rushmore. The Silchester shoe-makers' anvils resemble those still in use, and were supported on stems with shouldered tangs for wooden blocks. The mowers' anvils are from 7 to 11 ins. long, the upper third about 1 in. square in section, and tapering below to a point. The shoulder is per-forated for one or two strips of iron with their ends horizontally coiled to form supporting brackets. In the Caerwent example (Fig. 57, C) the brackets are of a single strip. Similar anvils are still used for beating the edges of scythes upon, in France, Spain, and Italy, and they are made at Birmingham for exporta-tion to South America. They are driven into the ground and flat stones or pieces of wood are placed under the brackets to give them a firm support.

The scythes of the Great Chesterford hoard were remarkable for their shape and length, which was little short of 7 ft. Like the modern scythes, they had a stiffening ridge at the back, but they differed in their curve. This, instead of being gentle throughout, made a rapid bend at about 17 ins. from the butt, causing this recurved portion to be turned somewhat in the direction of the point. This portion was narrow and ended in a turned-up tang for insertion in the sneed. There must, how-ever, have been some additional means for securing these large blades to their handles. Several scythes found at Newstead were shorter and wider, and their curves less accentuated towards the butt, thus approximating to the modern. A scythe found at Bokerly by General Pitt-Rivers, 2 ft. 5½ ins. long, differed again in its sickle-like shape and in having a socket for the sneed.

Curved knives of various shapes and sizes, and evidently used in agriculture, are of common occurrence. The larger of the form of Fig. 56, D, from Silchester, and E, F, from London, are certainly sickles, and the smaller may have been pruning-hooks. The small size of the Roman and the prehistoric sickles is due to the ancient custom of cutting the ears of corn from off the straw, handful by handful. A socketed tool less curved than the last and about 1 ft. long, found at Caerwent, may be de-

[1] Evans, *Ancient Bronze Implements*, p. 182.

scribed as a bill-hook, and was probably used for slashing off branches. The socketed tools from Rushmore, G and H, are usually described as spuds; they may, however, have been respectively the points of a wooden mattock and pick.

The ' hippo-sandal ' of the Silchester hoard of 1890 is a not uncommon object both in this country and in France. It has a remote resemblance to a slipper, with a portion of each side of its sole turned up to form a wing or clip, an ascending tongue with a loop at one end, and the other slightly rising and terminating in a loop or hook. In all these details, however, it varies considerably, and sometimes in lieu of the second, the wings are developed and coalesce with a loop at the junction. Others again may be regarded as half-' sandals,' being narrower, with one side straight and lacking the clip. Two of these—a right and a left—would make a complete ' sandal.' These articles have been regarded as lamp-stands, as skids for wheels, as shoes for the ends of the poles of the pole-car or sledge, but the prevailing opinion is that they were temporary shoes for horses with injured hoofs or when going over stony ground. Those in halves may have been for oxen.[1] Horse- and ox-shoes are found on Roman sites, and they differ from the modern chiefly in their smaller size, which is explainable by the well-known fact of the small size of the Romano-British horses and oxen. Horse-shoes with undulating or slightly scolloped sides are rather characteristic of the era.

The gridiron of the same hoard is about 17 by 18 ins. It consists of a rectangular frame, with bars arranged longitudinally and transversely (the central one expanding into a circle), resting on four legs and with a ring at each end. Gridirons are rarely found with Roman remains. There are two in the Lewes Museum, each about 1 ft. square, with four legs, parallel bars, and a straight handle. The curious object with chains in the Great Chesterford hoard was certainly a pot-hanger.[2] The swivel-piece was large and ornamented with a large ring on the summit to receive the supporting beam or bracket; and from it depended a chain, at

[1] *Brit. Arch. Assoc.* l, p. 251 ; *Archaeologia*, liv, p. 154. See also *Essex Arch. Soc.* i, p. 108.

[2] *Arch. Jour.* xiii, plate ii. See also *Archaeologia*, lvi, p. 242.

the foot of which was attached two shorter chains, each ending with a hook. There are the remains of a similar hanger in the Cirencester Museum. An iron folding tripod, 4 ft. 3 ins. high, found at Stanfordbury, Bedfordshire, had a swivelled pot-hanger suspended from its summit.[1] It was associated with a pair of fire-dogs and several bronze cooking utensils.

Other fire-dogs have been found associated with Roman remains at Mount Bures [2] near Colchester, Capel Garmon, Denbighshire,[3] and near Barton, Cambridgeshire.[4] They were all of one type, consisting of two uprights about 2½ ft. high, connected below with a horizontal bar, and resting on four feet, each pair of feet being formed of a curved piece attached to the bottom of the upright. Each upright terminated above in an ox's head with long horns, and facing outwards. The Capel Garmon dog was an elaborate example with the uprights ornamented with series of semicircular loops. These fire-dogs, having double fronts, were adapted for central hearths, in this respect unlike the medieval and later, which usually had single uprights and were placed on hearths in chimney recesses. With the Stanfordbury dogs, were two bars, 3 ft. 1½ ins. long, with terminal rings and hook-like projections on the inner sides of these. These were probably placed between the dogs, and held in position by being threaded on the horns, the hooks serving as supports for horizontal spits, and the intervening portions for hanging toasters and other cooking appliances. Bars resting upon the horizontal members of the dogs would usefully support pans and other cooking utensils.

Knives are almost invariably found on our Roman sites, but it is only where they have escaped the extreme effects of oxidization that their good quality and finish can be appreciated. Many have bone handles, but as most are without, it may be inferred that the majority were of wood. They were attached by three methods—by a narrow tang inserted into or passing through the handle ; by a plate-tang, the handle being in two halves, one on either side of the plate, and riveted through it ; and less frequently and only in the larger knives, by a socket, into which the handle was inserted. Occasionally the handle is of

[1] *Collect. Antiq.* ii, plate xi.   [2] *Ib.* ii, p. 25.
[3] *Arch. Camb.* 3, ii, p. 91.   [4] *Archaeologia*, xix, p. 57.

iron, blade and handle being in a single piece. Some are of bronze, usually in the form of an animal or terminating in an animal's head. Three prevailing shapes of blades can be distinguished, examples of which are shown in Fig. 58, A to I. Those with the curved blades of B, C, and I, and of the rarer shape A, all from London, are specially notable for their careful finish. The handles of these are mostly of bone, ornamented with incised lines or circles, and the plates to which they are riveted usually end in semicircular loops or rings. In rare instances these knives are tanged for tubular handles, as in E, from Rushmore. Knives of this type apparently answer to our table-knives, but they are smaller as a rule, and the handles rarely exceed 3 ins. in length.

Straight-bladed knives with tangs are more common. They vary considerably in shape and size, but G, from Rushmore, is representative of the majority. Occasionally they are leaf-shaped, or the back is straight from base to point. The handles were usually of wood, bone handles as in D, a large knife from Lydney, being uncommon ; and, to judge from the length of the tangs, they were generally long. We can hardly class with either group the little knives, A and H, both from London. The first is a rare example stamped with the maker's name—OLONDVS F., and its handle appears to have been of wood. The second has an iron handle, and was possibly a surgeon's implement.

Large knives with triangular blades of the shape of F have tangs or sockets, and there is a good example of the former with a bone handle from Arncliffe in the British Museum. They are probably butchers' knives, and this is corroborated by the fact that the knives carved on altars, with other sacrificial implements, are of this shape.

Clasp- or pocket-knives are mostly of the forms of J and K. The former is from Caerwent and has a turned cylindrical bronze handle. The latter is of more frequent occurrence, and its handle is of openwork bronze, representing a hound catching a hare. In the next example, L, from Lydney, the handle is of bone, ornamented incised circles, and furnished with a ring for suspension. The Roman clasp-knife lacked the back spring and the nail-groove of the modern.

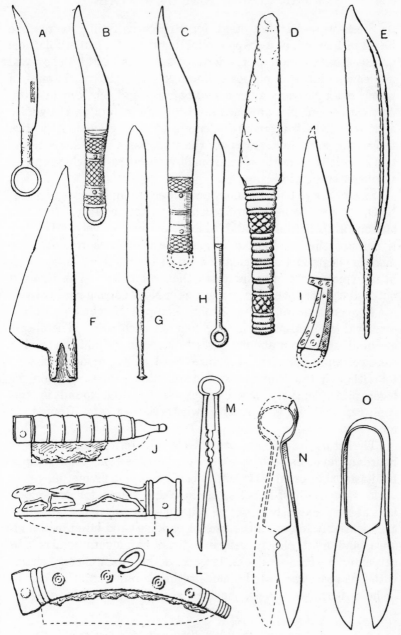

FIG. 58.—Knives and Shears.   (J, K, L, ⅔; the rest, ⅓)

Steels were certainly used, for Mr. Roach Smith figured one found in London, of a shape resembling that of a modern flat file, with a bronze handle in the form of a horse's head.[1] The usual implement for the purpose, however, was the whetstone, of which examples are almost invariably found on Roman sites. Any convenient piece of hard sandstone an inch or two in width, and from 4 to 8 or more in length, or a long silicious pebble, served the end ; but sometimes the stone was neatly shaped, and this especially so in the case of small whetstones, which often had a hole for suspension.

Shears are not uncommon, and three examples are given, M, N, O, the first being of bronze from Caerleon, and the other two of iron, from Rushmore and Aldborough respectively. The last is perhaps the more usual form. The other two resemble the modern shears in the circular sweep of their heads—an arrangement which materially increases their elasticity. The rounded notch at the base of each cutting edge of N for cutting cord or twigs is a frequent feature, but the bronze example, M, which possibly is medieval, is unusual in having four on each side. The shears are of all sizes from about 5 ins. to 1 ft. or more, and the smaller were certainly domestic appliances used as our modern scissors, for although the Romans were acquainted with scissors on the lever principle, very few examples have been found in this country, and it is doubtful whether they are Roman at all.

The list of the contents of the Great Chesterford and Silchester hoards by no means exhausts the varied uses of iron. Nails, straps, holdfasts, clamps, sheaths and sockets for door pivots, hinges of various types, hasps, bolts, latches, and joints for tree-pipes, indicate its extensive use in building-construction. The first are invariably found on the sites of buildings and often in abundance, and most closely resemble those of modern joiners and carpenters.[2] Iron padlocks, large keys, lock-escutcheons, chains with links as varied as the modern, bridle-bits and other details of horse-harness, swivels, shackles, goad-heads, swords, daggers,

---

[1] *Illustrations of Roman London*, p. 141.
[2] A series of these is illustrated in *Rom. Brit. Buildings and Earthworks*, chap. xi.

spear, arrow and bolt heads, and chain and plate-mail, have all been found, some plentifully, others rarely. Besides these, the excavations of large sites, as those of Silchester and Caerwent, have yielded many iron objects and fragments, the purposes of which are uncertain or quite unknown.

CHAPTER XII

MISCELLANEOUS IMPLEMENTS AND APPLIANCES

Spoons, *Ligulae*, and Forks—Lamps and Candlesticks—
Steelyards, Balances, and Measures—Bells—Objects
Used in Games — Spindles, Needles, and Netting-
tools — Strigils — Oculists' Stamps — Writing Appliances and Seal Boxes

SPOONS (*cochleare*) are frequently found on Roman sites.
The bowls are of three shapes—circular, as Fig. 59, C, D;
oval, as B; and one that may be described as fig-shaped
with a straight upper end, as A. The spoons of the first type
are mostly small and of bone, and they are generally regarded
as egg-spoons. Those of the second and third are larger and are
almost always of bronze and silver; neither, however, are so
frequently found as the first. The stems of all are slender and
pointed, and Martial refers to their use for extracting shell-fish from
their shells. Those of the metal spoons generally have a curious
crank at the base, whereas those of the bone spoons are usually
straight from point to base, C being exceptional in this respect.
This crank is a survival of a hinged joint by which the bowl
could be turned forwards upon the stem to render the spoon more
portable, and an example is figured in *Illustrations of Roman
London*.[1]

The slender spoon-like objects (*ligulae*), of which three are
shown, E, F, and G, are nearly always of bronze. They differ
from the spoons in their narrow bowls, and the expanded heads of
their stems to serve as counterpoises to their bowls. They were
probably used at the table for taking condiments out of narrow-
necked vessels, and for other like purposes.

[1] Plate xxxvii, 13.

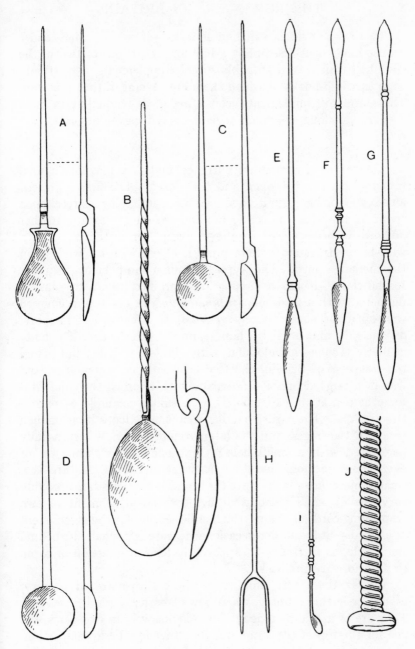

FIG. 59.—Spoons, *Ligulae*, etc.   (All ⅔)

There is no evidence that table-forks were used. The slender bronze implement resembling a hay-fork, H, is one of two in the Guildhall which were probably kitchen implements, as certainly were the flesh-hooks of which there are several in that museum. These are iron implements, consisting of a handled stem from 8 to 15 ins. long, to which several curved claw-like prongs are riveted.

Lamps are of common occurrence, and they may be divided into two classes, the open and the closed. The first represent an advance on the primitive saucer-lamps in having a lateral open spout for the wick to recline in : the second represent a further advance in being closed in above, except for a feed-hole and a wick-hole. In none is there provision for a vertical wick as in the modern lamps. The typical Roman lamp belongs to our second class. It has a circular oil-container from 2 to 3 ins. in diameter, with a feed-hole (*infundibulum*) in the top, a covered wick-spout or nozzle (*nasus, rostrum*) that varies considerably, on one side, and usually a handle, on the other side. The body at first was somewhat globular, with a large feed-hole ; but before the conquest of Britain, the feed-hole had become smaller, and was in a large depression (*discus*), which afforded the chief field for ornamentation. Fig. 60, C, is a simple example of one of these lamps. The earlier handles were simple loops large enough to admit the finger, and the later, rounded vertical lugs usually perforated with a small hole. Occasionally there are two, or even three or more, nozzles. Another occasional feature is a small projection on each side of the top, as in D. These are probably survivals of small perforated lugs for the attachment of two suspending cords or chains, the handle serving for the attachment of a third. Still another occasional feature is a small slit behind the nozzle, as in B and D, apparently for the insertion of a pin to push forward the wick.

By far the larger number of these lamps are of pottery, especially in this country, where few of bronze have been found. They are as a rule moulded. The moulds were in two parts, the one for the top of the lamp and the other for the lower portion. The clay was pressed into the half-moulds, and these being

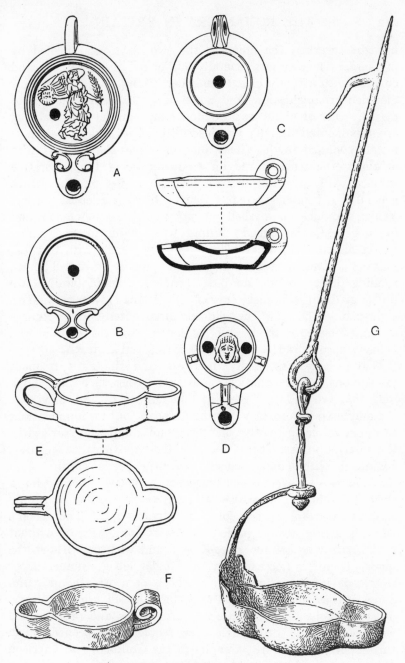

FIG. 60.—Lamps and Lamp-Stands.   (All ⅓)

brought together, the union of the two clays was effected by pressure. The clay was generally buff or red of fine texture, and covered with a ruddy or dark engobe. Many of the lamps bear moulded ornamentation, and not a few, the makers' names or marks. Out of about 105 London lamps in the Guildhall, 45 are ornamented and 23 are inscribed. The ornamentation is mostly confined to the *discus*, but sometimes the border is also or alone ornamented ; and an enumeration of the decorative subjects will give an idea of their diversity on the lamps generally — Jupiter seated; Diana (bust); Silenus (bust) ; Venus standing on a shell ; Victory (several) ; Actaeon and his dogs ; Cupid armed ; Cupid with a bunch of grapes ; Sol in his chariot ; Charon in a boat ; a female with torches ; busts of empresses ; a centaur with an amphora ; saddled horse ; running dog ; hound and boar ; eagle ; dolphin (two) ; two birds ; gladiatorial scenes ; crescent (for Diana ?) ; masks ; and an eight-petalled flower. The following ornamented borders occur— egg-and-tongue, meander, and ' mulberry ' patterns ; scrollwork ; helmets, spears, and shields ; oak-leaves ; and a wreath.

Lamps are occasionally inscribed, and the most frequent inscriptions are acclamations and good wishes, as VIVAS, ' Long life,' and AVE ET VALE, ' greeting and farewell ! ' As they were not only used for ordinary lighting purposes, but for illuminations at public rejoicings, votive offerings, tombs, and new year's gifts, the inscriptions sometimes indicate their destination. SAECVL, combined with circus scenes, evidently refers to the *Ludi Saeculares*. SACRVM VENERI suggests a votive offering for a shrine of Venus ; and ANNVM NOVVM FAVSTVM FILICEM, or simply FELICITAS, was appropriate for a new year's gift. The maker's name is nearly always placed on the bottom, with or without F for *fecit* or EX OF. for *ex officina* ; and with or without the name, there is occasionally a single letter, numeral, or simple device as a footprint, a wheel, or a wreath or palm. Some of these may indicate the patterns issued from a pottery, others may be of the nature of trade-marks, and others again workmen's marks. Although a few moulds have been found in this country—there are examples in the Guildhall and Caerleon Museums—the majority of our lamps were made abroad, and

Italy and other Mediterranean countries appear to have been the chief seat of the manufacture. In Italy and Africa, the later lamps were of the general form of those of the 3rd and 4th centuries, but those of the East were somewhat oval or kite-shaped, and in either case the handles were solid, the workmanship poor, and the ornamentation often included the ' chi-rho ' and other Christian symbols and subjects ; very few of these late lamps, however, have been found in this country.

Aberrant forms of lamps are rare. There is a remarkable example in the Guildhall collection, shaped above as a negro's head, the grotesquely projecting lower jaw of which serves as the nozzle, the lower surface having the form of a camel's head ; others in the form of a bird and of a helmet have been found at Colchester.[1] One found at Hexham was of normal character, but had a cylindrical stem below, which may have terminated in a foot or pedestal or have been intended for insertion into the sconce of a candlestick.[2] Bronze lamps resemble those of pottery, but differ in their finer manipulation. The handles especially are graceful, and are sometimes provided with ornamented plates or leaves to shield the hand from the smoke of the flame. Few have been found in this country, and there are several in the Guildhall collection.

Lamp-stands, or open lamps as they are often regarded, are shallow vessels with a rounded projection on one side and a handle on the other. E is an earthenware example in the Guild-hall, but is deeper than usual. They are often of lead, as F from Gellygaer ; and in the Guildhall there is one with three legs, which contained a small red-ware lamp when found. A fine bronze example, with an acanthus screen attached to the handle, was found with one of the Bartlow Hills interments. Iron examples are more frequent, and have been found with interments in the Bartlow Hills, at Rougham, Lockham, and elsewhere.[3] G from one of the first is typical. It consists of three parts, the stand, a swivel-piece, and a bar terminating with a spike and a lateral hook. The stand could be suspended by thrusting the spike into a crevice or hole in a wall or by catching the hook upon a shelf or over a nail. Iron and brass hanging-lamps with precisely

[1] *Proc. Soc. Ant.* 2, xv, p. 53.   [2] *Ib.* 2, xiv, p. 275.   [3] See Chap. VIII.

similar arrangements for suspension were in common use on the
Continent until half a century ago ; and the Scottish oil-cruisie
differs only in having two pans, an upper, the lamp proper, and
a lower to catch any dribble of oil from the former. The Roman
lamp-stand served the purpose of the latter, although it occasionally may have been used as a lamp, for in the Rougham example
were found the remains of a wick in its rounded projection.

Our Roman candlesticks are with few and doubtful exceptions
of iron and pottery. A common iron form consists of a tall and
tapering socket on three legs, as Fig. 61, A, a Caerwent example.
A variant of this form has a circular grease-plate at the base of
the socket, as in B, from Cirencester. Less frequent is the
‘ caltrop ’ candlestick, of which C is a Caerwent example, consisting of four sockets united at their bases and so arranged that,
however placed, three serve as legs. D and E, both from Silchester, are bracket candlesticks, having horizontal spikes to be
inserted into the wall. The former has in addition a downward
spike, which could be thrust into a hole in a table or shelf, or into
a wooden pedestal, the horizontal arm then serving as a handle—
a similar example has been found in London. J is a hanging
candle-holder from Silchester, the terminal hook of which is
missing. This and the bracket candlestick, E, are forms which
were in common use down to a century ago, and even more
recently in Scotland.

Earthenware candlesticks are rarely more than 4 ins. high, and
are usually of common red and buff wares. They vary considerably in shape and some resemble medieval forms. The Silchester
example, H, represents the prevailing form—a saucer-like vessel
on a tall foot, with a socket for the candle in the centre of the
cavity. The saucer was sometimes smaller and the foot more
spreading, or, as in F, an example at York, the former was larger
and deeper. Occasionally it was dispensed with, as in G, another
Silchester example. The object of the saucer was to catch any
molten fat from the candle. It is a common feature in the
medieval candlesticks, and it survived as a slightly concave or
flat disc in the earthenware, brass, and pewter candlesticks of
the 17th and 18th centuries.

I is a curious combination of iron open lamp and candle-socket

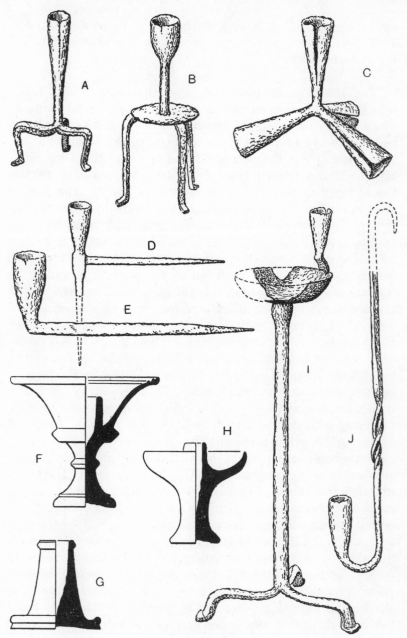

FIG. 61.—Candle-Holders of Iron and Pottery. (All ⅓)

215

resting upon a tall stem with a tripod base, found at Silchester. The oil-container is imperfect, and it is impossible to say whether it had a wick-spout.

The steelyard (*statera*) and the balance or scales (*libra, bilanx*) were in common use in Roman Britain. The examples which have survived are of bronze and of small sizes, the larger being probably of wood or iron. Fig. 62, A, is a small but typical example of the steelyard found at Kingsholm, Gloucestershire.[1] The graduated beam (*scapus*) is hexagonal in section, but as often as not it is quadrangular or round. The Roman steelyard differs from the modern in having two handles (*ansae*), consequently two fulcrums (*centra*) in different positions. The handles are in the form of hooks of flattened bronze, so that when hooked over the finger the instrument could be supported with comfort. Our example is shown in the position in which the fulcrum nearest the base is brought into operation, and in this position the instrument is adapted for weighing heavier articles than when reversed, with the other handle brought into use. From the base is suspended a hook—a double one in this case— or a pan for holding the articles to be weighed. The sliding weights are often of lead, but bronze examples in the form of busts or animals are not uncommon. The beams are graduated on both sides, the series of notches indicating progressive weights, beginning with that next the handle farthest from the base, and ending on the opposite side with the knob.

Scale-beams are perhaps more frequently found, and there are over twenty examples in the Guildhall Museum. They vary in length from about 4 to 14 ins., and are relatively slender. In its simplest form (as B from Lydney) the beam has a central eyelet to receive a finger-hook, and one at each end for the rings from which the pans were suspended. An improvement was the introduction of an index or pointer, as in the folding beam, C, from London ; and the handles of these beams were cleft as at present, for the passage of the index. An ornamented handle of the kind is figured by Mr. Roach Smith.[2] A Silchester beam has a small hole in the upper part of the index, which, when

---

[1] In Brit. Mus. [2] *Illustrations of Roman London*, plate xxxviii, 6.

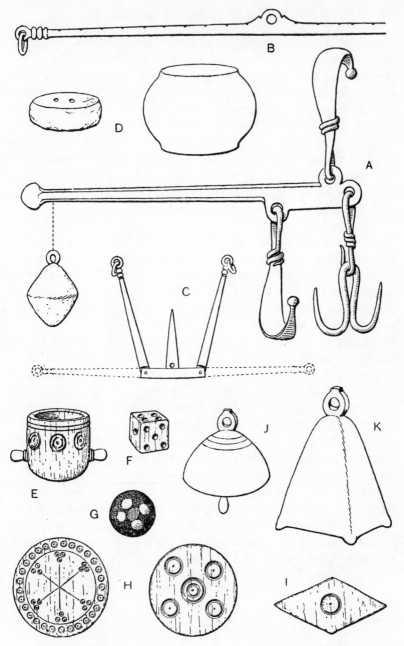

Fig. 62.—Weighing Apparatus, Bells, and Objects used in Games. (All ⅔)

217

coinciding with two corresponding holes in the handle, indicated that it was in a horizontal position.[1] The folding balances are of small size and were probably used for weighing money. The Lydney beam, like some others found elsewhere, is graduated on both arms ; and these are usually ounce graduations on the one, and half-ounce on the other, so that with a sliding-weight on each arm, and a pound-weight in one pan, it would be possible to weigh from an ounce by successive increments of half-ounces to two pounds. Scale-pans are rarely found. A small engraved one is figured by Mr. Roach Smith,[2] and there is a large iron one with four rings in the Cirencester Museum.

The smaller weights of the era are usually cheese-shaped, as the two shown in Fig. 62, D, the one a bronze pound from London, and the other a lead two-ounce from Melandra. The denominations are generally expressed by numerals, I standing for a pound or an ounce, and S (*semis*) for half a pound or ounce, or by punched dots and other symbols. Large weights of stone have been found, as two near Towcester.[3]

Nearly thirty lead weights have been found at Melandra Castle, most of which are of the cheese shape, the rest being flat discs, some perforated, squares, and a few of nondescript shapes. The marks, especially of the smaller, which are apparently coin weights, are intricate and in some instances obscure. The Roman subdivisions of the *uncia* were complicated by the introduction of the Greek *drachma*, but it is outside the province of this book to enter into the intricate subject of the Roman weights. For these the reader is referred to Smith's *Dictionary of Greek and Roman Antiquities*, Hill's *Handbook of Greek and Roman Coins*, and the important articles on the Melandra weights by Mr. Thomas May [4] and Prof. Conway.[5]

Examples of the Roman foot-rule (*regulus*) have been found at Caerleon,[6] Colchester, and Wilderspool.[7] They are of bronze and of identical construction, each having a single hinge, and a

[1] *Archaeologia*, liv, p. 156.   [2] *Illustrations*, plate xxxviii, 4.
[3] *Brit. Arch. Assoc.* vii, p. 107.
[4] Derbyshire Arch. and Nat. History Soc.'s *Journal*, xxv, p. 165.
[5] *Melandra Castle*, p. 99.   [6] *Arch. Jour.* viii, p. 160.
[7] *Warrington's Roman Remains*, p. 80.

riveted stay on the one arm, which, when the rule is opened, catches into a pin on the other, and so keeps it rigid.   Inches are marked by indentations, and the total length is approximately that of the estimated Roman *pes* of 11·649 English inches.

Bells are occasionally found on Roman sites.   They are of cast bronze and of small size, rarely being as large as our table-bells. The prevailing form is quadrangular with rounded corners, four little feet, and a perforated lug on the summit.   Fig. 62, K, is a typical example from London, but the feet are sometimes absent.   Hemispherical and conical bells, of which J is a London example of the former, are less frequent.   The clappers rarely remain and they appear to have been, as a rule, of iron.   The quadrangular form was derived from bells made of sheet metal bent into shape, with the edges riveted or soldered together, like the old-fashioned iron sheep and cow-bells which still linger in use, and many of the larger bells of the ancient Celtic Church of which St. Patrick's is a famous example.   Others of these ecclesiastical bells are in cast bronze, but, like the quadrangular Roman bells, retain the parent form, only with more rounded contours.   The small size and eyelets of the Roman bells render it unlikely that they were used for the table.   Their excellent finish is scarcely compatible with their being sheep- and cattle-bells, and the most feasible suggestion is that they were horse-bells and were attached to the harness in the same manner as at present.

Globular bells have also been found on Roman sites.   There are several plain ones in the Guildhall Museum pierced with circular holes and an oblong slit at the bottom ; and a small ornamented example was found at Headington, Oxfordshire, and others at Chesterford, Shefford, and Colchester.

Various objects used in games are of constant occurrence.   Dice (*tesserae, tessellae*), identical with the modern, have been found in sufficient number to prove that Roman Britain shared in the general passion for dice-playing.   Fig. 62, F, is a bone example, but occasionally they are of ivory and lead.   Dice-boxes seem to be rare in this country, but E is an undoubted example of bone in the Guildhall.   It is probable that small earthenware vases, like Fig. 50, Nos. 3 and 8, were used for the purpose.

Small discs of opaque glass or frit, flat below and convex above, made by pouring the molten material on a flat surface, are frequently found.   They are rarely less than $\frac{1}{3}$ in. or more than $\frac{3}{4}$ in. in diameter, white, deep blue, or black, usually plain, and when otherwise the upper surface has spots in white or red enamel, as in G.   The Romans had similar games to our draughts, and it is probable that these discs were used in these, the marked ones being superior pieces.   A stone draught-board, divided into 56 squares, has been found at Corbridge, and portions of others at Chesters and Maumbury Rings near Dorchester.

Wafer-like bone discs, ornamented on the face with concentric circles, are also of common occurrence.   The larger sizes are thicker and are often more elaborately ornamented, as two examples from Caerleon, H.   There is little doubt that these objects were used in games, the smaller as counters, and the larger as ' pieces ' like our draughtsmen.   We can hardly dissociate from these frit and bone discs, those made from potsherds and even glass, the former of which are of common occurrence, often with their edges neatly rounded by rubbing on stone, and mostly from $\frac{1}{2}$ to 1 in. in diameter.

Larger discs chipped out of stone or coarse pottery, ranging from about 2 to 5 ins. in diameter, were probably used in some game akin to quoits.   The stone ones are of common occurrence where thin flagstones abound, and considerable numbers made of the local pennant-stone have been found at Caerwent, Gellygaer, Llantwit Major, Merthyr Tydfil, and Ely near Cardiff. Small ornamented triangular, square, and lozenge-shaped (as I, from Lydney) plates of bone are occasionally found, and they may be ' pieces ' in some table-game.

There was a pastime, indulged in by Greek and Roman women and children, known by the Romans as *talus*.   It received this name because the game was ordinarily played with the knucklebones (*tali*) of sheep and goats.   Five were required, and they seem to be have been used precisely as in the modern game of ' five-stones,' now almost obsolete.   A Herculanean painting depicts two women playing the game, and one is shown in the act of catching three on the back of her hand, while two are falling to the ground. These knuckle-bones were imitated in ivory, bronze, agate, and other materials, and there are two of lead in the Guildhall Museum. The actual bones may also have been used in Britain, but it would not, of course, be easy to determine whether those found on our sites were thus used or were refuse of food.

That gladiatorial contests, combats with wild animals, chariot-racing, and other scenes of the amphitheatre were popular in Britain, are proved by the remains of amphitheatres and their frequent delineations on mosaics and pottery. Hunting, also, must have been extremely popular, for wild animals and hunting scenes were also favourite subjects. Inscriptions, too, bear witness to this, as also the bones and tusks of the wild boar and the antlers of the red-deer which are almost invariably found on Roman sites.

The art of spinning with the distaff and spindle is probably as old as the stone age, and it still survives, even as near to us as some of the outlying islands of Scotland. Of the ancient distaffs and spindles very few remain, but the perforated discs or whorls, the momentum of which prolonged the twirl given to the spindle by the finger and thumb, are common objects in our museums. These are mostly of stone, but also of other materials, as shale, steatite, Kimmeridge coal, lead, bone, and pottery ; flat or more or less convex or conical on one or both sides ; from 1 to 1½ ins. in diameter ; shaped by hand or turned in the lathe ; and plain or slightly ornamented. Fig. 63, A, is an example of a turned spindle-whorl. They are frequently found on Roman sites, but as a rule these cannot be distinguished from those of earlier or later times, unless they are made of pieces of recognizable pottery of the era. There are many bone and wooden spindles in the Guildhall that have been found in London, and one of these with its whorl, B, is shown. This whorl is the sawn-off upper portion of the head of a long bone, probably of an ox.

Bone and bronze needles and bodkins are seen in most collections of our Roman antiquities. They are, as a rule, carefully made, from 3 to 6 ins. long, and the eyes are nearly always in the form of narrow slots. Most of the examples in Fig. 68 are

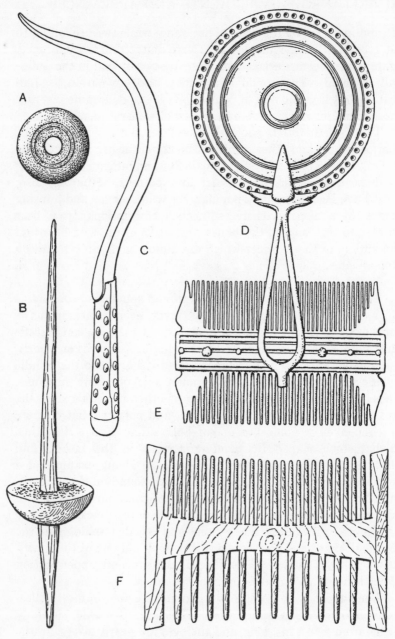

Fig. 63.—Spindle and Whorls, Strigil, Hand-Mirror, and Combs. (C, ⅓; the rest, ⅔)

from Silchester, the first group, F, being of bronze, and the second, G, of bone. Bronze netting-needles are rare, but several may be seen in the Guildhall. Thimbles are also rare, and they differ from the modern in being shorter and more hemispherical. Fig. 68, I, is a bronze one from Aldborough, and is perhaps unusual in being faceted.

The strigil or bath-scraper (see p. 95), the use of which was an occasional subject in Greek and Roman art, approached a sickle in general form, but with the point gently curved back, and in the Roman examples the blade may be described as an attenuated scoop. Few have been found in this country, and these are of bronze or iron. Of the former material is Fig. 63, C, from Reculver. Its handle is tubular, of sheet bronze, with oval bosses so as to ensure a firm grip in the hand. A pair of similar strigils were among the grave-goods of one of the Bartlow Hills (p. 143). In a more frequent form, the handle has two narrow openings or slots, one on each side, to serve the same purpose as the bosses, and there are several examples of these in the Guildhall.

Oculists' stamps have been found at St. Albans, Wroxeter, Cirencester, Kenchester, Gloucester, Bath, and several other places.[1] They are little oblong or tabular blocks of schist, slate, or other fine stone, engraved with names of medicaments and their makers, and often with those of the complaints for which they were specifics, the inscriptions of course being reversed. Ancient medical writers refer to a large number of *collyria*, some of which were the recipes of famous physicians and were known by their names, as the Collyria of Dionysius. Others were known by their chief ingredient or their colour. The Wroxeter example, which, contrary to the rule, is circular instead of rectangular, is inscribed on the face, TIB CL M DIALIBA AD OMNE VITIO EX O, " The dialibanum of Tiberius Claudius,· *Medicus* (?), for all complaints (of the eyes) to be used with egg." The Kenchester tablet has the name of the maker, Titus Vindax Ariovistus, on each of its four edges, followed by the name of a preparation—ANICET (*Anicetum*,

[1] Wright, *The Celt, Roman, and Saxon*, p. 298.

the ' Invincible ')   NARD (*Nardinum*, containing spikenard) ;
CHLORON (the ' green collyrium '), the fourth side being damaged.

Both Greeks and Romans were acquainted with pens, ink,
paper, and parchment, but these appear to have been chiefly
reserved for literary writing—ordinary correspondence, accounts,
memoranda, and even wills, being written on wax tablets
with the stile. Fig. 64, A, from a Pompeian mural painting,
illustrates these methods and materials. It depicts an inkstand,
pen, parchment roll, stile and writing tablets, one of the last
having leaves like a book and the other apparently being a single
leaf to hang on the wall.

The pen ordinarily used was made from the Egyptian reed,
whence its name, *calamus*, and it was cut precisely like the
modern quill pen. Bronze pens of the same size and shape of
the reed pens have been sparingly found on the Continent. The
ink, *atramentum*, was, like our liquid Indian inks, a preparation
of carbon, perhaps lamp-black. The inkstands were cylindrical
or hexagonal, of bronze or terra-cotta, mostly with contracted
mouths, and with or without handles and hinged lids. As might
be expected, no example of a reed pen or of a written paper or
parchment has survived to us in Britain ; but inkstands bear
witness to the fact that this mode of writing was in vogue. There
are five of bronze in the Guildhall Museum, one of which, D, is
shown. It has a contracted mouth, and riveted to its side is a
tongue of thin bronze, probably the base of a handle. Three
others have full-width mouths, and may have had loose lids with
contracted openings, which are lost. The remaining inkstand is
larger and has three feet of rather elaborate design. In the same
museum are several small bronze amphora-like vessels, which,
although intended for suspension, two are provided with small
bronze tripod stands. Similar vessels, in one instance a double
one, have been found elsewhere in this country. Their use is
unknown, and it is not certain whether they are Roman at all,
but possibly they were portable ink-bottles.

Writing-tablets (*tabulae, pugillares*) were ordinarily of beech,
fir, and box-wood, and rarely exceeded $5\frac{1}{2}$ ins. in length and $4\frac{1}{2}$ ins.
in width. They had a raised border, and over the sunk panel

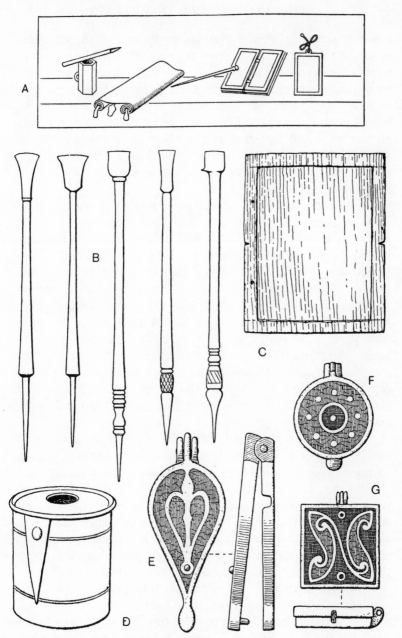

FIG. 64.—Writing Appliances and Seal-boxes. (B, D, ⅔; C, ⅓; E, F, G, ¼)

a film of soft wax, almost invariably coloured black, was spread. A set of tablets contained two or more of these leaves, hinged together with wire or thread, book-wise, the borders preventing the waxed surfaces coming into contact. The outer surfaces of the outside leaves were of plain wood. The *stilus* was usually of bronze or iron, from 3½ to 5 ins. long, pointed at one end for writing on the wax, and flattened at the other for smoothing the wax when again required for writing, or when it was necessary to make a correction, hence *vertere stilum*, to turn the pen, meant to make an erasure.

As stated above, the tablets were used for a variety of purposes. They were used in schools as slates are at present. Letters were written on them, and before they were dispatched by the letter-carrier or *tabellarius*, they were secured by pack-thread and sealed. They were used for accounts, private and public. Wills were written on them, and it was legally necessary that the outer borders should be pierced so that the leaves could be bound together with a triple thread upon which the testator first placed his seal, and then the witnesses their names and seals. After the decease of the testator, the thread was cut in the presence of the witnesses and a copy of the will made. The original was then sealed with the public seal and kept in the public *tabularium*, of which there was one in the chief town of every province, each in charge of a *tabularius*.

Owing to the perishable nature of wood, comparatively few writing-tablets remain. There are several London examples in the British and Guildhall Museums, and C is a perfect leaf in the latter. It is an outside leaf or cover, and its inner side is presented to show the recessed panel for the wax. In the border on the left are the two holes for the wire or string which bound the leaves together, and on either side is a central notch which apparently was not intentional, but was caused by the pressure of the string that tied the leaves together on the soft wood.

The *stili* vary little in form. In this country, the simplest and plainest are of iron, the more sumptuous of bronze. The examples shown in B are typical of the majority. The first two are of iron, from Rushmore and Caerwent, and the remaining three are of bronze, from London. These instruments have been found on most Roman sites, not merely of cities and the houses of the wealthy, but of out-of-the-way villages and settlements—Pitt-Rivers found them on the sites of these in Wiltshire and Dorset. This wide diffusion indicates that the art of writing was general in Roman Britain ; also that writing-tablets must have been extremely numerous, for whereas one *stilus* would meet the needs of a person or even of a household, tablets would be required for many purposes.

Seal-boxes are shallow bronze boxes rarely more than $1\frac{3}{4}$ ins. long, with hinged lids, bottoms pierced with small holes, and two notches or slots, one in each side, but in rare instances these are absent. They were formerly regarded as lockets to hold perfumes or aromatics in a solid form, the holes allowing of the dispersal of the aroma. Two difficulties, however, beset this view. While the lid is invariably ornamented, the under side is plain and the holes are often arranged in a careless manner, the two indicating that this side of the box was not intended to be seen. The side notches or slots also would be useless in a perfume-locket, whereas they have a definite function in a seal-box.

In using the seal-box, the cord or tape which tied the article to be sealed, was so arranged that the knot lay in its cavity, with the cord on either side resting in the slots. Wax was then placed in the cavity and was impressed from a signet-ring or other matrix. The article, now tied and sealed, could not be opened without cutting the cord or breaking the seal. The wax used was evidently of such a nature as to become soft enough by the warmth of the hand to be pressed into the cavity, hence, not having the hard surface of our sealing-wax, the need of a lid to protect the impression from accidental abrasion.

The seal-box was probably a fixture on the article to be sealed, and it has been suggested that it was held in position by rivets or small nails passing through the holes in the bottom. It seems unreasonable that so small an object should require so many rivets or nails to fasten it, for the number of holes is never less than three, and is often four or even more ; besides, out of the many seal-boxes that have been found, a few should certainly have retained some remains of these fastenings, but this does not appear

to have been the case.   They are invariably found as loose objects.
This suggests the question, what the articles were that required
sealing ?   Trinket- and toilet-boxes seem to have always had
locks, so it would hardly be necessary for them to be sealed.
On the other hand, writing-tablets had to be secured against
prying eyes, and we have the evidence of classical writers that
when used for correspondence and wills they were sealed.   The
tablets, however, that remain to us lack any indications that
seal-boxes were ever attached to them, and as ordinarily they
were of plain wood the presence of these decorated objects upon
them would be rather incongruous.   One ventures to suggest
that the tablets were carried in sealed satchels of leather or
woven fabric, each having a seal-box sewn to it (hence the holes)
to hold the seal of its cord.

Seal-boxes afforded considerable scope for the exercise of
their makers' ingenuity.   In this country, pear- or bellows-
shaped, circular and square are the most frequent examples of
which, Fig. 64, E, F, and G respectively, from Caerwent,
London, and Humby in Lincolnshire, are given.   The vesica-
shaped are rare.   The ornamentation of the lids is usually in *champlevé* enamel.   The designs vary considerably, and, as is usual in
Romano-British enamels, they often exhibit Late-Celtic influence,
and this is especially noticeable in our square example.   In this
the lid overlaps the sides of the box ; but usually it does not.
Sometimes it has a small pin or stud, which fitted tightly into
a socket in the box and secured it from accidentally opening, as
in our first example.

CHAPTER XIII

LOCKS AND KEYS

THAT locks were in general use is proved by the keys found on most of our Roman sites. Of the actual locks, few remain, and these are of two kinds, small fixed locks with hasps for boxes and caskets, and padlocks of a peculiar type which have survived, but not without change, in some Eastern countries. Locks suitable for doors have not been identified, yet they must have been common enough, for many of the keys could not have been used for padlocks and are too large for the hasped locks just referred to. It is probable that these larger locks were wholly or partly of wood. For the exact mechanism, with the exception of that of the padlocks, we have to rely more upon a comparison of the keys with those of old forms of locks that have survived, than upon their actual remains.

The padlocks shown in Fig. 65 are all upon the same principle, and may be termed spring padlocks. A is a typical example of the larger sort found at Great Chesterford in 1854. It is of iron, and consists of two separable parts,—(1) a rectangular box, *a*, with a long rod attached to the upper surface and bent back as indicated, and (2) a bolt, *b*, one portion of which inserts into the case and is provided with catch-springs, the other having two arms ending with eyes. The rod served the purpose of the shackle on the modern padlock; and the bolt pushed home, sliding its eyes upon the rod in so doing, the catch-springs prevented its removal until compressed by a key. B is a transverse section of the case to show its construction. The sides are a

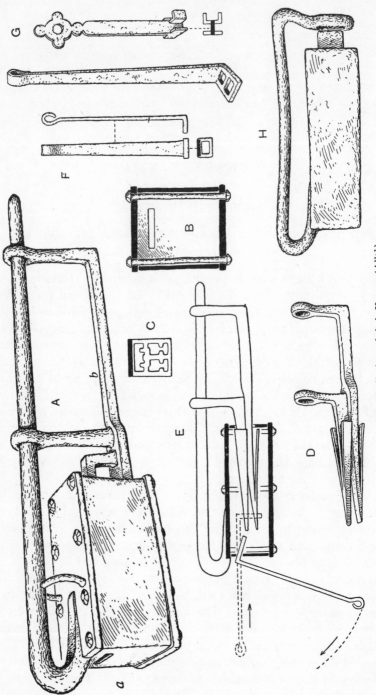

FIG. 65.—Padlocks and their Keys. (All ⅓)

230

continuous piece of iron, and the whole is secured by rivets passing through the top and bottom. D is a bolt of simpler construction from Llantwit Major. The portion to enter the case is doubled and each piece is pointed, the upper having two lateral springs arranged like the barbs of an arrow, and the lower a single one on the under side. In E, we have provided this bolt with a case and rod of the usual form, the former shown in section. Two examples of keys for these padlocks are given (F), and one to compress the Llantwit Major springs would require two rectangular openings in its foot as in the second. The foot being introduced into a narrow slit in the end of the case opposite the bolt-hole, was wholly inserted by a movement indicated in E. In pushing the key forward, its openings invested the springs and compressed them, when the bolt could be withdrawn by hand. The bolt of the Great Chesterford padlock is more complicated, having two parallel arms and eight springs, and thus required a key with intricate openings (C). Padlocks of the above type have been found at Silchester, Caerwent, Irchester, Cirencester, and elsewhere, but the keys are more numerous.

At Great Chesterford, two padlocks of a more compact form were also found, of which H is one. The rod ends with an eye, and is turned down so that the latter faces the bolt-hole, but with an interval to allow of the passage of the links of the chain to be secured. The bolt is straight and sufficiently long to project through the eye and so close the interval. Padlocks of this type were in use in medieval times and still survive in the East.[1] The key, G, found at Swanscombe, is almost certainly that of a padlock with a keyhole of the shape of its foot.

Turning now to the fixed locks : it is probable that locks akin to the well-known wooden locks of Scandinavia and Scotland were used in Roman Britain. The essentials of these locks are a bolt and two or more falling pegs, known as tumblers. These freely move in vertical grooves in the back of the case, and when the bolt is shot they fall into notches in it, and it cannot be drawn until they are raised by a key. The key has two lateral teeth, and upon being inserted into a horizontal groove in the back of

---

[1] Examples are shown on plates v to ix, Pitt-Rivers' *Primitive Locks and Keys*.

the case and of the tumblers, the teeth coincide with the latter, and by lifting the key these are raised, when the bolt can be drawn by hand. Fig. 66, A, presents the front, side, back, and longitudinal section of one of these locks, and B is its key. C is the key for a similar lock with three tumblers.

An old improvement upon these locks consists in the tumblers falling into holes in the bolt, in which case the key is inserted *below* the latter. The key being lifted, its teeth enter the holes and push up the tumblers, thus taking their place, and the bolt is drawn by a lateral movement or slide of the key. Locks of this type are in use in Egypt and elsewhere in the East. We thus have two types of primitive locks. In the one the bolt is hand-drawn, and, in the other, key-drawn. In either case, all the tumblers must be raised before the bolt is free, hence the key must have a corresponding number of teeth and arranged in the same manner. Keys of precisely the same form as the above have been sparingly found on our Roman sites, and imply that locks of the principle just described were in use in Roman Britain. D is a bronze example in the British Museum from Kingsholm, Gloucestershire, and a portion of a bone one has been found at Gellygaer.[1]

The defect of the above locks is that in order to allow of the key being inserted they have to be attached to the front of the door ; but before the Roman conquest of Britain, keys had been devised to operate locks placed on the back. Keys of the form of E and I, which are found on both Roman and Anglo-Saxon sites, were adapted for this purpose. Similar keys are still used in Norway for wooden spring locks.[2] The spring is nailed to the door and its free end, which is towards the staple, strikes into a recess in the bolt when shot. The keyhole is a horizontal slit passing through door, spring, and bolt, and the key, pushed far enough through, is given a quarter-turn, then pulled forwards so that its teeth enter two holes in the back of the bolt and press down the spring, and the bolt is then drawn by sliding the key along the slit. It is not unlikely that these

[1] Two similar bone keys are shown in the Limes Report on Zugmantel, plate xx.

[2] One is figured in *Primitive Locks and Keys*, plate iv.

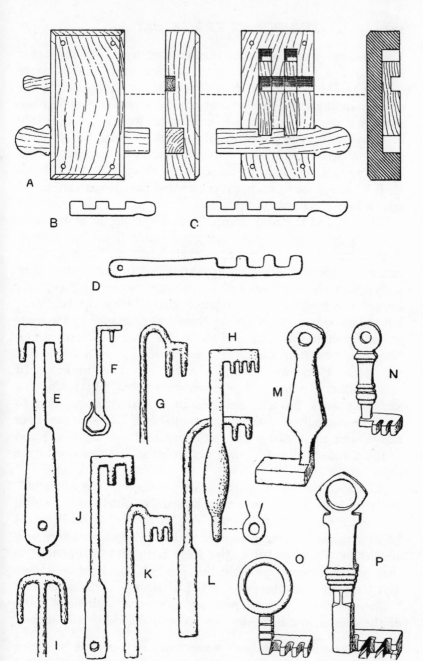

FIG. 66.—Old Scottish Tumbler Lock and Keys, and Roman Keys. (The latter ⅔)

Roman keys operated locks of this principle. On the other hand, it has been thought that they operated tumbler locks similar to the Scandinavian, only placed on the backs of the doors. In this case, the keyhole would be vertical,[1] and giving the key a quarter-turn as before, its teeth would be drawn into holes in the tumblers, and so allow of them being raised. The bolt now free would have to be drawn by some simple contrivance, as a cord passing through the door. The keys, F, G, H, J, K, L, are found on both Roman and post-Roman sites, and are evidently variants of the above.

The keys of the next group, M to P, belong to a large and distinctively Roman class, and they differ from the modern in their bitts being transverse to their handles. They operated tumbler locks of the second type referred to above, but with keyholes in the front instead of the side, hence their peculiar form. The keyhole was not immediately below the tumblers, but on one side, so as to render them less accessible to the lockpicker ; and it was L-shaped as in the bronze lock-plate and hasp of a box from Colchester, shown in Fig. 68, A. The bitt was inserted sideways through the wider end of the hole. In this position the teeth were downwards ; but by turning the key they were brought upwards in a horizontal position to the left immediately below the tumblers. The key was then raised, and in so doing the teeth displaced the tumblers ; and finally the bolt, now free, was drawn by sliding the key to the right.

The first key of the group has no teeth, but the whole projecting side of the bitt may be regarded as a single tooth, which, of course, would fit an oblong hole in the bolt. As it would be easy to raise a single tumbler with a piece of bent wire or a smaller key, it is probable that there were several tumblers, so that unless all were raised together the bolt could not be drawn. The teeth of the other keys fitted a corresponding number of holes and raised a corresponding number of tumblers, those of the fourth key being in two series and of different shapes.

---

[1] A lock-plate with an I-shaped hole from Rushmore is figured in Pitt-Rivers' *Excavations*, i, plate xxiv ; and another by Liger with a horizontal slit, perhaps for a small knob by which the bolt was drawn when released by the key.

Fig. 67, A, presents the upper surface of a metal bolt in the Guildhall Museum, and B, the under surface of a more complex bolt from Caerwent, which would require a key similar to the last to fit it. Most of the keys of the present type were for the locks of caskets and boxes, but the larger were apparently for doors, as certainly were the large iron keys with their teeth arranged in a zigzag, as in C.

While the tumblers in the door-locks may have been simply falling ones, it would be necessary for those in box and casket locks to be pressed down by springs. In restorations of these locks, this is shown as accomplished by a single spring.[1] This could hardly have been the case, for by raising one tumbler— no difficult matter—the spring would be released from the others, and, by turning the box upside down, these would fall back from the bolt, which could then be easily drawn. To be really effective, each tumbler should have its own spring.

Our next examples, Fig. 67, D to F, also belong to a large class of Roman keys which have a familiar look to modern eyes, but are more akin to medieval keys than ours. They are true revolving keys, and mark an advance in the locksmith's art, as a simple revolution one way or the other shot the bolt or drew it. It is not surprising that this advantage, combining simplicity of movement with expedition, should have secured the eventual victory of the revolving-key lock over its rivals. This lock had already reached a stage that persisted far into medieval times— until, in fact, the 15th century, when the craft of the locksmith attained an unsurpassed perfection in Germany and France. It was not a tumbler lock, and it was not until about a century and a half ago that the revolving key was made to operate tumblers, but of a different form from the ancient.

The Roman revolving keys, like the medieval and modern, are of two varieties, the 'pin' and the 'pipe,' the one having the stem solid and projecting beyond the bitt, and the other having it tubular. The principle of the lock is simple. The outer or fore-edge of the bitt presses, during part of its revolution, against a projection or stop on the bolt, and so propels it for a short but sufficient distance—the movement is that of the rack and pinion,

[1] There is such a restoration in the Guildhall Museum.

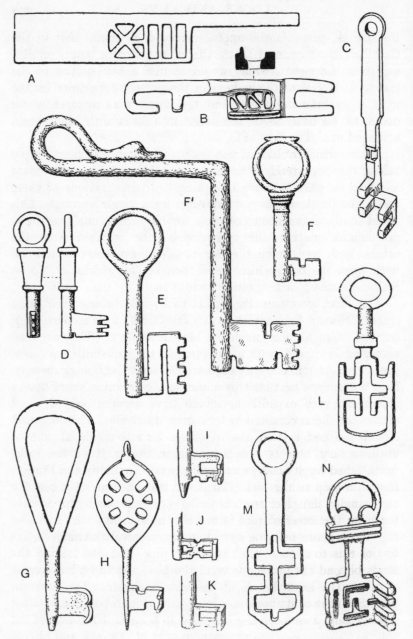

FIG. 67.—Tumbler Bolts, and Keys of several types.   (A, B, ½; the rest, ⅓)

the key being a pinion with one cog. If the mechanism of the
lock went no further than this, it is obvious that any key with
a bitt of the right length and sufficiently narrow to turn in the
case would operate the bolt. To render this difficult or impossible, obstructions or wards were introduced into the case, which
could not be passed by the bitt unless it had corresponding slits
or openings. The key, Fig. 67, F, from Silchester, has two of
these slits which would correspond with two little pegs or curved
plates, the one attached to the front of the case and the other
to the back. The keys D and E, from Caerwent, have, in addition
to these slits, a number of notches on the fore-edge of the bitt.
These imply a toothed ward-plate which would bar access to the
bolt unless the notches corresponded with the teeth. Roman
wards rarely went further in intricacy, in this respect contrasting
with those of the later medieval locks. The curious iron key,
F', from Bath, is almost certainly Roman.

The keys of the next group, G to K, are less frequently
found than the last. They chiefly differ in the fore-edge
of the bitt having a right-angled flange or one or more
teeth. It is probable that they answered to the modern latch-
keys, that is, that by a half-turn a key of this type pressed
back a bolt that was shot by a spring. This is confirmed by the
fact that many of these keys have 'island' ward-holes. It is
obvious that if a complete revolution was intended, the ward such
a hole was designed to pass, could have had no support. If, on
the contrary, only a half-turn was necessary, the ward could
be fastened by its end to a transverse plate which would serve
also as a stop to the bitt. The most feasible explanation of the
right-angled flange or teeth is that they caught against a stud or
studs on the lower surface of the bolt and so propelled it *beyond*
the plate, there being a corresponding notch or notches in the
top of this to allow of their passage. If a key failed to carry the
studs beyond the plate, the bolt, of course, would be only partly
drawn. The examples shown are from London, and it is noticeable that keys of the type usually have long loop bows, as in G.[1]

Our next two keys, Fig. 67, L and M, resemble those of the

[1] Pitt-Rivers, in *Primitive Locks and Keys*, considered that these keys raised
tumblers, but it is inconceivable how they could have done so.

French latches which were in vogue until a generation ago. The keyhole of the French latch is of this shape—⊥. The key is inserted in the bottom slit and is then raised, the short stem sliding up the vertical slit. In doing this, the bitt has to pass a horizontal plate-ward, as also a narrow vertical plate to the foot of which the ward is riveted. This vertical plate is just within the vertical slit, and it serves as a screen to prevent access to the lock above the ward. The key, having passed the ward, comes into contact with a descending arm from the latch, and so raises the latter. The bronze plate of a hasped lock in the Guildhall, Fig. 68, B, would require a key of this form. There is no doubt that the movement of the Roman keys of the type was identical with that of the French latch-keys, but it is doubtful whether they lifted latches. It is more likely that their locks had bolts, and that in lifting the key the bolt was freed from tumblers of some special form. The key, however, would not be competent to draw or shoot the bolt, and the horizontal hole above the keyhole in the lock-plate just referred to indicates how this may have been accomplished. If the bolt had a small knob protruding through it, it could then be moved with the one hand while the key was raised with the other. The keys are rather rare, and the two shown are Guildhall examples.

Our next key, Fig. 67, N, is a rarer form of lifting key, which differs from the foregoing in having a marginal row of long teeth. The teeth seem to have raised tumblers that passed through the bolt; but beyond proving that the lock had both wards and tumblers, it is difficult to understand its operation. Probably it moved the bolt by a sliding movement.[1]

There yet remains another key of a very unkey-like appearance, which, although frequently occurring on Roman sites here and in France, is also found with Late-Celtic remains in both countries, for which reason it has been called the Celtic key. It is a bar of iron bent somewhat into the form of a sickle, with a flat handle. Fig. 68, C, is a typical example from Rushmore, and is 12 ins. long, which rather exceeds the average. There have been several suggestions as to how it was used, one being that it

[1] Liger figures lock-plates with ſ-shaped holes, probably intended for keys of this type.

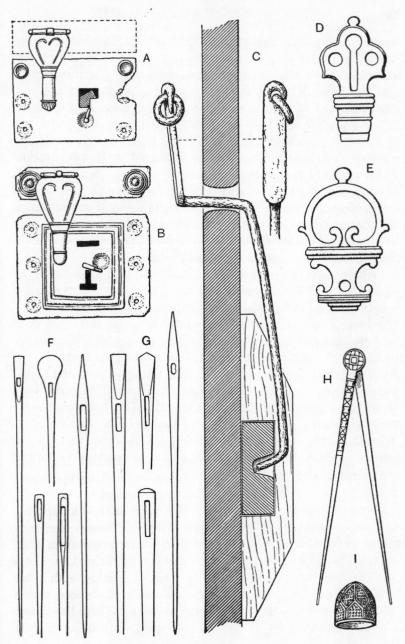

FIG. 68.—Lock-Plates, Keys, Needles, etc.   (A, B, C, ⅓; the rest, ⅔)

worked a bolt with a single tumbler, and another that the hand was thrust through a hole in the door and the key was used as a hook to pull the bolt. Neither, however, accounts for the curious shape of the key. We offer another suggestion—that it was pushed through a small hole in the door at a distance above or below the bolt equal to that between the point and the turn or ' neck ' at the foot of the handle, the point being inserted in a hole in the bolt, as indicated in the illustration, which presents the section of part of a door. In this position the key became a lever with the key hole as the fulcrum, and by pressing the handle to the left or right the bolt was moved in the contrary direction. It is a simple contrivance, and may seem to afford little security ; but it is evident that only a key of the right length from neck to tip would be effective.

Whether plain or ornamented, the locks and keys that have survived almost invariably exhibit the good workmanship common to all the productions of the metal-worker of the era. The hasped lock-plates are comparatively plain, but were often held by bronze nails with more or less ornamented disc-shaped heads. One found at Rushmore had a hinged keyhole-cover decorated with a youthful head in a Phrygian cap, the covers usually being internal and turned by a small external lever as will be observed in Fig. 68, A and B. The keys were sometimes elaborate, as the two typical bronze bows, Fig. 68, D, E, indicate. The keys of small trinket boxes were often in the form of ring-keys to be worn on the finger, of which two examples are shown in Fig. 76, P, Q.

CHAPTER XIV

DRESS AND THE TOILET

FOOTGEAR—PINS, BROOCHES AND OTHER DRESS-FASTENERS—
TWEEZERS, NAIL-CLEANERS, EAR-PICKS, MIRRORS, COMBS,
AND DRESSING-BOXES—BRACELETS AND ARMLETS, FINGER-
RINGS, EAR-RINGS, BEADS AND NECKLACES

EXAMPLES of the footgear of Roman Britain have been found in many places where the conditions were favourable for the preservation of the leather, notably in London and at Bar Hill and Newstead. Roman writers distinguished several varieties. The *solea* or sandal, bound to the foot by straps, was not ordinarily used out of doors. The *calceus*, the close-fitting boot which completely covered the foot, was the national foot-attire for public occasions, and etiquette ordered that it should be worn with the toga in the city. It was secured by straps, which were wound round the lower part of the leg and tied in front ; and their number, colour, and other details marked the rank of the wearer. The boots of the ordinary citizens were not so high, and were fastened over the instep by tongues or latchets extending from the sides. Between the sandal and the boot were various transitional forms which may be generically classed as shoes. The *gallica* had low sides with loops, through which a thong was laced to secure it to the foot, and the *crepida* appears to have been similar ; and both were sometimes classed as *soleae*. The *caliga* was the strongly made sandal-like shoe with open sides, worn by soldiers, and held by straps wound round the leg. It was also worn by the inferior officers, but the higher officers wore the *calceus*. The *soccus* was a light low shoe answering to our slipper. The *carbatina*, apparently made of a single piece of leather, was used by rustics. The *cothurnus* was a hunting-boot, and custom demanded that it should be worn by tragic actors, as the *soccus* by comic actors.   The differences between some of these have not been satisfactorily determined ; still less can the Roman names, and the classification they imply, be satisfactorily applied to the footgear of Roman Britain. If by *solea* is understood a simple sole held to the foot by straps, it was rarely used in this country, for the large 'find' at Bar Hill yielded only one.   On the other hand, a large number of shoes with low openwork sides or borders have been found, and these are usually described as sandals. They appear to correspond with the *gallica* and *crepida*—half-sandal, half-shoe. These pass, however, into the shoe which wholly enclosed the foot, some with openwork and others with solid uppers, and the shoe passes into the boot, of which only few examples have been found in this country.   The shoes are of several types, and one of these may be the *carbatina*.   Many of the Bar Hill shoes were certainly worn by soldiers, but none quite answers to the classical *caliga*.[1]

The shoe was evolved from the sandal.   The addition of a heel-piece and toe-cap gave the sandal a firmer hold to the foot ; and by extending the heel-piece forward on either side as a tongue-like projection with an eye to receive a thong or lace passing over the instep, the strap could be dispensed with. Fig. 69, A, a child's shoe in the Guildhall, illustrates the outcome.   The uppers are of two pieces of leather sewn together at the heel and the toe. They are solid for nearly an inch all round to serve as a sheath to protect the foot against stones and mud ; but above that level, portions are cut out so as to leave a framework of narrow bands, apparently a survival of the straps of the sandal. From the lace-holes, the bands radiate to various points between the top of the back and the ' waist ' of the sole, so that the pull of the lace is well distributed.   Over the toe they run transversely, just in the direction where strength is required. An elaborate man's shoe of the form was found at Bar Hill ; and in the Guildhall is an unusual variant in which the whole of the uppers is reduced to a mere skeleton of slender bands reaching down to the sole.

It is obvious that shoes like these, with their uppers reduced

---

[1] *Roman Forts on Bar Hill*, p. 101.

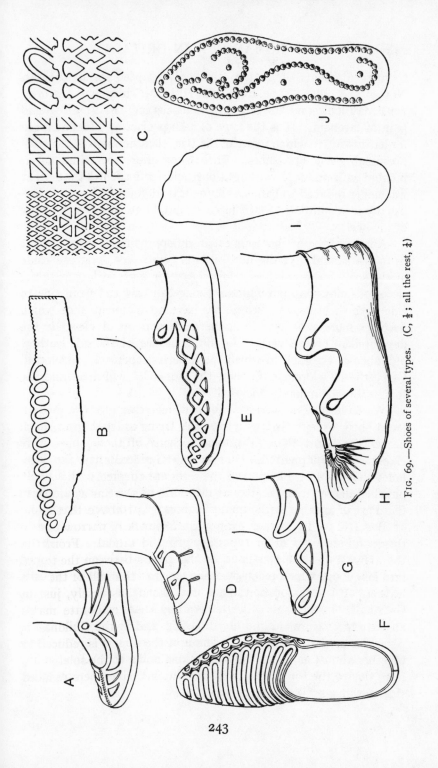

FIG. 69.—Shoes of several types. (C, ½; all the rest, ¼)

to mere filaments of leather, were only adapted for light wear. Not so the child's shoe from Bar Hill, D, which has a sturdy workaday look, and its grip to the foot is increased by a second pair of latchets. It is the type of a large class of shoes adapted for hard wear, to which many of the Bar Hill specimens belonged—presumably soldiers' shoes. These shoes were sometimes ornamented with punched work, but only sparingly so, and the leather was never reduced to bands. Those intended for heavy wear had usually a ' counter '—a stiff piece of leather to support the back of the heel.

Another type of shoe suggests a different line of development from the sandal. If the heel-piece is continued along each side of the sole to the point as a low sheath or kerb with a marginal series of holes, through which a thong can be laced from side to side over the toes and instep, we have an incipient shoe which becomes more shoe-like, from the modern point of view, by the development of the kerb. Fig. 69, B, is one of the side leathers of a shoe of the kind in which the kerb is moderately developed. Carry the development further, the lace-holes will meet and the foot will be completely enclosed.

We have now arrived at a form which resembles the modern laced shoe, except that as a rule the lacing started from much nearer the point than at present. Some of these shoes were elaborately ornamented. One in the Guildhall has the lace-holes elongated into loops and the sides are covered with a finely punched diaper with rosettes at intervals, as the first example in C. Part of another with equally elaborate patterning was found at Bar Hill. Two other examples of punched work found in these and shoes of other types are given in C. In a variant of the above type, the lace-holes of the one leather are developed into long loops which reach over the foot to those of the opposite leather. F is a restoration of a woman's shoe of the kind, in the Guildhall. In the same collection is a boy's boot, which represents an extreme variant in another direction, and remarkably anticipates the modern laced boot. The upper, which is solid, is sewn together almost as far as the bottom of the instep, and extending from this to the top of the boot are oval lace-holes, ten on either side, within a scalloped margin as in B.

Some shoes may be regarded as of mixed type. The boy's shoe from Bar Hill, G, has two heel latchets in the form of long loops, a pair of side loops, and a pair at the point. E, in the Guildhall, is a more elaborate example, and Mr. Roach Smith figures another still more advanced which combines the side-laced form of F, with heel-latchets.[1]

In another and primitive type of shoe, sole and uppers are made of a single piece of leather, but occasionally the sole is fortified by an additional leather. Several examples have been found at Bar Hill, one at Netherby, and another at Birdoswald on the Wall of Hadrian. In these shoes the only seam is up the back of the heel; each side is cut into two latchets with lace-holes; but the distinguishing feature is the manner in which the toe-cap was formed. This, as will be seen in the Birdoswald shoe, H, was accomplished by cutting the leather into a series of wedge-shaped strips, each with an eyelet at the end. These strips were then bent back, and the eyelets threaded together, presumably by the lace. Dr. Haverfield suggests that this kind of shoe was the *carbatina*, and mentions that it is still used by the Carpathian hillmen and by peasants in Italy, Roumania, and Bulgaria.[2]

The soles of the sandals, shoes and boots closely approximate to that of the foot. Not seldom the first or the first and second toes were indicated, and occasionally all the toes as in I, a sole in the Guildhall Museum. J, another Guildhall example, is a typical sole of the coarser shoes intended for rough wear, and it will be noticed that it still conforms to the natural shape. The sole is usually of three or four layers of leather with a thinner insole, and the heel is never raised by additional layers. In sandal-like shoes with low openwork sides, the upper is sometimes of a single piece of leather continuing across the sole; but most often, the upper is of two leathers with their lower margins tucked in between the insole and the sole. The whole fabric was fastened together by nails clenched on the insole, but this was occasionally done by stitches in the lighter shoes.

A notable feature of the soles of the era is the armature of hob-nails on the under surface, not merely of men's, but

[1] *Illustrations Rom. Lond.* p. 132.
[2] *Cumb. and West. Archaeo. Soc.* xv, p. 183.

of women's and children's footgear. Even the lightest and most elaborate shoes usually have it, and the exceptions are comparatively few. The nails are arranged in a variety of ways. Occasionally they are loosely scattered all over the sole, or are scattered in clusters of threes ; or they are confined to a marginal row all round the sole. Men's soles were usually thickly studded, the nails within the marginal row being often arranged in some pattern as indicated in J, or in close rows leaving little of the leather visible. The custom of thickly studding soles with nails was common in Italy, and Pliny in describing a peculiar fish likened its scales to the nails of a sandal. Pitt-Rivers found, with the hob-nails at the feet of two skeletons at Rotherley, several cleats from $1\frac{1}{2}$ to $1\frac{3}{4}$ ins. long, the use of which he compared with that of Blakey's boot protectors.[1]

We now consider some articles for fastening the attire. Of these, pins are the simplest, perhaps the most ancient, and are among the most numerous objects found on our Roman sites. They are mostly of bone and bronze, the exceptional materials being ivory, jet, silver, iron, and even glass. They are rarely less than $2\frac{1}{2}$ ins. or more than 6 ins. long, and while the general form is necessarily constant, they differ greatly in the form and ornamentation of their heads. The simplest are mere skewers of bone shaped by hand and with ill-formed heads ; but the majority have been turned in the lathe, and in the more elaborate the heads are enriched with carving, sometimes taking the form of statuettes, busts, animals, and birds, and occasionally those of the bronze pins are enamelled. The York Museum contains a fine collection of these articles, and among its rarities are bronze pins with glass heads, bone and ivory pins with jet, agate, and silver heads, and another with a gold head. The pins shown in the two groups, A and B, Fig. 70, respectively of bronze and bone, are selected from London, Silchester, Caerwent, Rushmore, Woodyates, and Spring-head (Kent) specimens. The hooked head of the last bronze pin but one is unusual, and the last bone pin, in the Guildhall, is remarkably large, and the bust is supposed to be that of the Empress Sabina.

[1] *Excavations*, ii, p. 190 ; also iii, p. 102.

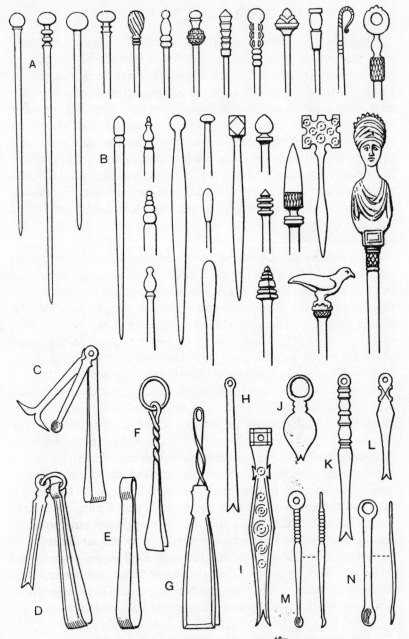

FIG. 70.—Pins, Tweezers, Nail-cleaners, and Ear-picks. (All ⅔)

Pins were used for the hair as well as the dress, but there does not appear to be any special feature, either in the general form or the ornamentation, by which they can be distinguished. Probably they were used to some extent indiscriminately. We may, however, draw the broad distinction that the smaller and more attenuated were dress-pins, and that the larger and stouter were hair-pins, and from this conclude that as a rule bronze pins fall under the one head, and bone and jet pins under the other. The materials of the latter being light would render them specially appropriate for the coiffure ; as also the entasis of many of them, which, by increasing their hold, anticipated the advantages of the modern ' curved ' and ' falcon ' hair-pins.

Pins are frequently found in the graves of the ladies of the era, and their positions often indicate whether they were used in the dress or the coiffure. There are two good examples of the latter in the York Museum. In the one, the lady's hair is still intact, and is plaited and made into a coil on the back of the head and held in position by two jet pins. In the other, there are three jet hair-pins, two small ones and a third, 7 ins. long, with a perforation near the point. Apparently this pin was threaded with a fine cord, which, being drawn over the hair and caught under the knob and tied, effectually secured it to the head. Similar large pins with eyes have been found elsewhere. In Smith's *Dictionary of Greek and Roman Antiquities* is shown, under ' Acus,' a female head in marble at Apt in the South of France, with the hair plaited and coiled at the back, the coil being kept in position by a single large pin. This simple style of coiffure was characteristic of the third and fourth centuries, and it contrasted with the extravagant head-dresses of the earlier Imperial period, which met with strong disapproval from the early Christian writers, as expressed in 1 Tim. ii. 9 and 1 Pet. iii. 3. In these elaborate productions many pins must have been used. The Apt treatment of the hair lingered to our own times in Italy and some parts of Germany.

Brooches are almost as frequently found as pins. The older antiquaries regard the brooch as a Roman introduction, but there is abundant evidence that the natives were familiar with it before the conquest, not only as an imported article, but as a product of the native metal-worker. Most of the early Continental forms have been found in Britain, and most of the forms associated with Roman remains had already been developed before the Romans appeared on the scene.

The brooches of Roman Britain may be conveniently, and on the whole satisfactorily, classified as bow-, plate-, and ring-brooches. The first were the most numerous, and, divested of their ornamental and other non-essential features, resembled the modern safety-pin. The second were an extreme variant of these, in which the bow or arch was replaced by a more or less flattened disc, rosette, or some other geometrical or animal

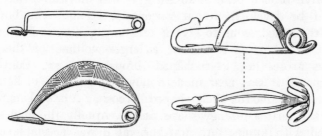

FIG. 71.—Modern Safety-Pin, Italian 'Leech-shaped' Brooch, and Late-Celtic Brooch. (⅔)

figure, in this respect foreshadowing the generality of modern brooches. The last stand markedly apart, were apparently derived from the buckle, and have no modern representatives except in Algeria and elsewhere in northern Africa. These various brooches were mostly of bronze ; sometimes of bronze-gilt, of silver, and even of gold. Enamelled enrichments were frequent. As a rule their workmanship was excellent, such as could only have been accomplished by craftsmen of skill and experience. Many certainly were imported ; but there is little doubt that the majority were made in Britain, and these indicate that in this particular branch of industry the home metal-worker rivalled, if indeed he did not surpass, his Continental brother. The ornamentation sometimes consists of Late-Celtic designs of considerable purity, and these are most frequently seen on

brooches found in the north and west, where Roman influence
was less felt than elsewhere. But even in a small collection of
the brooches of the era, an experienced eye will hardly fail to
detect survivals of these designs and a general Late-Celtic feeling

The Bow-brooch, or *fibula* as it is customarily called—an
arbitrary but convenient limitation of the word—was of ancient
lineage and varied form and construction ; and its history
has received much attention of recent years, in this country
especially from General Pitt-Rivers, Dr. Arthur J. Evans, Prof
Ridgeway, and Mr. Reginald Smith. It appears to have been
derived from a simple Italian form of the Bronze Age,
which anticipated the modern safety-pin in its earlier form
when it was made of a single piece of wire, Fig. 71. This
primitive brooch once established, it was inevitable that there
should be developments in various directions. The bow was
soon thickened so as to give it greater rigidity, and it became
more arched so as to enclose a larger volume of the dress
—thus arose the ' leech-shaped ' brooch, Fig. 71. Continuing
to expand, it was next made hollow for the sake of lightness
and thus became the ' boat-shaped ' brooch. A lateral angularity
gave the boat a lozengy shape, and eventually the angles were
capped with knobs. At first the catch was a simple crook
then it was developed in a forward direction into a horizonta
spiral for the point of the pin to lie upon, thus answering to
the guard-loop of our safety-pins, and this eventually became
a solid disc. Meanwhile a new form of catch arose, by beating
out the foot of the bow and curling up its lower margin to form
a hollow to receive the pin, and this was soon extended anteriorly
to cover its point. The spring-coil, which at first was of a single
turn, was given a double turn to increase its elasticity. All these
Italian developments had long been accomplished before the
conquest of Britain, but a few examples have been found in
this country, probably importations of an earlier period.

While forms that appear to be *later* developments of the
Italian brooch are found on our Roman sites, the ancestors of
the generality of the Romano-British *fibulae* are to be sough
in those of the Iron Age of the Swiss lake-dwellings and of centra
Europe generally. Their type, which is generally known to

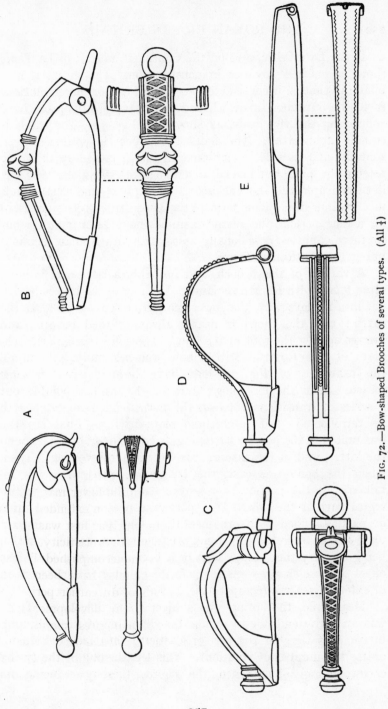

FIG. 72.—Bow-shaped Brooches of several types. (All ¼)

251

us as the Late-Celtic, and on the Continent as that of La Tene, shows a marked advance in construction. The spring is now bilateral, that is, it consists of two coils of two or more volutions each, the outermost of which end in a transverse loop or chord connecting the two coils, as shown in Fig. 71. The catch is equally noteworthy. The foot of the bow is produced horizontally, and its side is manipulated into a curled-up flange to receive the pin; but instead of ending with the point, the bar is turned upwards and backwards to the bow, and usually ends in a knob or disc. This form of the Late-Celtic brooch persisted for a long period, and many examples have been found in our southern counties, occasionally associated with Roman remains; but it is a pre-Roman form.

A variety of this brooch, and probably a later one, is more often found with Roman remains. The foot of the bow is beaten out into a plate with the lower margin curled up to form the catch; and the chord is nearly always turned inwards and presses against the root of the bow. The solid triangular catch-plate of the Romano-British bow-brooches, noticeable in all the examples of Fig. 72, may have been derived in some measure from the foregoing; but Dr. Evans has pointed out a series of transitions between the normal La Tene catch with its retroflected 'tail' and these plate-catches. First the tail was united to the bow by flattening its end and wrapping it round the latter, and in the case of iron brooches by welding. Then, when the body was cast, the triangular open space was retained, but the portion representing the 'tail' became an integral part of the bow. The space was next encroached upon or partially filled with ornamentation, and it then assumed a plate-like character with pierced ornamentation, its sole function being to carry the catch. Finally it became a solid plate. The effect of these changes was to make the catch an internal, instead of external, feature (compare Figs. 71 and 72).

Meanwhile, the spring was subject to modification. There was an early tendency to reduce the diameter of the coils, and, in compensation for the loss of elasticity thus incurred, to increase the number of volutions. This lengthening of the spring correspondingly lengthened the chord, thereby reducing its resistence to torsion, hence, upon closing the brooch, its ' play ' resulted in some displacement of the coils. One early remedy for this weakness was the insertion of a rivet through the coils. Another and more effectual remedy was the introduction of two wing-like plates or bars, one on each side of the head of the bow and immediately over each coil. In order to tighten up the coils to these, the chord was caught over a small spur at the back of the head, and this was eventually converted into a loop or eyelet by being lengthened and hammered back to the bow, the point being often secured by a rivet. Presently the plates became semi-cylindrical so as to sheathe the upper halves of the coils. Then their ends were boxed-in and drilled to receive a rivet which passed through the coils, the pin and spring being now a separate entity held in position by this rivet. At this stage the eyelet was drilled in a small cast lug, with an ascending tail reminiscent of the upturned portion of the spur.[1] We now leave the **T**-*fibula* to follow up a cognate line of development.

We return to the short La Tene spring with the chord turned inwards. The first development was an expansion of the root of the bow to cover the spring, and this generally took the form of an inverted trumpet-bell, as in Fig. 73, A, B, both from Caerwent. At first the pin was in one piece with the bow, but eventually it was separately made and held in position by a central lug under the ' bell ' with two perforations, a forward one for the chord and the other for the axle which held the coils. Later, this gave place to two lateral lugs to hold the axle, the spring being between them. We have now arrived at the transition of the spring and hinged pins. The chord no longer attached to the head, allowed of the pin being rotated, until, in the act of closing it, the chord came into contact with the margin of the head and brought the spring into operation, as in Fig. 73, A. Perhaps this development of the trumpet-headed *fibula* suggested a corresponding modification of the

---

[1] The pyramidal ornament with its terminal boss in Fig. 72, A, a *fibula* found in Deepdale Cave, Buxton, and the projection at the back of C with a disc of red enamel held by a small pin above it, are legacies of the ascending tail and its rivet, but are purely ornamental, as the pins are hinged.

T-*fibula*.   By dispensing with the eyelet at the back and placing the straight chord on the opposite side, the same action was attained as in Fig. 73, D.   In either case the step to the true hinged pin was a short one ; but its introduction wrought a modification of the coil-sheaths of the **T**-*fibula*, which were now made solid and perforated longitudinally for the rivet. These were unnecessarily long for the purpose, but continued to be a prominent feature as they contributed to keep the bow at right angles with the surface of the dress.   Still there was a trend of modifications in which they diminished in length, and this was correlated with a compensating change in the bow in which it ceased to be bar-like and assumed a light and strap-like form, as in Fig. 72, D, E.

It was a British custom, both before and during the Roman era, to wear brooches in pairs.   Several examples have been found with their components linked together with chains, and rings for their attachment, or the attachment of cords, are common enough.   The ring was either manipulated out of the rivet wire of the spring, as in Figs. 72, C, and 73, A ; or was in one piece with the bow, that is, cast with it, as in Figs. 72, B, and 73, B, C.   In the former, the neck of the loop was confined by a small ring, but more usually with an oblong clamp, as in Fig. 73, A.   In order to keep these wire loops in a horizontal position, there was a small spur projecting from the back of the root of the bow.   It is seen in Fig. 72, A, in which the loop is lost, and has been replaced by a simple rivet for the pin.

We have now carried the evolution of the bow brooch through two concurrent types—the ' **T** ' and the ' trumpet,' each beginning as a spring brooch and ending as a hinged one. To these in their later developments belong most of the Romano-British *fibulae*.   True it is, that there are many forms which do not at the first sight seem to conform with these types, but they generally prove to be of intermediate character, or their fundamental identity is obscured by abnormal developments of the bow, the head, or the foot.   In every large collection of these objects there are forms so fundamentally different as to suggest some other origin altogether, and they may prove to have been evolved on the Continent.

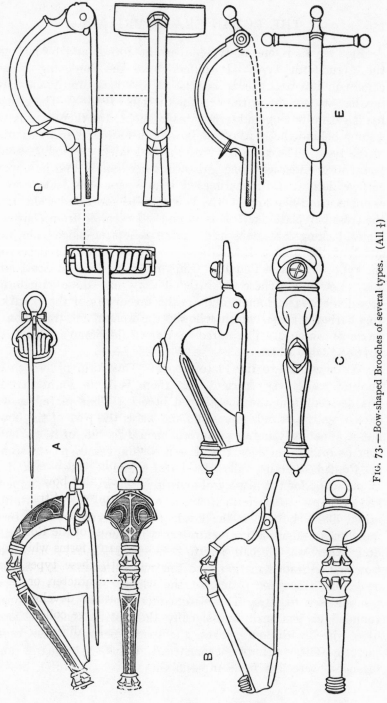

Fig. 73.—Bow-shaped Brooches of several types. (All ¼)

Fig. 73, E, is one of these aberrant forms, and belongs to the 'cruciform type.' It differs from the foregoing types chiefly in its catch being *external* to the bow, and somewhat box-like with a slit in the side for the pin to enter. The cross-bar is generally long and terminates in knobs, and there is usually a knob behind the head of the bow. There are several variants of the type. The catch-bar is especially subject to modification, being often wider and longer than in our example, and its upper surface decorated. Sometimes it is a conspicuous feature and assumes a fan-like form. The bow may be short and wide, and the cross-bar plate-like. D is an unusual example from Charter-house, lacking the knobs and having a 'spring-hinge' pin, instead of the almost invariable hinged pin. Gold brooches of the type have been found at Odiham, Hampshire, in Scotland, and elsewhere. There is little doubt that these cruciform brooches are late Roman, and are the precursors of the remarkable barbaric *fibulae* which followed the Roman era, transitional forms of which are illustrated in Hans Hildebrand's *Industrial Arts of Scandinavia*.

We now pass to the Plate-brooch. This form of brooch is unquestionably very ancient, but there is little doubt that it was derived from the bow-shaped brooch. The 'plate,' as we have already noticed, represents and plays the part of the bow, but it apparently began as an ornamental feature of it. Whatever its origin, however, the plate-brooch appeared on the scene of Roman Britain fully developed. The 'plate' afforded ample scope for the display of artistic ingenuity. In its simpler, and perhaps earlier, form it was a metal disc, flat or centrally raised like a button or the head of a large stud, with turned mouldings and usually a central boss or knob. In a favourite design there was a broad cavetto between the central ornamentation and a beaded margin, and this was sometimes relieved by spoke-like ridges or plates, or the whole central portion was treated as a rosette. The margin often had a series of small rounded projections. Occasionally the 'plate' had the form of a wheel with four spokes, the spaces between these being pierced. Other simple geometrical forms, as squares and lozenges, were less frequent, and these also were often bossed

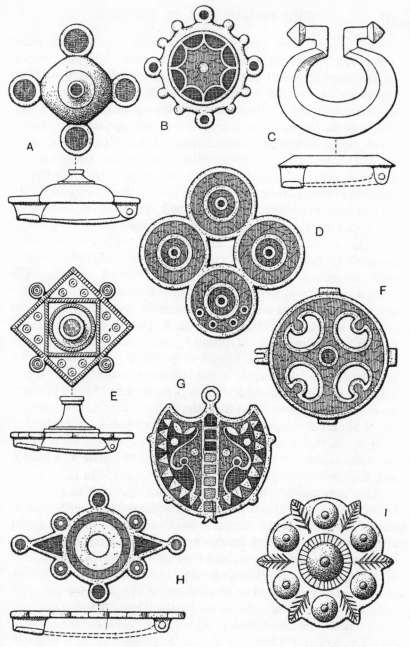

FIG. 74.—'Plate' Brooches, mostly enamelled. (All ¼)

or domed and their margins relieved with roundlets or other ornaments. Combinations gave rise to more elaborate forms, as four discs arranged quatrefoil fashion, and elongated patterns consisting of two discs or lozenges united side by side, or of one central disc or square with two triangular or peltate wings. Brooches in the form of animals were not uncommon, horses, hares, birds, and fishes often displaying a barbaric quaintness, being the favourite subjects. Many were enamelled, and on no other class of objects is the art of the Romano-British enameller better seen or studied. With few exceptions the enamel was *champlevé*, that is, it was deposited in cavities in the metal basis. Sometimes a considerable expanse of metal was visible, and served as the ground of the enamelled ornamentation ; but usually the visible metal was reduced to narrow walls or ridges which separated the different colours. The designs were mostly geometrical, as ' checks ' of two colours arranged chessboard-fashion, concentric zones of different colours, roundlets of one colour on a ground of another, and so forth. Delineations of animals seem never to have been attempted, and those of foliage only rarely. Occasionally the brooches were decorated with ' mosaic ' enamel. In these, metal walls were dispensed with, or were confined to the primary divisions of the design, and the chief feature was the fine patterning of minute rosettes, squares, crosses, spirals, dots, and ' checks,' built up in the same manner as millefiori glass (p. 180). Fine examples of these brooches have been found at Caerleon, Lydney, and Rushmore.

The examples of plate brooches in Fig. 74 will give the reader an idea of the diversity of their forms and decoration. In A, from Caerwent, the projecting roundels contain green enamel and the central knob one of darker colour. B, from London, has blue and green enamels. C, from Caerwent, is of unusual form, representing the Greek *omega*, and without enamel. D is a Lydney example bearing traces of enamel, and with an open centre. E, from Richborough, has an inset of white enamel in its raised centre. F is an openwork brooch from Caerleon, with remains of rich blue enamel. G, a peculiar peltate form, is enamelled in red, blue, green, and yellow, and its design has a marked Late-Celtic feeling. It was found at Wolvershill near Banwell, and similar brooches have been found at Castor, Irchester, and Leicester. H is another Caerwent example with red and green enamels and a pierced centre. I, from Wappenham, Northamptonshire, is of tinned bronze, with seven studs of bone held by bronze rivets, the intervening portions of the plate being engraved. A quatrefoil brooch of the same unusual decoration was found near Ipswich. Fig. 75, A, B, are two examples of enamelled zoomorphic brooches, the one found in Gloucestershire and the other at Rotherley.

Our next is a typical example, Fig. 75, F, of the **S**-shaped or dragonesque brooches, a small but highly interesting class which may be regarded as a connecting link between the plate-brooches and the ring-brooches next to be described. It was found at Faversham, Kent, and resembles the letter S with its serifs developed into grotesque and somewhat horsy heads with large ears and attenuated necks. The curved pin is loosely coiled, as in the ring-brooches, round one of the necks. In using the brooch, the pin was thrust through a sufficient volume of the dress, and its point was passed between the lower neck and the body, the pressure of the dress keeping it in that position. All· these brooches appear to have been enamelled, the usual colours being red, blue, green, and yellow, and in both shape and decoration they have a strong Late-Celtic feeling. There are about eighteen known examples found in this country, and a few have also been found on the Continent.

The Ring- or Penannular- Brooch is a common object in almost every collection of Romano-British antiquities. It is a simple yet ingenious contrivance. After inserting the pin in the dress, the ring was revolved until its gap was above the point ; then the pin was pressed down, and the pin having passed through the gap, the brooch was ' locked ' by giving it a quarter-turn, the pressure of the dress within the brooch maintaining the ring in this position. These brooches were rarely larger than 1½ ins. in diameter, and their decoration was almost exclusively confined to the terminals of their rings. The simplest terminals were effected by hammering back the ends of the wire of the ring, as in Fig. 75, C, the returns being slightly ornamented

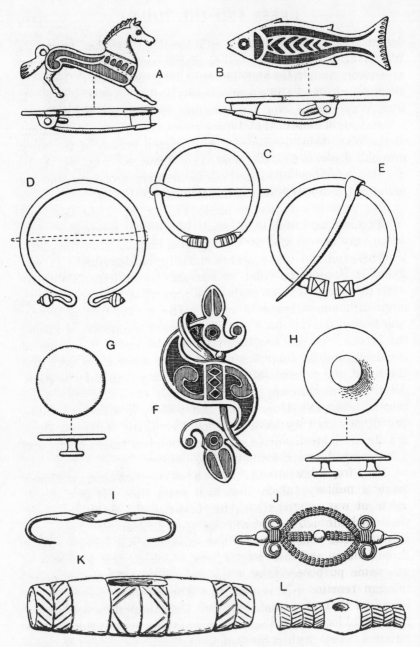

FIG. 75.—'Plate' and 'Ring' Brooches, Studs, and other Dress Fasteners. (All ¼)

by groovings. More pleasing terminals were knobs, which were usually grooved longitudinally. In a variant of this, as in D, a Guildhall example, the knobs are bent back, and the ends of the wire were sometimes flattened and made to imitate serpents' heads. In E, from West Coker, the terminals are rectangular plates.

It is remarkable that the ring-brooch should not have got beyond an elementary stage in Roman times, considering its wonderful developments a few centuries later, especially in Ireland and Scotland; but these developments, it must be admitted, seriously reduced the usefulness of this form of brooch.

Besides pins and brooches, other forms of dress-fasteners have been found on our Roman sites, but they are far from common. About half a dozen bronze studs have been turned up at Silchester, with flat (as Fig. 75, G), convex, and conical circular heads, H being unusual in having two shanks. There are several in the Guildhall, one with an enamelled head. In the same museum are about eighteen double hooks of bronze, which are described as dress-fasteners and might well be called hook-links. The simpler are of a single piece of bronze wire, flattened and twisted in the middle with the ends pointed and bent into hooks, as I. Others are more or less elaborate productions in wirework, as J, the framework of which is wrapped with thin coiled wire and ornamented with three beads. Small dumb-bell-shaped objects of bronze and bone have been found at Newstead and elsewhere, which appear to have been used as the 'frog' buttons or 'olivets' attached to the 'loops' of modern military tunics, that is, a cord from one side of the garment was secured round the middle, and the dumb-bell was buttoned through a cord-loop attached to the other side. The curious bone objects, shaped like a corkscrew handle, K and L, from London and the Victoria Cave at Settle, were probably for the same purpose. They are found with both Late-Celtic and Roman remains. A variant of these fasteners consisted of a disc like that of a stud, but with the shank developed into a horizontal loop by which it was attached to the dress by a braid or cord. Two with enamelled discs have been found at Slack, and it is probable that some of the small enamelled discs, which have been described as the fronts of brooches, were really the heads of studs or these dress-fasteners.

Of toilet requisites, tweezers, nail-cleaners and ear-picks are seen in most collections of British Roman antiquities. The first (*volsellae*) were used for removing superfluous hairs, and are ordinarily a narrow band of bronze bent into the form shown in Fig. 70, E, the looped head serving the double purpose of increasing the elasticity of the arms and of providing an eye for a ring or cord. More elaborate examples have solid handles, turned and finished off with a knob. F, from Rotherley, is of wire doubled upon itself and twisted to form a handle, the free ends being flattened to form the arms. Nail-cleaners are usually narrow plates of bronze notched at one end to form two sharp points and with an eye at the other for suspension, as in H, L, and J. I, from Cirencester, is unusually large and is ornamented with engraved lines and concentric circles. K, from Lydney, has a handle turned with many mouldings ; and others are of wire hammered flat below, and twisted above to form a handle with a loop at the end. Occasionally they have only a single point. Ear-picks resemble diminutive spoons with minute bowls, and the simpler sort are made of bone or of flat strips of bronze as in N. M, from Rushmore, has a bar-like handle, turned above and ending as usual with an eye.

These instruments are often in sets of two or all three, threaded on a ring, like the tweezers and nail-cleaner, D, found in London. The rings are as a rule quite plain, but sometimes they are ornamented, or one side is developed into an ornamental plate ; or a bronze band bent into an arch and united at the base by a bar takes the place of a ring. In another London set, C, the nail-cleaner of which is of unusual shape, the instruments are riveted together. Very rarely two functions may be combined in a single instrument, as the combined tweezers and ear-pick, G, also found in London.[1]

Mirrors (*specula*) are rarely found, but the Colchester cemeteries have yielded a considerable number. Although looking-glass—

[1] *Illustrations of Roman London*, plate xxxiii, 8, 11, 10.

glass backed with a metallic film—was known to the ancients, its use was exceptional, and no example of it has been found in this country. The Roman mirrors were ordinarily of white bronze or yellow bronze plated with tin or silver, and were highly polished. They were, as a rule, circular discs with handles, which, although of excellent workmanship, were rarely if ever ornamented to the same degree as the Etruscan and Late-Celtic mirrors, and compared with the latter the examples found in this country are much smaller.

There are twenty-three hand-mirrors in the Colchester Museum, of which more than half retain their handles. According to Mr. A. G. Wright, they range from 2½ to 5 ins. in diameter, and are mostly of white bronze, the rest being of pale yellow bronze plated with tin, and several apparently with silver. The reflecting surface is slightly convex in order that the image of the face or the head, being reduced, may be seen as a whole within the field. The front is in some cases bordered with an engraved band, a row of ring-and-dot ornaments, or a row of small perforations ; while the back is generally relieved with concentric groovings. Fig. 63, D, presents the back of one of these mirrors, which is further ornamented with a marginal row of conical depressions. Its looped handle is thoroughly typical, and is surmounted with a trilobed plate which is soldered to the back of the disc.

Another form of Roman mirror—the box or pocket mirror— is of rarer occurrence. A fine example was found at Coddenham, Suffolk, in 1823.[1] It was nearly 2½ ins. in diameter and ¼ in. in thickness, and the two halves—the lid and the box—were made of a bronze medallion of Nero, each half containing a small convex tinned reflector. In the Colchester Museum there are four rectangular mirrors ranging from 3¾ by 3¼ ins. to 6 by 5 ins., which are quite plain, and with little doubt were fitted in the lids of toilet-boxes.

The comb (*pecten*) was in common use among the Greeks and Romans. Those of the latter were mostly of bone and box-wood, and the employment of this wood for the purpose was so pre-

[1] *Archaeologia*, xxvii, p. 359.

valent that *buxus* was an alternative name for this toilet appliance. Wooden combs were used in Roman Britain, but, as might be expected, only a few specimens have survived, those usually found being of bone. The ordinary form was double, that is, it had two rows of teeth, one on either side of the body, the teeth of the one being coarse and of the other fine—a form that continued throughout the Middle Ages and still survives in our ' tooth-combs.' Fig. 63, F, is a wooden example in the Guildhall Museum. The bone combs were often made in several pieces held together between two strips or cleats by means of rivets; and if made of a single piece, the cleats were used as stiffeners. E is a typical example from Woodyates,[1] both in form and construction. It appears to have been originally held together by bronze rivets, but was afterwards repaired by iron ones. The cleats are the only portions which offer a field for ornamentation, and in this case it consists of parallel grooves. One found at Wroxeter has a row of concentric circles between two beads; but the ornamentation is never elaborate. Combs of similar forms and like construction are frequently found with Anglo-Saxon remains, and it is sometimes difficult to distinguish them from the Roman. Metal combs are rare. One of bronze exactly resembling a modern tooth-comb, only larger, and a similar iron one, were found at Chesterford.[2]

Small combs with a single row of teeth and flat triangular backs are occasionally found on Roman sites, and a plain example was turned up at the last place. Similar Continental examples, more or less ornamented and with cases to sheathe the teeth, were evidently pocket-combs. They are regarded as late Roman, and were apparently the prototypes of the larger Anglo-Saxon combs of the form. A small comb with an ornately shaped back and converging teeth found at Wroxeter [3] may have been worn in the hair, as part of the coiffure. A comb and a large hairpin were found adhering to the hair of a lady in a coffin at York.

The remains of small ornamented boxes have been frequently found in the graves of women, and their scattered contents, which

[1] Pitt-Rivers, *Excavations*, iii, p. 132.
[2] *Brit. Arch. Assoc.* iii, p. 208. [3] *Uriconium*, p. 278.

usually include brooches, bracelets, and other articles of the toilet, show that they were dressing- or trinket-boxes. One is sculptured on the tombstone of the Palmyrene woman at South Shields, Fig. 39. Fragments of many derived from the local cemeteries are to be seen in the Colchester Museum, and the woodwork of one of these has so far survived as to show that it was neatly dovetailed at the angles. The mountings of these caskets, mostly of bronze, consist of ornate corner-pieces and plates, held in position like their lock-plates (of which two are shown in Fig. 68) with ornamented nails, ring and other hinged handles, bosses, and various ornaments. The mountings of a casket found at Icklingham are replaced on a modern box in the British Museum ; and those of another, including its contents, found at Rushmore, are figured by General Pitt-Rivers.[1] The keyhole cover of the latter was in the form of a hinged boss ornamented with a bust in a Phrygian cap. Several of the Colchester caskets appear to have had mirrors fitted within their lids, as mentioned in a paragraph above.

Of articles of pure adornment, those which are comprised under the general term *armillae* are conspicuous in our Romano-British collections. The term is convenient, for it is often impossible to decide whether a given specimen is a bracelet, armlet, or anklet, as they are not distinguishable by peculiarities of form or pattern. Relative size helps us, but not much. If one is too large for a bracelet, it may be reasonably concluded that it encircled the arm ; but a child's armlet may be as small as the mother's bracelet. The women of the era certainly wore them as bracelets and less frequently as armlets, for they have been found in graves occupying these positions on the skeleton ; but whether they were used as anklets is not so clear. If, then, these articles are specified below as bracelets and armlets, the reader must keep in mind these limitations and uncertainties.

As a class, the Romano-British *armillae* are not conspicuous for variety of form, construction or ornamentation. They are resolvable into few types, and the decoration, when present, is of a simple sort, never including enamel, and this is remarkable

[1] *Excavations*, i, p. 61.

because they could easily have been designed to present an admirable field for its display. They are rarely in other material than bronze and jet, and if a precious metal is used in their construction, it is used sparingly. Those of metal are light and slender, and many would now be designated bangles. The massive gold *armillae* with Late-Celtic ornamentation, which are occasionally figured as Roman, are almost certainly the productions of contemporary Scottish or Irish metal-workers, or are pre-Roman.

The bracelets most frequently found are of two bronze wires twisted into a cable, one wire being manipulated into a small hook at one end, and into an eye at the other, the free wire being coiled to form a collar, or instead of this, the ends may be confined by tubular collars, as in Fig. 76, A, a Lydney example. The component wires were often attenuated towards their ends so as to produce a pleasing swell in the cable. Sometimes these bracelets were not made to open, as a small example in the Guildhall Museum composed of a bronze and an iron wire twisted and looped together at the ends to form a central ornament.

Our next example, B, from Rushmore, is of less frequent occurrence. It is made of a single bronze wire, expanded about the middle, and sliding on itself, each end being coiled round the wire at some distance from the opposite end. Its large size is suggestive that it was an armlet, for which it would be well adapted, its elasticity exerting a pressure on the arm which would keep it in place. The unusual bronze armlet (it is too large for a bracelet), C, was found with a skeleton at Deepdale Cave near Buxton. The hoop is square in section, and each attenuated portion is bent into a row of loops, the two rows being parallel and held in position by the surplus wire being wound round the contiguous parts of the hoop. Similar *armillae* have been found elsewhere, and a finger-ring of similar manipulation at Silchester. The slender bracelet, E, from Caerwent, is transversely ribbed and has three bead-like swellings and a hook-and-eye clasp. Bracelets of this type have been sparingly found, and are apparently derived from a prototype in which several beads were threaded on a wire, the intervals being wound with finer wire.

Our next example, F, from Richborough, stands for a large

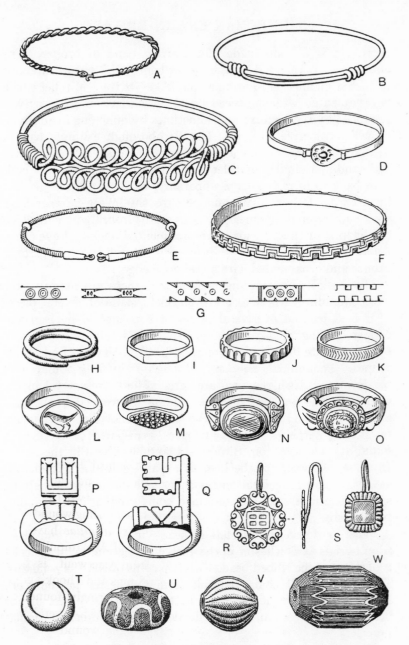

FIG. 76.—Bracelets and Armlets, Finger-rings, Ear-rings, and Beads.
(A to G, ⅔; the rest, ¼)

267

class. It is a hoop made of a narrow band of bronze. The exterior is ornamented by the angles being filed out at intervals in such a manner as to leave a simple key-pattern in relief which is ornamented with engraved lines. A variety of patterns was produced by these means and sometimes by punching in addition, of which we give five, G. The Richborough example has an overlapping joint so that it could be sprung open in passing over the hand. A similar bracelet found at Aldborough had its ends bent back to form two loops apparently to allow of its being tied by a cord. Others again and perhaps the larger number have their ends riveted together. D is a variant from Lydney in which the hoop is plain and ends in an ornamented hook-and-eye clasp. Another type of bangle was apparently cut out of a thin plate of bronze and ornamented with a scalloped edge.

Jet bangles are not uncommon, and there are many in the York Museum ; where also are bracelets made of several pieces of carved jet and of several pieces of bone united by lead and copper bindings ; also two glass bangles, a small green one with blue and white lines, and a larger, dark red, with white and purple stripes. Penannular *armillae*, although frequently found with pre-Roman British remains, are rare. There are several in the Guildhall Museum, one of silver ending in grooved knobs, and another of tinned bronze with the ends expanded into ornaments resembling serpents' heads. Bronze ' arm-purses ' [1] have been found at Thorngrapton, Birdoswald, and elsewhere in the north. In these, a portion of the hoop is expanded into a boat-shaped cavity, with a hinged lid on the inner side closing with a spring snap. The first example contained coins ranging from Claudius to Hadrian.

There are several bracelets of beads, mostly of jet and glass, from burials at Colchester in the Joslyn Collection. One bracelet is of sixteen blue ribbed beads with two coins of Nero as pendants. There is a small chain bracelet from Colchester in the York Museum, and it is not unlikely that some of the pieces of fine bronze chain seen in most collections are portions of similar bracelets.

It is noteworthy that the *armillae* found on our Roman sites

[1] *Arch. Jour.* viii, p. 88 ; xvi, p. 84.

show little, if any, Roman influence ; on the contrary, they seem as a class to have been derived from indigenous prototypes of pre-Roman times. The cabled bracelets so closely resemble the British neck-torcs that one can hardly hesitate to trace them to that source ; as also the wire and ribbon examples to similar pre-Roman forms. The ancient Britons also had jet *armillae*, and it has already been noticed that their penannular form survived into Roman times, while jet, amber, and glass beads are of common occurrence in their graves. Another noteworthy point is that while not few of the British *armillae* were of gold and highly decorated, the precious metals are singularly wanting in the Romano-British. This is remarkable when we consider that the 3rd and 4th centuries were characterized by a love of display and personal adornment, and it seems to indicate that the wearing of *armillae* was not fashionable with the wealthy, but was mainly confined to the poorer classes, during these centuries.

Finger-rings are of great antiquity, and were at first objects of utility rather than of pure adornment, being seals adapted to be carried on the finger or thumb. Among the Romans the earliest rings appear to have been of iron or stone ; but gold rings were early conferred as a military distinction, and the privilege of wearing them was afterwards extended to ambassadors, to senators and chief magistrates, and then to knights. Tiberius next extended the *jus annuli aurei* to all who had a certain property qualification, and his successors to all whom they willed. Severus conceded the right to all Roman soldiers, after which the gold ring gradually ceased to carry with it any distinction. The devices engraved upon the signet-rings were varied, and included mythological subjects, portraits, and allusions to the family history of the wearers, thus in a sense answering to our crests. Originally the men wore only a signet-ring and the wedded women a marriage ring ; but under the later emperors, rings, often of a costly sort, were worn in great profusion.

Finger-rings are frequently found on our Roman sites, and they appear to have been worn by all classes. They are not confined to the sites of towns and country mansions : even the small and remote Romano-British village at Rushmore yielded twenty to the spade of General Pitt-Rivers.[1] Bronze is their usual material, then follow in descending order, jet, silver, iron, gold, amber, and glass. Such is their diversity of form and ornamentation that it is scarcely possible to classify them. Many are hoops which, if ornamented, have their ornamentation diffused all round ; many have their ornamentation concentrated to one spot, the rest of the circuit being a hoop, and to these belong the signet-rings and the forms derived therefrom ; while the residue consists of rings of intermediate character or of aberrant forms.

The simplest Roman 'hoops' are of bronze wire bent into a circular shape with the ends meeting, but more often overlapping, and more often still the wire is made into a double coil—as Fig. 76, H, or even a coil of three turns. Such rings were probably home-made ; but in skilful hands the ends of the penannular ring were ornamented, or, if they overlapped, each was bent back and assumed the shape of a serpent's head, while the double coil sometimes took the form of a serpent twined round the wearer's finger. Of endless hoops, two found at Rushmore are simple examples, one being of bronze wire with the ends brazed together, and the other of white metal square in section. Another Rushmore example, I, which is not uncommon, is of base silver, circular within and octagonal without, and it provides us with a starting-point for continuous ornamentation. The periphery of a Silchester ring, J, is cut into a series of concavities, that of another, K, is punched with a fine herring-bone pattern, while that of a third is diagonally grooved.

We now turn to the more interesting class of signet-rings and rings of kindred form suggested by or imitating them. In the bronze ring, L, found in London, the hoop swells into the bezel, which contains a paste intaglio of a bird. There is a similar ring in silver with a jasper intaglio of Mars in the Caerleon Museum, and two of bronze in the Guildhall Museum ; in fact, these rings are not uncommon, and probably represent an old form which died out in the 2nd century. Iron rings are occasionally found, and they all appear to be of this form. There are two in the

[1] *Excavations*, i, p. 51.

Guildhall Museum, the one with a jasper intaglio of a man holding
a *patera* and *cornucopiae*, and the other engraved with a galley
in some other stone.   A Wroxeter example has its stone engraved
with a fawn springing out of a nautilus,[1] and a Melandra Castle
one has a ram.[2]   Iron was not used for these rings on account of
its cheapness.   From Roman writers we know that many had a
preference for iron signet-rings long after those of more costly
metals and alloys had become general.   In the imitation or
bastard signet-rings of the form, the bezel lacks an intaglio, and
the ring is wholly of metal, as M, a Silchester example, or instead
of an intaglio there is an inset of unengraved glass or stone, or of
enamel.

In the more elaborate rings of this type, the shoulders of the
bezel are ornamented and the setting of the stone takes the form
of a rim or border often also ornamented, hoop, shoulders and
setting now ceasing to flow into one another and appearing as
separate ornamental entities.   Usually the setting is highly
raised, in order that the impression from the intaglio should not
be disfigured by the impress of the shoulders.   The highly
ornamented rings are, as a rule, of silver and gold, but their
technique varies considerably, many of them being of decadent
execution and reflecting a taste for display.   Instead of intaglios,
their settings sometimes contain cameos, which again are often
of inferior workmanship.   Two examples of these ornate rings
are given,—one of silver, N, from Great Chesters, containing a stone
with a bevelled edge,[3] and the other of gold, O, from Sully near
Cardiff, with an onyx cameo of Medusa's head.[4]   The last was
associated with three other gold rings of similar character and a
large number of coins which proved that the hoard was buried
in the first quarter of the 4th century, and this confirms the
attribution of this class of rings to the 3rd and 4th centuries.

We have already described some examples of engraved gems,
and as it is unlikely that this delicate art was practised in Britain
it is unnecessary to give it more than the briefest notice.   This
art was at first confined to the production of seals, but under the

---

[1] *Uriconium*, p. 318.
[2] *Melandra Castle*, p. 113.
[3] *Archaeo. Aeliana*, xxiv, p. 42.
[4] *Numismatic Chron.* xx, p. 64.

Greeks it attained such perfection and was so appreciated that precious stones were not only carved in intaglio but also in relief (cameos), as pure works of art for the connoisseur and collector. The Romans equally esteemed them, and they were produced in large numbers by Greek artists settled in Italy, but from the first century the glyptic art gradually declined. The examples found in this country, whether in rings or loose, are in both precious stones and paste, and are mostly intaglios. Few belong to the best Roman period, the larger number being mediocre and some even barbaric, the work probably of provincials. Some of the loose gems may have fallen from rings, but many, and especially the cameos, are too large to have ever adorned these articles. It is probable that these were appreciated for their own sake, as also for the various virtues they were supposed to possess—these virtues depending in part upon the kind of stone (a superstition not yet extinct) and in part upon their subjects. The number found in this country, however, is not great. There are thirty-three intaglios in the Pump Room at Bath, which were obtained from the main outfall drain of the baths in 1895, where they were apparently all dropped together in the 2nd century, perhaps accidentally by a jeweller. Eight different stones are represented in the series, nearly half being sardonyx, and the rest onyx, sard, agate, chalcedony, amethyst, heliotrope, and plasma. Nearly one-third of the subjects are taken from the animal world, and include a gryphon and a crane. Next in point of number are gods and goddesses and other mythological personages, the residue being charioteers, athletes, a horseman, a shepherd, a youth making an oblation, two heads, and a trophy. There are some good examples of engraved gems in the York and Shrewsbury Museums.

Few ear-rings of the era remain, and as these are mostly of gold, it may be that being small and delicate objects, those of inferior metals and alloys have perished beyond recognition. The prevailing form is a small disk or a precious stone in a setting, with a wire hook attached to the back. Fig. 76, R, is a Silchester example, with a circular gold plate of delicate pierced work, and S, in the Chesters Museum, is a rectangular blue stone in a ribbed setting. There are several set with stones in the York Museum, and another from Silchester has the form of a serpent holding an emerald in its mouth. One in the Pump Room at Bath has a pear-shaped carbuncle, and linked to its setting are two gold wires, which probably terminated in small ornaments. Much more elaborate was a gold ear-pendant found at Housesteads. The base of the hook was expanded in the form of a small leaf, and from it depended successively two *acanthi* and two S-spirals, all linked together and having a total length of $2\frac{3}{4}$ ins.[1] Two found at Gellygaer are of a different type, each being a fusiform piece of metal ending in fine points and bent into the form of a penannular ring. The larger is of bronze and the smaller, T, of base silver. The points being pressed together into the perforation of the ear-lobe, the ear-ring was necessarily worn permanently. There are several ancient gold ear-rings of this type in the collection of the Royal Irish Academy, and similar are still worn in northern Africa. Two in the Colchester Museum, found with the remains of a child in a lead coffin in the vicinity, are of gold wire bent into the form of the bracelet shown in Fig. 76, B. In the Guildhall collection is another of pewter in the form of a simple ring with the ends twisted together. It is probable that some of the small penannular rings, which have been described from time to time as children's finger-rings, were worn as ear-rings.

Glass beads, of two prevailing shapes, cylindrical and globular, are of common occurrence on Roman sites. The ordinary cylindrical beads appear to have been made from round or polygonal tubular canes of blue or green glass of about the thickness of a thin tobacco-pipe stem, broken into the requisite lengths, and rounded at the ends by partial fusion. In a larger and elaborate variety, the cane was clothed with several layers of different colours, and the shoulders of the bead were bevelled off with a series of facets, thus exposing the edges of the layers as a succession of zigzag bands, as indicated in Fig. 76, W. The globular beads are usually somewhat flattened, varying from $\frac{1}{4}$ to $\frac{3}{4}$ in. in diameter. The larger sizes are generally decorated

[1] Bruce, *Roman Wall*, p. 200.

with superficial zigzags, meanders, stripes, or 'eyes' of white
or yellow, the body usually being dark blue. U is a Gellygaer
example. Other shapes are also met with, a frequent one being
an oblong or oval plate of coloured glass perforated longitudinally.
Many of the glass beads are hardly distinguishable from those
found with Anglo-Saxon remains ; but a characteristic Roman
variety, V, is somewhat melon-shaped and ribbed, and made of a
pale blue vitreous frit. Of beads of other materials, those of
jet are not uncommon. They are of various shapes, and are
sometimes carved with incised ornamentation. Amber, coral,
ivory, and bone beads are sparingly found, and those of stone
are rare—there are an alabaster bead with projecting spines and
another of chalcedony in the Guildhall Museum.

Now and again sets of beads of necklaces and bracelets have
been recovered, mostly from graves, and several examples of
these may be seen in the York and Colchester Museums. In the
former museum are two necklaces still intact, the one of yellow
and green glass beads and the other of blue glass and coral beads,
strung on fine silver wires. A necklace in the Guildhall consists
of twenty-four bone and ivory beads with a perforated piece of
tusk for a pendant. Many small objects have been found,
mostly of jet and bronze and perforated for suspension, which
may have been pendants of necklaces, as for instance a jet bear
and Medusa's head at York, and a bronze drop ornamented
with a violet stone at Colchester. Most of these were probably
regarded as amulets. Coins were sometimes used as pendants,
and probably also the larger and more enriched beads.

CHAPTER XV

COINS AND ROMAN BRITAIN

ALLUSIONS TO BRITAIN—MINTS IN BRITAIN—ARCHAEOLOGICAL
VALUE OF COINS—HOARDS AND THEIR EVIDENCE

BRITAIN shared in the monetary system of the western portion of the Empire generally, and with comparatively few exceptions the coins that circulated here were struck in Continental mints. The subject of the Roman coinage is too large and intricate to be even reduced to a mere sketch in this book, and it is unnecessary, as there are many works which treat of this branch of numismatics. The coins, however, which were struck in Britain, and those which, wherever struck, commemorate events in Britain,[1] come within our purview, as also certain points of archaeological interest arising from the occurrence of coins generally on Roman sites.

The first allusion to Britain on the Roman money was a triumphal arch bearing the inscription, DE BRITANN, on some of the coins of Claudius to commemorate his triumph after his successful invasion of our shores. Hadrian's visit in A.D. 120 gave rise to a type, which with variations appeared not only on some of his coins, but on some of those of his successors, Antoninus Pius and Commodus. Britannia is personified by a draped female or male, seated on a rock, and holding a spear, javelin, or standard. By the rock is usually a spiked shield, and in most instances the free hand rests upon it. The male figure is wearing trousers, showing that he represents a barbarian. The female in one

---

[1] For list and description of these see Akerman, *Coins of the Romans relating to Britain.*

instance has her right foot on a globe ; in another she is seated on a large globe surrounded by waves. The female figures are of special interest, as they are the prototypes of the ' Brittannia ' introduced by Charles II on our coins. The Caledonian victories of Severus, in which his sons Caracalla and Geta were associated, were commemorated on their coins, the usual type being Victory with the inscription VICTORIAEBRIT TANICAE. After these, direct reference to Britain ceases on the Roman coinage.

The earliest evidence of a Roman mint in Britain is under Carausius (A.D. 287–293). The mint-letters on the coins of this emperor and his successor Allectus, prove that there were several minting places. L. and M.L. are identified as London (*Londinium* and *Moneta Londinensis*) ; C., CL., and MC., as Camulodunum or Clausentum (Bitterne), or possibly both places ; and RSR., the most frequent combination, as Richborough (Rutupiae). The meaning of the last letters is obscure, but they may stand for *Rutupiae Statio Romana*. RSP. and MRS. appear to refer to the same mint. There are also other obscure initials which may relate to other places. LON. and ML. occur on coins of Diocletian and Maximianus, and PLON. (*Pecunia Londinensis*) on many coins of Constantine the Great and his family. These indicate that the London mint was in operation down to the middle of the 4th century ; but there is evidence that it was revived during the short reign of Magnus Maximus (A.D. 383–388). It is probable that the other mints ceased with Allectus.[1]

The coins found on sites inhabited in Roman times are often helpful in determining the approximate period of their occupation ; but without the exercise of caution they are liable to mislead. Then, as now, some of the money in daily circulation was old. In almost every hoard of the era, the coins cover several or many reigns, and it is not unusual for a few to be a century or more older than the latest. Hence the presence of coins of emperors before the conquest of Britain and of republican coins of the 1st and 2nd centuries B.C., on the sites of our Roman towns, forts, and villages, is no evidence that these places were in existence before the Claudian conquest : these early

[1] For list of coins struck in Britain, *Arch. Jour.* xxiv, p. 149.

coins may very well have been in circulation for some time after that event. The latest coins on a site more definitely indicate the approximate close of its occupation, provided these are not the latest that were in general circulation in Britain. The latest on the sites of most towns of the era are those of Arcadius and Honorius (A.D. 383–423), but we know that some of these towns survived the English conquest and that those which were eventually deserted or destroyed continued a century or more after these reigns. The absence of the coins of later emperors is due to the conquest of northern Gaul by the barbarians, which brought about the severance of Britain from the rest of the Empire.

The proportional numbers of the coins of the different emperors is of service to the archaeologist. The coins found at Richborough, Caerleon, Cirencester, Lydney, and in Pitt-Rivers' excavations at Rushmore and Woodyates cover all or most of the era, and a comparison of their lists shows that the proportionate numbers substantially agree. The coins of the Constantine period are the most numerous, and those of the ' Thirty Tyrants ' (A.D. 254–284) follow next. Or, taking the emperors whose coins are the more numerous,—Constantine the Great heads the list ; then follow, Gallienus, Claudius Gothicus, Carausius and Constans ; next, Tetricus and Constantius II. ; next, Victorinus, Probus, Valens and Gratian ; and finally, Vespasian, Trajan, Hadrian, Antoninus Pius and Faustina I. This enumeration must be accepted as somewhat tentative : a tabulation of the coins found at Silchester and Caerwent would certainly give more precise results.

Buried hoards of Roman coins have been found in all parts of the country, not only in the vicinity of the dwellings of the time, but in places remote from these—on moors, in woods, and among rocks. They are usually in earthen vessels, sometimes in those of bronze or lead, or in wooden boxes, and if found loose in the soil they were probably placed in bags or wrapped up in cloth. Hoards of bronze coins are the most numerous, and those of silver come next, while those of the two together are few. Gold coins in hoards are comparatively rare, and they appear to be always associated with silver. In several instances gold rings and other articles of jewellery have been found with the coins. The number of the coins varies exceedingly. It may be anything from a dozen or so to tens of thousands. A hoard found at Baconsthorpe, Norfolk, contained about 17,000 coins ; one at Bishopswood in the Forest of Dean, 17,226 ; one at Blackmore, Selbourne, 30,000 ; while the quantity in one near Falmouth could only be estimated as 25 gallons ! A hoard of one or two thousand coins is not unusual, but these and higher numbers are bronze coins, occasionally with a few of silver mixed with them, the hoards of silver coins alone or with a few gold ones rarely exceeding five or six hundred.

The burial of treasure for safety is perhaps as ancient as man himself. The dog, for the same reason, buries a bone, yet not for the benefit of other dogs that may chance to find it, but for his own enjoyment at a convenient season. That any of these coin hoards should remain to us is accidental, and probably due in most instances to the untimely death of the hider ; but the large number so remaining indicates how common the practice must have been in Roman Britain. The approximate dates of the hoards, as indicated by their latest coins, prove that while the practice was continuous, there were times when more hoards than usual were buried or more hiders than usual failed to secure them, but probably both contributed to the result. That these were times of strife and disquiet is confirmed by history. The first of these hoard-periods was shortly after the reign of Aurelius. It coincides with a troubled state of affairs under his successor, Commodus, which began with a serious inroad of the Caledonians, was followed in A.D. 184 by a mutiny of the army in Britain and the murder of Perennis, the Pretorian Prefect, who had been sent to quell it, and it was not suppressed until A.D. 187, under a new legate, Pertinax. The death of Commodus in A.D. 192 was followed by a struggle between claimants to the purple, which ended with the victory of Severus over his rivals in A.D. 197. The next hoard-period, and the one to which the highest number of hoards belong, was a century later. During the last thirty years of this century, confusion and strife prevailed in most parts of the Empire, especially in the west, where pretender after pretender, most of obscure origin and the creatures of the military, seized the supreme power, the last two of whom, Carausius and Allectus, successfully and on the whole tranquilly held Britain for nine years. The defeat of Allectus in A.D. 296 left Diocletian and his colleagues masters of the Empire, and ended this period of confusion. The hoards fall into two series, those without and those with coins of Carausius and Allectus, the one series apparently being secreted during a few years before the accession of the former emperor, and the other during the struggle between Constantius and Allectus. A considerable number of hoards have for their latest coins those of Constantine the Great and his family (A.D. 306–350), and it is probable that they were secreted when Magnentius seized the supreme power, first in Britain and then in Gaul, in A.D. 350, or was dispossessed of it in 353. History is silent as to what transpired in the former country on that occasion, but these hoards seem to indicate a disturbed state of affairs. The last great hoard-period followed the reign of Honorius (A.D. 395–423), when Britain, cut off from the rest of the Empire, had to fight single-handed her own battles with the over-sea barbarians, and with results that are well known.

Coin-moulds have been found at Edington in Somerset,[1] Lingwell Gate in Yorkshire,[2] Wroxeter and Candover in Shropshire, Castor in Northamptonshire, and elsewhere. They were undoubtedly used for the production of false and debased money, but they occurred in such large numbers at the first two places, as also on several sites in France, as to suggest official connivance. The moulds were built up in two or three piles or columns in such a manner that a dozen or more coins could be cast at a time. In making the moulds, discs of fine clay were prepared, about six going to a pile ; and between every two discs a coin was pressed. The pile completed, a notch was cut in the side so as to expose the edges of the coins. These were then removed, and the discs were fired at a low temperature. The discs replaced, the pile was ready for use. Two or three such piles were placed together notch to notch, which thus formed a channel or tube. The angles between the piles were than luted with

---

[1] *Archaeologia*, xiv, p. 97. [2] *Phil. Trans.* xxiv ; *Numis. Jour.* ii.

clay, and the molten metal was poured into the channel and entered the cavities which had been occupied by the coins. Most of the moulds appear to date from the 3rd century, a period when a large amount of spurious and base money was in circulation.

MAP OF ROMAN BRITAIN SHOWING THE CHIEF ROADS AND PLACES

INDEX

Addy, S. O., 87
Adzes, 198
Aedicula, 119
Agricola, 42, 44, 61–2, 70; camps attributed to, 42, 44
Altars, 13, 122–35; examples, 123–7; general form and parts, 122–3; inscriptions, 131–5; ornamentation and symbols, 127, 131
Altars at Appleby, 104; Auchindavy, 103; Bath, 102, 104, 108, 134; Benwell, 108; Binchester, 102; Birrens, 103, 107, 108–9, 126, 130, 131; Bitterne, 108; Caerleon, 102, 104; Caerwent, 105; Carlisle, 102, 105, 127; Carrawburgh, 106; Carvoran, 104, 108, 110, 133; Castlehill, 103; Chester, 103, 107, 126, 130; Chesterholm, 102, 103, 126, 131–2; Chester-le-Street, 105; Chichester, 103; Cirencester, 108; Colchester, 108; Corbridge, 126; Ellenborough, 101, 109; Elsden, 108; Folly, 109; Glasgow, 105; Greta Bridge, 107; Haddon Hall, 126; High Rochester, 102–3, 123, 126–7; Housesteads, 110, 126, 132, 134; Inveresk, 106; Lanchester, 102, 106; near Lanercost, 130; Lincoln, 102; London, 107; Kings Stanley, 127; Kirk Haugh, 101; Maryport, 102, 127, 130, 134; Netherby, 106; Newcastle, 102, 107, 127, 132; Newstead, 102; Old Carlisle, 102, 105, 126; Old Penrith, 106; Overborough, 109; Plumpton Wall, 109; Port Carlisle, 107; Ribchester, 102; Risingham, 103–4, 126, 130–1; Rutchester, 126–7; Stanwix, 103; Walton Hall, 103–4, 130–1; York, 103, 105, 107, 133
Amphitheatres at Aldborough, Caerleon, Caerwent, Charterhouse, Colchester, Dorchester, Maryborough, Richborough, Silchester, Wroxeter, 93–4

Anicetum, 223
Annexes of forts, 60–1
Antonine Itinerary, 15
Anvils, 195, 200
Apodyterium, 95, 99
Apuleius, 110
Aqueducts, 59
Arm-purses, 268
Armillae, 265–9
Armlets, 265-9
Arretine ware, 154
Artis, Mr., 178
Athanasius, 112
Atrebates, 10, 12
Awls, 198
Axes, 195

Barbaric deities, 101
Balances, 216
Ballistaria, 64
Barns and barn-like buildings, 81, 84, 85, 88
Barracks, 57–8
Bartlow Hills, 223
Base money, 279
Basilical houses, 85–91. *See* Houses
Basilicas. *See* Forums
Bastioned forts, 45, 53–4
Bastions, 45, 53
Baths, 94–100; examples described, 96–100; process and comparison with the modern Turkish, 94–6; public, private, and military, 96
Baths, domestic, at Bignor, 82; Brading, 84–6; Caerwent, 96; Mansfield Woodhouse, 85–6; Petersfield, 87; Spoonley Wood, 81; Woodchester, 84
Baths, military, 60–1; at Chesters, Gellygaer, and Great Chesters, 99
Baths, public, at Silchester, 12, 79, 99; Wroxeter, 12, 99
Beads, 268, 273–4
Bede, 64, 113, 146
Belgae, 10